BEYOND PIAGET

A Philosophical Psychology

BEYOND PIAGET

A Philosophical Psychology

JEAN-CLAUDE BRIEF
University of Quebec at Montreal

Teachers College, Columbia University
New York and London 1983

Published by Teachers College Press, 1234 Amsterdam Avenue,
New York, N.Y. 10027

Library of Congress Cataloging in Publication Data

Brief, Jean-Claude.
  Beyond Piaget.

  Bibliography: p.
  Includes index.
  1. Cognition. 2. Knowledge, Theory of.
I. Title.
BF311.B727   1983   153.4   83-4662

ISBN 0-8077-2739-3

Manufactured in the United States of America

88 87 86 85 84 83   1 2 3 4 5 6

To Joy, Dominique and Michelle

Contents

Preface

One of the most persistent tendencies of our Western culture has been its bias toward the thinking, knowledge, and reality of its own adults. Philosophers were prone to concentrate their analyses on culturally privileged sets of concepts, while psychologists would articulate the causal links between phenomena identified with their own environment. Alien civilizations and so-called primitive societies were left aside, with dire consequences for the understanding of the adult world.

More crucially, the progenitors of the mature mind now covered by developmental psychology were disregarded, mainly because of Thomistic influences. The loss was twofold: the adult's Western world was not set up as being just one of the possible alternatives along a broad spectrum, and a lateral (cross-cultural and inter-individual) or longitudinal (along the growing child) explanatory framework was not delineated. This second omission is felt particularly in the lack of dynamism inherent in the conservatively unique status given to the three domains indicated above, namely, the adult's knowledge, reality, and thinking.

Appraisal of their identity as well as their continuous progression has to be part and parcel of a neo-Piagetian analysis. This text offers such an analysis and, to provide it, deals with the claim that the adult mind has privileged access to an external world. The fact that this claim has yet to be substantiated remains, in Kant's words, "a scandal."

One of the major problems posed by the external world is its all-embracing nature. In effect, it overflows any one of its appearances as they are perceived at any given moment. This problem is acute enough to warrant the attention of psychologists, philosophers, and educators alike. It is therefore reasonable to seek fresh lines of inquiry in Piaget, who is reputed to wear all three hats. Nevertheless, a conscientious reader of his numerous writings will have great difficulty choosing between the psychologist that Piaget admits to being, and the reluctant philosopher. One must not be too quick to dismiss Piaget's contribution just because he sometimes slurs over the distinction between philosophy and psychology. Typically, his psychological dialogue on sensations, perceptions, and environment is intertwined with a philosophical discourse on properties, object, and knowledge. The former set underscores the way in which we come to believe certain propositions, while the second settles the grounds for the truth of those asserted propositions. Specifically, a contrast is drawn between the perceptual object composed of a complex of sensations, and the object scheme which legitimizes the logical possibility for the object. Accordingly, he uses his findings concerning intellectual capacities and their products to reject criterial claims to truths.

Any epistemological effort has to establish solid bases for its claim to knowledge. Chief among those stands the status of objects and the world they inhabit. Their properties, of course, are many, and to determine their relative importance is crucial to any theory of knowledge. On that account, a prime target of investigation has to be the very conditions under which one can vouch for objects and their externality relative to a knowing person.

To my mind, Piaget's work excels in providing the proper framework to satisfy the needs just mentioned. In short, I work out in detail a transposition of his genetic studies into conceptual priorities. As a result, I am drawn into the odd position of extracting the primitive concepts of an epistemology from among the notions given by a particular psychology. Piaget's cognitive psychology, however, is so pregnant with heuristics explaining the birth and growth of knowledge that one is forced into erecting upon them a viable theory of knowledge.

Although it could be held that philosophical analysis begins where psychological studies end, I argue that it is opportune to accept a neo-Piagetian synthesis as being astride the two domains. Admittedly, by going beyond the letter of his work, which centers on a genetic structuralism, I am led to identify a conceptual holism as the real Piagetian message.

Acknowledgments

It is a pleasure to acknowledge the help from many quarters that led to this book's completion. First and foremost, a special testimony of appreciation is due Professor Patrick Suppes, whose formative influence at Stanford University should, but may not, have resulted in stylistic sobriety and methodological exactness.

My personal thanks are extended to Professors Jules Vuillemin, Maurice Natanson, Zoltan Domotor, and Anne Fagot. They were the sources of helpful suggestions, and their support always came at the most opportune moments.

To David Llewellyn, my admiration for his exemplary translating talent, which ensured that the right word found its way to the right place. Also appreciated were the editorial skills of Gloria Hall, whose painstaking corrections eliminated ambiguities and introduced clarity.

For their diligence and accuracy in typing the manuscript, I am grateful to Jennifer King and Lois Valliant. My warmest appreciation and a lifelong obligation go to my wife, Joy Penso-Brief. Her selfless task consisted in deciphering, collating, typing, and rechecking the successive handwritten drafts.

I am most grateful to editor Kerry Kern and copy editor V. Rangel-Ribeiro for correcting and improving the text. Their competence was essential for turning out a completed book.

For its financial assistance in the preparation of this book, I should like to mention the University of Quebec in Montreal and in particular

Denis Bertrand, dean of Graduate Studies. This book has been published with the help of a grant from the Social Science Federation of Canada, using funds provided by the Social Sciences and Humanities Research Council of Canada. My thanks to its officer, Denise Lachance, who inserted a human touch in all our official dealings.

Introduction

THE PROBLEM AND ITS SOLUTION

A most deceptive puzzle is evident throughout this work. Whereas human beings are all subject to a singular development, they also progress toward a quasi-universal intellect. As individuals they have to integrate into their total functioning system the foreign bodies constituted by their life experiences, while as rational minds they bring order into a seemingly chaotic world. The search for a common front, around which these dual facets can be united, is found in the progressive evolution characterizing cognition.

The cognitive progression is to be viewed as a trend toward a greater stability of the intellectual equilibrium. The origin of the progression is acknowledged by Piaget to be the very conflicts that mar the operation of cognitive structures. At one and the same time, conflicts indicate the stable limits at any one level and concurrently initiate the next phase, where they are reabsorbed. Consequently, conflicts only disturb the schemes used at that moment; they play toward them the role of obstacle, and do not confront some absolute knowledge. Such a view really means that any given phenomenon, perceived by an individual, must first submit to the organization proper to each one of his cognitive levels.

In his pre–1975 writings, Piaget adopted a probabilistic stance regarding both cognitive evolution and adapted knowledge of reality.

As a consequence, his problem was to delimit the conditions leading to the cognitive definition of the permanent features of reality. His genetic studies showed that the first central feature was an invariant that he called the object.

Piaget's original analyses indicate that an individual does not begin with sets of reflexes; they are too specific. He starts with instinctive drives or general forms of activities, such as avoiding danger or foraging for food. Reflexes are defined within the activity of the organism, and acquire their modalities in encounters with reality. Prohibitive conditions repress the appearance of some forms, while a successful payoff relative to some expected sensation favors the repetition of others. These repetitions become reproductions as they reappear under various environmental conditions. It is as though the varied phenomena of nature, having been apprehended by means of a specific modality, are then reduced to a repeated uniform manifestation. This repetitive assimilation suggests a restriction on knowledge, where the reflex has a history created by the confrontation of the organism with its environment.

The first cognitive lesson to be drawn is that reflexes are defined in use, and are therefore modified not by disuse but by misuse. They gradually become obsolete as they are functionally modified by the absence of the expected sensorial payoff. Innate predispositions render the organism receptive to stimuli that, acting as indices, orient general activities. Theses predispositions become dispositions when they take on specific characteristics, and graduate to genuine reflexes in actual encounters with the environment. The tuning occurs under the appropriate sense-data that fit in with the instinctual predisposition.

Piaget elaborates from this basis, and is then able to clarify the fundamental concepts of his cognitive psychology and genetic epistemology. The main idea is that the semantics of reflexes is rooted in the sensorial field. For instance, proprioception acquires its meaning within the tactilo-kinesthetic realm.

To progress from mere physiological reactivity to the cognitive level, reflexes must allow specific stimuli to be significant for their onset. Reflexes therefore take on some of the characteristics of actions by picking up the what, whether, how, when, and where of their occurrences.

Instinctive drives, viewed as ways of behaving guided by sensations, permit the modification of reflexes. A possibility is thus uncovered of using sensations significantly within an organism's activities. Interpreting it as the generalizing assimilation reveals how the original automatism of instinctual drives becomes the behavior of a system. Actions are then repeatable and, if successful, are repeated and reinforced. This repetitive assimilation is a source of regularity, order, and permanence, both for sensations and for reflexes. The various interplays between sensations and reflexes permit us to hint at a semiotics which constitutes the basis for believing in a continuum where reflexes major into actions. In fact, we are delimiting a semiotics of action where three relations hold between reflexes and/or sensations:

1. Sensations occur at the onset of actions, thus typifying the semantics of action.
2. Sensations conclude the outcome of the motor part of actions, and are thus able to determine the next segment in the overall behavior. This discloses the pragmatics of action.
3. Sensations are events that are fed back and influence the future of the corresponding type of action. This transaction is indicative of the meaning of action.

Within the Piagetian framework, meaning—where reality influences the future of reflexes—corresponds to the generalizing assimilation; pragmatics, representing the continuation of behaviors, sanctions the existence of a repetitive assimilation. This position is fraught with momentous consequences concerning the central notions of action, identity, and objects. It thus establishes the basis for an epistemology beyond Piaget's own cognitive psychology.

Action is to be defined as a sequence of movements characterized by tactilo-kinesthetic and proprioceptive qualities conjoined with mental predicates such as intentionality, purposefulness, and goal-directedness. The sequence consists of a motor phase whose limits are operationally significant in the sense that they determine the structures at play in any one action. In turn, the modes of operation essential for the dynamism of these structures acquire the properties characteristic of Piaget's logico-mathematical network, such as reversibility or inversion.

The essential view here is that it is not the sensations which are structurally significant but the mobile linkages of sequences leading to these sensations. In turn, the semantics of any object dwells in the goal-motivated sequence. The intentional aspect lies in the open-ended expectancy of sensations inherent in the chains formed by a sequence of acts. Essential properties of cognition stem from these features. At the first few levels, and before the intercoordination of actions, a chain involves only one sense. Thus, sensations become cognitively significant much later, when they are part of distinctly different sense-modalities. Other-ness, out-ness, objectivity, obstacle permanence, and substantiality, which subtend any reality, are all properties ensuing from such a position.

Intercoordinations of behavioral chains build up the spatial frame and, if constant, are the origin of a collation of distinct sensations (belonging even to several modalities) attached to a single postulated entity. This is a source of enrichment and complexity of the object. Occurrences of a sensation under repetitive use of chains give rise to the temporal identity of the object. Moreover, the various properties of a specific object are tied within the semiotics of actions that have epistemological relevance. Accordingly, properties are conceptually linked by a relation of entailment, and are not events which exist within a causal network.

The continuity of a prolonged behavior is transformed into the basic modes of permanence and externality when the fulfilment of expectations terminates purposeful acts. Identity thus obtained bestows an ontological status on objects through the goals inherent in every action. An instrumentalism belonging to achievement is introduced, along with the intimate cohesion between the motor chains and their dependent sensations. Therein lies an additional argument for the cognitive role of sensations. In turn, the expectancy implicit in an existent chain of acts suggests a permanent entity standing apart at its terminal, but—as will be shown in Chapters 3 and 4—the world is cognitively exposed within the frame determined by at least two sense modalities. Using one modality to reach the other gives it the aura of an anticipated goal which, under constant repetition, obtains an objective status; only then can we aim through our expectancies toward the outside, and find obstacles. Representation of sensations becomes accredited in the form of a foresight. Herein lies the true sense of Piaget's virtual actions, which, through their representation, promote the transfer of temporally distributed sensations to simultaneous spatial presentations. In other words, expectations set up by a sequence of acts will be translated, under appropriate circumstances, into recognitions that cognitively appear as a set of differentiated, and yet simultaneous, operations.

From the set of simultaneous operations which share common features, invariance of actions is extracted, in terms of sensations and operational linkage. This interpretation does not limit us to the structures that Piaget's clinical studies have disclosed. A study of all degrees of freedom, interconnections, and coordinations provides mater-

ial for the discovery of new operational sequences within an intentional, and thus creative, dimension. These sequences when consolidated
will yield invariance of sensations and define structures. *Expectancy is
the key to intellectual structures, since it is the source of the invariance that
knits the variations into operational combinations of acts.*

PHILOSOPHICAL PRELIMINARIES

So far it has been hinted that the world is not aimed at, or reached for,
as a realist would have us believe. Rather it becomes known to us in a
constructive and dual manner:

> *Constructive*, because the pattern inherited from the instinctual
> drives provides a frame whose segments remain in disarray
> within the generalizing assimilation. Soon these segments are
> assembled under the recognitory scheme, and finally become
> consolidated by repetitive assimilation.
>
> *Dualistic*, because nature, being the original architect of the here
> ditary stock, retains the same role in the breaking and rearrang
> ing of these segments. On the other hand, thought processes
> provide the dynamism that consolidates what we ultimately call
> our knowledge of the world.

Here it is worth observing that it is the scientific bent in Piaget that
forces him to use a dualistic discourse, while the constructivism described above reflects his monistic epistemology. For Piaget, the universe must therefore be cognitively defined: it thus depends on the
combined activities of mind and body. Accordingly, there is a powerful
reason for Piaget to oppose empiricism.

An exploration of the notion of constructivism reveals that, under
the influence of the environment, certain forms of activity become
specific, are repeated, and then pay off as expected. Here lies the crux
of the matter.

A reflex becomes cemented to a sensation by reinforcement and
repetition. Conversely, the sensation integrates within established
reflexes, and by the same token becomes cognitively relevant. More
forcefully, one can argue that a sensation has to terminate a reflexive
behavior to be acknowledged as part of the organism. That point
provides us with the first inklings of an important epistemological
message: namely, that behavior is goal-directed. Moreover, that quality is inescapable if behaviors enmesh the organism into its environment. Specifically, a reflexive act is shaped out of an instinctual drive
through various encounters with the milieu in which it manages to

attach itself to specific sense-data. Those sense-data become stimuli for subsequent segments of the general activity. Thereafter, through repetitive assimilation, they belong to the onset of those segments. It is plausible from there on to grant, to those sense-data that have become stimuli, the added status of sensations, because they are supposed to follow from the reflexive behavior. Having a cognitive role to play, sensations are expected, so to speak. More importantly, they make an act out of the behavior. In other words, the cognitive orientation taken by an activity borrows from the quasi-goal that the sensation has become. The directedness and the purpose of the act stem from here.

A good example is vision where at first we have an extended field for visual impressions, stationary for resting objects, oscillatory for slowly moving ones, and dynamic for swift transitions. The use of these schemas results in a specific visual performance which will use the recognitory assimilation toward a given category of visual impressions. This purposefulness defines the "looking act," which goes beyond mere seeing. Hence, within this cognitive framework, visual sensation, which concludes an oculomotor action, also gives it goal-directedness!

Only in the context of action schemas are objects manifest. Similarly, externality and predictability supporting their appearances are conquered via the coordination of acts. The coordination essentially occurs through a generalizing assimilation, because any stimulus is bound to be significant in some degree to various actions. A child will hear a sound and be visually excited; or "the child tries to listen to the face and to look at the voice," as Piaget so aptly described it.

We have to remember that the continuity inherent in the cognitive growth of all individuals requires the integration of new experiences within existing schemas rather than random associations. As I have already noted, *hindsight is vital to foresight*. The complexity of action coordinations favors conceptualization, which enhances the role of meanings among actions proper. Hierarchical sequences of motor segments, linked through their onset and outcome, are adaptively confirmed through some strategically directed intentions toward reality. Hence, to achieve adequacy to the real, we utilize the rules available at the competence level, and not the immediately accessible performances of the senses. The flavor of this remark is strongly Piagetian because, by framing reality more through competence than via performances, it emphasizes form over content. At the same time, it gives preeminence to the mechanisms of intelligence or capacity, and pushes aside the immediate influence of a data base. As it should be when knowledge is implicated, epistemology, in its weak sense of being concerned with competence at the conceptual level, governs the analysis over and above any psychological studies that survey events or performances.

Piaget's concern for knowledge indicates for us a constant epistemological interpretation of cognitive and behavioral terms. Whenever a stimulation provokes a response, or a sensation organizes around a deportment, then a property emerges out of an action. Specifically, stimuli from various sources integrate to form the semantics or the onset of a movement. Together they form an action that, once exercised, pays off in a new set of sensations. There lies the pragmatics of that action, but only if those sensations match the expected set. In that case there is recognition, which provokes the resumption of the behavior by the repetition of the next segment, if such was previously established. *Recognition is therefore a prerequisite to the repetitive use of selected acts.* A sensation must fall within an ongoing activity to be of any relevance to the organism, which means that, cognitively speaking, there cannot be totally "new" sensations. Undifferentiated groping about betrays a lack of pragmatics. The resumption of a behavior indicates that the sensation that proceeds from the pragmatics of an act becomes a means for a transaction, and is thus part of the semantics of another act. Here we have our first break toward cognitive invariance, which is that particular sensation belonging to two acts by virtue of being their linkage and the source of their coordination.

A critical feature of Piaget's epistemology is the discovery of these cognitive invariants. They are due to an acquired adaptation by coordination of actions. Hence, *the world must be mediated by the conceptually based assimilatory schemas in order to gain its stability.* For example, at first everything grasped is sucked: later, sucked things are grasped. In this particular case, tactile sensations are the invariants that give birth to something independent and therefore possibly real.

I define recognitory assimilation as the fulfilment of a sensorial expectation. It anticipates that, through environmental encounters, there will be an asymptotic convergence between the assimilatory schemes and reality. By gaining some specificity in the field of actions, consciousness is restricted to the tail-end of a behavior, and should consequently be associated with an "intention to" and not with intentionality. On the contrary, we will see that the latter is related to the complexity of actions. It follows that the pragmatics or outcome of an action is a source of permanency, since it is conditional on the convergence of a behavioral sequence for its entrenchment.

An explanatory comment is in order here. It is pertinent to recall that the pragmatics of an act was defined relative to the resumption of a behavior containing that act. The interchangeability of motor segments introduces the distinction of means from ends in the goal-oriented world of cognition. Consciousness, attached to the pragmatics of a behavior, to that end refers to the exclusion of the various intermediaries provided by the linkages within the behavior. *The formation of various accesses to a conscious end ties the permanency resulting from recognition to the mean-ends dichotomy, and generates the notion of an external world.* Sensations, incorporated under recognition, connote adaptation of the organism to the environment, and single out the cognitively relevant and constant features of a reality.

The constant need for equilibrium, so prevalent in Piaget's work, demands that the ever-expanding experiential field be internally tied by relational constraints. The generalizing assimilation accounts for this systemic expansion through the tentative linkages that it establishes between potential actions under the impact of new environmental conditions. Fortunately the environment is diverse enough to press the generalizing assimilation into play, and to open to investigation the whole field of potential sensations. The accommodation of conflicting schemas occurs within action intercoordinations, and, being still nonspecific, this accommodation takes the form of a strategy proper to a competence characterization.

An adequate set of linked actions is achieved through the matching of the expectancy with the sensorial encounter. Thereafter, recognitory and repetitive assimilation stabilize the acquisitions and ensure the regularity of specific behavioral performances. Purposefulness ensues, and exacts achievement from behavior ar the cost of the open-endedness of unadapted actions.

It is within the coordination of actions that we find the source of permanence and invariance, and it is therefore within the conceptual dimension that "objectification" and coherence can be circumscribed. Accordingly, the conception of the object as an aggregate of properties is gratuitous and renders the notion of observability cognitively irrelevant.

We must note that it is not the object that is delimited, but characteristically the conditions for its existence, or (in Piaget's terminology) the object's scheme. It can then be asserted that Piagetian thought, permeated by his psychological findings, is ineluctably drawn to a constructive conceptualism. Hence it ensues conclusively that his cognitive psychology is not only the inspiration, but more importantly the essential grounds for an epistemology.

Properties, objects, and their interrelations inhabit the world and also man's consciousness. Traditional views have been that the latter brings order into the chaotic diversity of the former, or conversely, that nature regulates the composition of thought processes.

A reappraisal, inspired by Piaget's cognitive interpretation, shows that the conditions under which the notion of an external reality appears do validate the various claims to knowledge about a world which preexists the knower. Specifically, Piaget tells us that organizing various actions so as to operate on the environment yields common properties. Their general and invariant features form a conceptual presentation of the world. An individual gives a cognitive status to his action as a function of its results on the environment, but he understands objects when they are inserted within intercoordinations of actions. There remains implicit a classical line whose dual allegiance promotes a will to understand and a desire for practical results. Both subtend a fear that the world may pass us by if we do not conceive of it in some way or other. Piaget's modern follow-up is to emphasize cognition, whose organizing function branches out toward achieving success on one side, and realizing understanding on the other. For the first type, a chain of temporally distributed acts reaches a goal as a function of the various contexts. For the second, a self-regulated set of transformations reveals the structural properties of the world. By coordinating transformations, the intellect imposes a nontemporal presentation of general concepts (constant food value in vegetables). On the other hand, by establishing correspondences, the individual enacts possible strategies to effect some gains (pulling and grabbing a toy). In the first instance, the child explains, while through the second he resolves problems.

All those cognitive aspects transpose straightforwardly into epistemological desires such as to know, to comprehend, and to be aware of. On that account, it is not the predominant role of concepts to simplify, but rather to link conceptualization to complexity with the added advantage that it provides a framework for awareness, understanding, and knowledge. By shifting the discussion from parallel role-playing to a continuous development, one avoids reductionist talk where intricate events are broken down into their elementary components. Instead one surveys the genetic process underlying concept organization which accompanies consciousness. There is a strong sense in which a neo-Piagetian position flies in the face of common sense by accepting that abstraction is understanding by satellization of concepts, rather than that it is a simplification through a hierarchy of definitions. Allusion is made here to Warren Quine's cobweb interpretation of knowledge which sides with Piaget's constructivist thesis. In fact, both defend the continuous evolvement of concepts against the descriptive use of key words. It is in that sense that a Piagetian follower should assert that man constructs more than he invents, more than he creates, and definitely more than he observes. Owing to the continuous and progressive buildup of coherent realities, the child cannot be said to be misinformed, but on the other hand he can be judged to operate at a more primitive level than any adult. The issue can be broadened to mean that the child, subject to ontogenetic evolution, is immature, not only with respect to a modern man, but equally in comparison with a paleolithic one.

In view of these paradoxical remarks, it is proper to verify whether a constructivist thesis truly emerges from Piaget's cognitive psychology and genetic epistemology. One can expect that it develops along two main axes. The first is dominated by structural criteria which govern the viability of objects and events, while the other looks at the sequence of intellectual schemes that reveal the evolution of cognitive presentations of the world. The first can be inserted among the various theories of knowledge, while the second falls within the scope of psychology. Hence, Piaget's position promotes primarily a philosophical psychology and secondarily a philosophy of psychology.

My Solution

My aim is to contribute to the neo-Piagetian movement which, by making full use of his insights, is presently shedding some light on various central problems:

> How are bodily movements psychologized?
> Where do the coherence and stability of the mind come from?
> Why does the world turn out to be not only permanent but also external to the conceiver?
> What makes the distinction between competence and performance so crucial?

In order to address these questions, I find it interesting to ascertain the status, role, and interrelations of a few notions such as action, intention, representation, consciousness, imagination, conflict, creativity, and ignorance.

From these one can begin to narrow down Piaget to three more manageable credos: epistemological, psychological, and educational.

EPISTEMOLOGICAL CREDO. Acting cannot be separated from thinking and even less from seeing the world as it is. What this really means is that the mind, together with its brain support, does not simply inhabit the body, and therefore cannot be transferred or transplanted.

The mind's fundamental dependence on the body seems to preclude its reduction to a computer, partially because in the latter case its formal representation renders any model independent of any particular computer. With respect to knowledge of the world, the intimacy between mind and body reinforces the importance of the contacts with that world, and locates there the origin of mental progression. Of course, it does not stop at mere manipulations leading to abstraction of qualities, but evolves through reflection on actions. An object is not sensed or something one "becomes acquainted with," it is compared and operated on. "To sense" and "to be acquainted with" are passive while "comparing" and "operating" (transforming) entail actions. Both activities reveal a mental gymnastics that contrasts with the mere reception denoted by the first two verbs. Moreover, comparing and transforming constitute the basic tools of assimilation used to build properties. They ensure that cognition prevails so that to comprehend supercedes to describe. This explains the importance of an assimilatory logic of action to bring about an understanding which, for Piaget, foreshadows any accommodative explaining in terms of mere sensorial descriptions. *One must think of thinking in order to progress, and this implies tying percepts, linking acts, relating ideas.*

PSYCHOLOGICAL CREDO. This credo contains a belief in a continuous intellectual development that functionally equates the adult to the child. It jeopardizes the view, apparently held by Piaget, that cognition is a ladder-like sequence of stages. But this does not create long-term problems because, as the sequel will show, the achievement of universal structures is eclipsed by contextually dependent reequilibration procedures that integrate continuity and discontinuity.

Once more, the essential role of contacts with the milieu is introduced as a link between the cognitive and the productive modes. It also traces to the environment the source of mental development, which leaves aside the maturationally inspired views that intelligence is either homeostatically controlled by physiological determinants, or homeorhesically guided by biological principles. In both cases, it would not matter what content is fed to the child in order to shape his mind, since his ways of coping with the world would be either universal or so personal that he would endure undisturbed. Still, the preeminence of directed thinking suggests a close tie between cognitive and motor developments, and between structured thinking and procedural acting.

A natural question to ask, since maturation is ruled out, concerns the role played by motivation and need, bearing in mind that Piaget rejects the behaviorist drive-reduction solution. To explain the forward march of the developing intellect, many cognitive psychologists rely on a motivation activated by needs. This ranges from a need to weaken dissonance (Festinger), a need for knowledge that resolves conflicts (Berlyne), a need to assimilate (Mischel), to a need for equilibrium (Piaget).

Chapter 1 details the reason for abandoning the crutch constituted by the use of needs. This notion is quite superfluous for a march forward which evolves, not from intraconceptual or organismic species-dependent principles, but intrinsically through contacts with the environment. Quite simply, Piaget's need for equilibrium is uncalled for if equilibrium means a search for the stable, the coherent, the relevant, and the reversible. The main reason is that cognitive cohesiveness stems directly from encounters with the world using intentional acts which are goal-directed and not teleologically organized. Thus, a transposition of the main themes governing gradual development is welcomed when it relates the concepts of intention, purpose, and awareness to a theory of knowledge.

EDUCATIONAL CREDO. While strictly outside the scope of this work, this credo appears to reject implicitly the validity of the "American question" about accelerating intellectual development. The main reason for this is that global expected contexts are essential to increased competence and these cannot be replicated since the person concerned must himself define the prerequisites for any fruitful contact. For example, the social demands of a particular adolescent determine the specific peer interactions generating conflicts, disequilibrium, and subsequently progressive equilibrium. Hence, to ask how fast a fractioned intelligence can grow plays second fiddle to how far it can be helped.

My next task is to justify the prominent and central role played by the notion of object. Its importance is mostly due to the fact that for Piaget it is the source of the objective-subjective and physical-psychological dualisms. Specifically, the particular cognitive status of the object renders us independent of the contextual present and points to the fact that we start at the body's periphery while slowly spreading out into the world through actions. By reproducing these actions and their coordinations in a conceptual framework, which is more and more removed from the immediate sensorial input, we constitute the real. A stripping process reveals the real structures against the backdrop of inner feelings. *Our reality is not built by association but by dissociation! The outside is not set upon, seen, or heard. It is constructed within our actions network, which makes us look at and listen to it.*

In addition, I find that as a consequence of the progressive match-ing-up process, that which is repeatable slowly emerges within the schemes of intercoordinated actions. The permanent comes forth, jus-tifying Piaget's characterization of cognitive development as a flight from egocentrism. It explains his predilection for a scientific epis-temology, traditionally biased toward common—predictable—features.

Beginning with a study of reflexes, I establish a developmental and conceptual continuity leading to a theory of action which explains the emergence of a stable reality. A reflex leads to action as an impover-ished version of it. They are both essentially dependent on encounters with the milieu, but the reflex is specified out of an innate activity. The position adopted is that stimuli graduate to sensations when they become significant in the field of activities. This is rendered possible through a three-pronged correlation between sensation and action, which constitute a semiotics closely linked to the generalizing, repeti-tive, and recognitory assimilations so familiar in Piaget.

Modifications under sensorial guidance of reflexes and/or actions mean that sensations come within the very activity of the organism, and this stands as the generalizing assimilation. The new acquisitions are then repeated and, if successful, are reinforced under the repetitive assimilation which indicates regularity. There are two domains with polarized allegiance, one to the outside world and the other to inner mentation. One must not forget that whereas representation comes from a perceptual accommodation that internalizes what is exact and specific, conceptualization by contrast is an assimilation of acts that interiorizes what is global and general.

The recurrence of appropriate sensations is in fact an exogenous imposition of permanence on the mind via recognitory and repetitive assimilations, called adaptation by Piaget. By contrast, intercoordina-tions of actions, becoming structures, are explained by the various interplays occurring among the three assimilatory schemes. Of course, accommodation is subservient to assimilation because, being tied to motor changes, it follows the lead of the latter which reflects the sensorial components of an action. Thus, the well-known analogy of accommodation and assimilation to a digestive process is simplistic at best, since accommodation differentiates within the process of assim-ilation, and does not operate in opposition to it, nor complementarily with it. Objectivity follows by dissociation and not association, be-cause it is the differentiation which multiplies the linkages between acts and proportionally separates the object from the percipient.

A further analysis shows that awareness is proportional to the complexity of required acts in a given situation. It is therefore not toward the instantaneous present that one must turn, but to a wealthy past which contextualizes events. In the contemporary literature, the present is overrated and does not qualify as a worthy defender of reflective man. Indeed, man is never a neophyte—he is always historical and relies on his past to encounter a meaningful reality.

An interpretation within Piaget's notion of action reveals that complexity favors the occurrence of new sensations, and gives increasing play to generalizing assimilation. Hence, intentionality can be located in the complexity of actions, and is dependent on a sequence of adjustments to the world, which ultimately defines it, not by a representation, but within a correct presentation of reality. Moreover, I am able to recognize that under this analysis Piaget attaches consciousness to the generalizing assimilation via the semiotics of actions, forcing the intuitively coherent view that consciousness is of the real, but is once-removed from acting through its conceptual dependency.

Consciousness does not surge out of a direct acquaintance either with the world or the inner self. It stems from the play of cognitive processes interacting with the environment through actions. The act obtains henceforth the special privilege of being at the origin of both the concept and reality. Accordingly, knowledge and awareness make one!

I can then sharpen the distinction among representation, re-presentation, and presentation. The last-named is a genuine carrier of a semiotics, while the others denote the lower status granted respectively to perception and figurative knowledge. Beliefs and representations may fluctuate under the diversity of the environment, but it still matters that presentations depend on our mode of being relative to the global world.

By differentiating the means from the ends of actions, I come to realize that externality is not found in a direct access to the remote real, but is grounded in the means utilized to reach for it. It is relative to this aspect that I am able to point out in the text that whereas consciousness is centripetal, externality is centrifugal.

The flight from egocentrism, which defines cognitive development, is rooted in the clear-cut distinction of means from ends. This in turn is paradoxically dependent on the mobility of intercoordinations of actions, which are the bases for the awareness of the permanence of selected sensations, thus the determination of objects. It becomes obvious that the object as a permanent substantive entity must conceptually precede its sensorial attributes; even more so, in view of the exclusively assertive nature of direct encounters that perforce leaves negation, inversion, and cancellation to mentation. Moreover, regularity and predictability within intercoordination of actions yield security, and could explain various rhythmical gestures such as drumming fingers, swinging children, or even polite social formulas.

PLAN OF THE BOOK

Chapter 1 succinctly summarizes Piaget's genetic psychology, cognitive psychology, and genetic epistemology in relation both to intellectual progress and to knowledge claims. Of course, I do not intend to recapitulate or even reexamine his findings, since this has been done excellently by Piagetian scholars such as P. Cowan, H. Furth, H. Maier, D. Elkind, and R. Vuyk.

In Chapter 2, I show that Piaget's method is to proceed through a cautious, step-by-step matching of our representations with the results given by our actions on the environment. In fact, epistemology for Piaget consists in delimiting the relations between the cognitive tools of the individual and the objects that are accessible through direct encounters. This means that one of his contentions is that one must rely on genetic epistemology as the foundation of a viable theory of knowledge.

In Chapter 3, I maintain that recognition precedes repetition of behavior, thus obviating the cognitive relevance of new phenomena. This last point is reinforced by the fact that the integration of sensorial ends with motor means under repetition gives goal-directedness to actions, and implies that there are no ways for an action to depart suddenly from its original schema without becoming cognitively irrelevant. On that topic, as Bruner daringly asserts, the use of a concept avoids surprises. Thus, one must seriously consider whether there can be foresight without hindsight. After these preliminaries, I determine a cognitive meaning for the notions of coherence, consistency, cohesiveness, and invariance, which are fundamental for the constructivity inherent in the performance of an act. Accordingly, this warrants an acceptance of genuine intellectual activities such as expecting and predicting. Oddly enough, it is on this basis that Piaget can argue that we, as human beings, can look with our ears and listen with our fingers, and that the blind can see. An understanding of cognitive invariance, which denotes the interface between a chain of acts and the start of an action, can help us explain the sequence linking the various sense-organs such as eyes to hand or to mouth.

By attaching the complexity of action to generalizing assimilation, I elucidate in Chapter 4 the notion of intentionality, and make explicit the open-endedness of complex behavior, while restricting achievement and purposefulness of actions to the recognitory and repetitive assimilations. It is due to this dual allegiance to intention and goal-directedness that human beings proceed with fluid gestures, while robots, lacking both, move haltingly. Thus, I can stress at this point the importance of giving a psychological dimension to bodily movements, and can lodge in the action-oriented aspect of our intentions a fore-check that blocks any possible loafing through life.

Chapter 5 provides a presentation and an analysis of Piaget's latest thinking on the concept of equilibration, conflicts, and intellectual progress. I establish that my critical emphasis on the cognitive importance of the "encounter" of the organism with its environment is vindicated by Piaget's detailed study of the origin of cognitive structures. Moreover, the semiotics of action developed in the first four chapters adequately fits the new models presented.

Beginning with a sketch of the Piagetian position on the mind and the objective real, I contrast it to the traditional epistemologies. In so doing, I define the conceptual network inspired by Piaget's genetic psychology, which explains the construction of reality in the context of our actions on the environment. I then identify the succession of concepts that satisfies the structural demands of the developing person, relative to the chronological distribution of cognitive realities and their dynamic transitions. The obstacle that the world can proffer leads to readjustments of a total model of that reality or alternatively is the source of intellectual progressions toward various states of equilibrium. It follows that conceptual stability has a much more profound cognitive meaning for Piaget than conflicts.

Next, the study centers specifically on the origin of a progression toward the intellectual stability of objects. It has to be decided whether or not the environment spoils our representations and is the source of adjustments. I point out the interesting result that optimal creativity occurs at the interface between competence and performance, immediately preceding each and every mastery of the various intellectual operations. Under these conditions, conflict for me has a more fruitful effect on the person than does equilibrium.

Finally, to elucidate Piaget's structural constructivism, I have to pry into the notion of schema, its ties with actions, its birth out of conflicts, its equilibrated synthesis by regulated activities, and ultimately its role in cognitive development.

CHAPTER 1

Piaget's Theory

It is not pure chance that an analysis of the evolution of intelligence precedes in Piagetian writings the problem of how knowledge is articulated. Unlike various theories of knowledge, particularly the empirical tradition, and in spite of his psychological bias, the polarity that opposes object first to reflective subject second is reversed for Piaget. This means that first the cognitive tools are detailed, and subsequently they justify various adapted realities.

There is a latent conceptualism that postulates an anteriority, not only causal and genetic, but also logical, of intellectual structures relative to the reality which they generate. This position could be considered a Copernican revolution since it relegates the paradigm of an all-encompassing adult universe to the peripheral status of one among several possible worlds. Knowledge is then identifiable with the multiplicity of possible worlds where the reality conceived by an adult is only probable.

Piagetian psychology subjects the world to control by the intellect. The reality thus produced takes on a dynamic form due to an intelligence which steadily develops. The path is staked out by structures whose birth and obsolescence are the result of interactions between its predecessor and the environment. Successive structures culminate in a system of imagined actions whose interrelations possess logico-mathematical properties that render these structures operational and equilibrated. In other words, the final intellectual system is composed

1

of totally reversible actions and thus immunized against errors. Intelligence is therefore restricted to a form of thinking which operates in a structural format defined by actions on objects, their properties, and the relations between these properties.

KNOWLEDGE AND INTELLIGENCE

Dealing with Piaget's enormous output is a tremendous challenge and requires that one divide in order to conquer. Since the main purpose of this work is to frame a philosophical psychology out of Piaget, but nevertheless beyond him, we must master initially the philosophical and the psychological aspects of his thought. To do so, we have to understand their interrelations rather than attempt to recover the details contained in his clinical studies.

Throughout his works four main trends are distinguishable:

1. *A genetic epistemology* where philosophy and psychology are thoroughly mixed, and that centers on the evolution of knowledge as a function of the child's successive views of the world.
2. *A genetic psychology* that emphasizes, through psychology, the stepwise acquisition of concepts.
3. *A cognitive psychology* whose functional analysis of cognition reveals an original philosophy.
4. *A scientific epistemology* where the notions uncovered by psychology are especially chosen to characterize the scientific mind.

To clarify this division, a fourfold analysis of memory can be envisioned. It submits to genetic psychology through a study of the recall process, while cognitive psychology is interested in the function of memory itself. The role of genetic epistemology is to uncover the development of souvenirs. Finally, a strict epistemology analyzes how souvenirs sustain claims to knowledge by memory.

GENETIC EPISTEMOLOGY

It is in his early writings that one finds Piaget's clearest account of how knowledge develops in direct relation to one's reality.[1] Indeed, the mechanisms that are used to know the world constitute genetic epistemology and, some say, all Piagetian epistemology.[2]

1. According to Piaget, the child starts with a "realistic" view of the universe, which means that he is completely immersed in it. He does

not distinguish between the physical and the psychical, the external and the internal, objects and their names.

In the first case, dreams and thoughts make one with smoke, air, or matter. The second confusion ties all things to thoughts and only slowly do imagined objects move from the room to the eye, and end up within the head. The identification of the third kind places names in the object; for instance, a child will call a cow a "cow" because it is part of its natural property to sound "cow" to him. In other circumstances, the cow gives milk, which is a property on a par with the name. The same reasoning would hold for the existence of God, which follows from the simple fact that it has a name.

The "realistic" phase is signaled by four main traits: all personal perspectives are absolute; there is no dualism opposing the self to the world; thoughts cannot be traced back for lack of a self; lastly, there is a centripetal evolution where the mind ultimately recovers ownership of its goods.

The child betrays these traits by his odd behaviors. For example, he assumes every known idea is absolutely his own and he had simply forgotten it. We may have many little Platos in our midst since children seem to give a psychological origin to Plato's theory of memory. The lack of dualism shows up in the curious phenomenon that accompanies a child's hurt when he blames his mother for not caring: after all, she must feel his pain since it is located everywhere. As for the third trait, the favorite examples show that the child is prone to look outside for the dog that he has just dreamt of; or when thoughts are expressed in words, they participate in objects and make things happen as if by magic. Who knows whether the sacred value of the "verb," as uttered by the pharaohs of yesteryear, cannot be traced to this oral power?

Fourthly, in dealing with the means used to achieve knowledge, Piaget noticed that they all progress in a centripetal fashion. Accordingly, dreams are at first everywhere, then outside, and finally in the eyes or in the head. Names are in things, then in the voice, then in the air within the head. Visual percepts come from the object; later they meet it halfway, and lastly they emanate from the eye.

Conclusions about the "realistic" child must contain the idea that consciousness of his self evolves not by construction of experiences, but by dissociation of his thoughts from things and of the outside from the inner self. Indeed, psychical events are first the thing, then in the thing; after that they are anywhere in between; finally they land in the head. To help this progression, opposing the child's will might appear a fruitful ploy.

The paradoxical phenomenon is that mental events that had invaded the outside world have to return one by one within the mind. Having involuntarily loaned all subjectivity, one regains it by depleting the outside of its features, and by the same token one grants it objectivity. The self emerges as the world appears. In the process egocentrism diminishes proportionally as objects gain a rightful status and the self retrieves its legitimate qualities. Thinking about oneself holds the self apart from the world. Hence, dissociation is cognitively preceded by indivisibility and not by association.

2. The child moves to an "animist" phase after objects gain their legitimate status separate from subjective thoughts, images, and names. However, they still keep some of the subjective qualities that the child shares with them, rather than attributes to them. Objects are alive, feel, want to do things, and are fully conscious. As a matter of fact, the "why" of a child is directed at the intentions looming behind teleologically-minded active things. A cloud following him, water knowing how and wanting to boil at 100° C., a hammer that aims to hurt him—all are examples of such animism. Its participatory aspect resembles the American Indian's myths governing properties enjoyed by animals and humans alike. By contrast, a more mature thinking would, like African magic, attribute traits to individuals before identifying them.

Being egocentric compels the child to foresee the sun going to bed, rain announcing clouds, stones standing purposefully in the way. His animism consists in granting life to everything that is active, aware, and morally willful rather than obeying physical laws. For example, the sun wants to move because it has to keep us warm.

Once again, this phase follows the centripetal process of bringing home the properties shared by nature. The principle of universal activity, life, and consciousness is slowly restricted to inert objects, then to moving ones, and lastly to self-moving entities like a falling leaf which is followed by animals and man.

3. Having cleared the hurdles of distinguishing the two domains constituting knowledge and the real, and then their respective properties, the child next masters the range of their separate activities. Piaget baptized that phase the "artificialism" of children. In it, man is supposed to have created all things, including mountains, stars, and himself. Of course, everything has a purpose and so all of nature is causally ordered. But, as against the animist who saw reasons inside the object in a typical Aristotelian manner, artificialism promotes a universal order. Accordingly, instead of things "being for" some reason, they are now "made by" utilitarian doers. At this stage a child finds his parents all-powerful. The usual centripetal move goes from

universal finality of nature serving man, to detailed mechanistic designs of objects surrounding us.

Each of the three phases defines a special reality whose knowledge depends strongly on the mind's workings for a genetic epistemology in the Piagetian mode. From the above, the details about reality indicate that perceived events migrate from realism to animism, and on to artificialism, only after gaining vital qualities. In the first place, they obtain an objective status; then they acquire various properties which they can call their own, while losing their subjective markings; finally, they are inserted within causal networks and abandon the artificial human origin bestowed on all of them.

On the side of knowledge, egocentrism—which was strongest when the mind "saw" itself in all things—weakens by blurring that "vision" successively in objects, in properties, and lastly in activities. Strikingly, the object that is initially all-embracing cannot be something assembled. Indeed, it contains pell-mell the whole range of psychical elements at play during its conception. Intellectual growth consists of the object drying up, so to speak. The mind separates the qualities proper to the subject from the recurring properties belonging to the object. For instance, pain will ultimately be housed in the body instead of being lodged in the mother or in the table that is struck.

Two distinct chains of attributes come out of the mind's evolution: one is psychical and the other appears physical. Regarding the first, there is a phenomenological distinction between an objective real and subjective affectivity reminiscent of William James's stream of consciousness.[3] Equally important, the second chain reflects the primacy given to conceptual grids over the socioaffective aspect, and reveals a debt to Ernst Mach,[4] precursor of Logical Positivism. Piaget's dual allegiance to a governing intellect and to a preeminent world is already quite obvious. The epistemological lesson tells us that all and any knowledge acquired throughout one's existence evolves from a realist phase to animism and to artificialism.

GENETIC PSYCHOLOGY

Piaget's claim to fame relies partly on his relentless pursuit of structures which, in a three-pronged attack, he centers on intelligence, reality, and knowledge. The previous section revealed that this pursuit could establish some relation among the three domains; but it also uncovered a constant progression characterized as a flight from egocentrism, whose path in all instances is to move inward, or in a centripetal fashion. This phenomenon occurs when the mind ebbs after invading reality. Further studies searched for the final pattern adopted by the mind, and this was found to be structural. As a result, specific formal structures control behaviors as well as consciousness. They take the form of a progressively more perfect logico-mathematical framing which Piaget extends to all his psychological findings.

Intellectual development thus follows the two axes of an immediate determination of the object and a lifelong sequence of structures. In the first case, it resumes the successive appearance of cognitive schemes and their very crucial transitional mechanisms, while in the second it represents the continuous formation of knowledge. In brief, from a psychogenetic examination of causally related constructions, Piaget draws the main lines of conceptual solidarities. Among the constructions his genetic psychology introduced a chronological hierarchy broken down into four main stages: sensorimotor (0–2 years); preoperational (2–7 years); concrete operational (7–11 years); and formal (11–16 years).[5]

The sensorimotor stage divides into six phases beginning with reflexes (0–1 month old), which are truly activities rather than simple reactions. To be active by simply repeating some hereditary movements is in itself a primitive form of organization. Obviously, the constant use of vision, prehension, audition, suction, vocalization, and proprioception, imposes some regularity on a variable environment.

The progression to his first habitual movements (1–4 months old) provides the baby with a systematic form of exercise. Mere reproduction without goals leads from reflex to movements, as seen in the Babinski reflex becoming a grasp. The point is momentous because it means that for the first time the outside environment influences fixed hereditary patterns of activities. Thereafter, combinations of behaviors can and do happen, but only because reflexes have acquired the flexibility of movements. Objects grasped are viewed, indicating that the baby sees; then he grasps and brings to his mouth the thing that is thereby to be sucked. Coordinations between the various sense organs eliminate simple contemplation of an object in favor of that object being acted on. Of course, for various objects to be used they have to submit to repeated movements (assimilations), and at the same time they impose their own physical conditions on the appropriate coordinations (accommodation). For instance, a thumb is "sucked" by assimilation, but the baby sucks a "thumb" by accommodation. However, an object is at this stage only a series of pictorial scenes whose controls depend on the sense organs. To remember anything is to feel as correct a sequence of various sensations tied to some activity that imparts to them a total unity.

When the baby begins to notice the sensorial components of his activities, he tends to repeat those interesting effects (4–9 months old). Being able to produce a sensation almost at will confers on it the constancy of a result. On the other hand, not to get an expected result jeopardizes the whole activity, and under the impact its unity breaks down. Only when object-to-suck separates from object-not-to-suck does grasping split from sucking. Once freed, these activities recombine, allowing such a motion as grasping to connect with seeing rather than extending into it as in the preceding phase. The fact that grasping connects to sucking and at other times to seeing bestows on it the quality of invariance. An object that until then was seen is looked at from now on while in the line of sight, but ignored as soon as it disappears. However, the original impetus for connections is accidentally provoked by the use of a movement together with haphazard presentations by the milieu. The baby strikes a string with a jerky hand, and thereafter repeats the motion to see his hand swing the butterfly.

The next phase consists of by-passing the mere satisfaction of being active and enjoying its results instead (8–12 months old). Handling things has some kind of effect which is read as being both provoked and a resultant: the baby rejects a disagreeable object. Accordingly, intentional behavior begins to replace bare movements. For that enrichment to occur, it should be possible to aim at a result through an activity that occurs in a variety of situations. For Piaget, the baby has acquired a schema whose main applications are to generalize and to expect. In fact, he will search for an object hidden from sight, but still where it was found before, and not where it disappears. There is a radical shift from hearing to listening, and from seeing to looking. The crucial cognitive progress takes place because, while hearing does not combine with seeing, listening does link up with looking. It is all rendered possible due to the baby's ability to repeat, recognize, and generalize. Those qualities are respectively mastered in phases two, three, and four.

The fifth phase consolidates and extends the wealth of coordinated activities (12–18 months old). Any new phenomenon is subjected to multiple experiments where new ways of reaching it are devised. The body is an instrument for the mind seeking acquaintance with its environment, but (for full mastery) activities have to espouse the particularities of the milieu (accommodation). The object is truly born as it is at last defined by goal-oriented and means-controlled behaviors.

For example, the baby removes obstacles blocking the view of a disappearing object, but does not yet suspect invisible displacements.

The sensorimotor stage concludes with the instrumental means taking on the heavy role of representing the very objects they are supposed to reach for (18–24 months old). For instance, the baby spreads his arms, opens wide his eyelids, or leaves his jaw agape to indicate a large object. He is even able to vary and combine his movements so as to extend his own organs by the use of external "instruments." At that level, children are prone to use sticks in order to draw desired toys nearer. They are able to imagine virtual displacements that they extend in relational space, constant time, and causal sequences.

Progress at the sensorimotor level is fundamentally tied to the evolution of behavior as it relates to the world. Issued out of a total immersion in the real, a series of sensorimotor attachments between the body and the milieu slowly emerges. They are the means used to realize that there is a world and there is a body. The dichotomy gains a tremendous boost from the organism's ability to coordinate the attachments under environmental pressure. From repetitions to variations and to coordinations, the mind elects to differentiate and to integrate. The resulting gains center on the design of strategies where means and goals are distinguished, and where aiming at objectives loads any behavior with intentions. Naturally, the infant inhabited by these intentions can be their locus and so originates activities. This polarization marks the distance between his body as an object and those objects around him. Only then can he reach out toward the qualitative state of an object that is distinct from its position. By varying the means touching on the first aspect the baby plays while assimilating. On the other hand, modifying the ways to copy the positions of objects leads to accommodation by imitation.

The preoperational stage pursues the important representational shift begun at the end of the sensorimotor level. By intercoordinating the various activities adapted to the world, there emerges a way of symbolizing events (2–4 years old). The progress evolves from physical, to behavioral, perceptual, and representational processes, but it does not yet escape the infant's limiting egocentrism, syncretism, and centration.

To begin with, the baby accommodates himself through adjusted movements to be able to handle various imposed as well as intruding phenomena. Having to physically refine his trials at reaching out, grasping, following with eyes and hands, the infant becomes conscious of the variety among objects. The main point is that by differentiating the initial coarse corporeal effort of reaching out into the later more tractable grabs, the body explores the details of objects and identifies with them. From this quasi-molding process there originates the resemblance between object and motions. Herewith lies the most important aspect of symbolization where common features tie the signifier to the significant. Activity of the body is thus at the source of symbols. However, the imitative movement is differentiated out of an overall behavior rather than as a facsimile produced by an intellectual faculty. It follows that to symbolize is not a matter of establishing an identical semiotics, but more correctly of having a common one for both the object and its imitation. To complete the symbol Piaget attaches the appropriate image on perception to an imitation. The door is henceforth open to perceptual variations around the symbol which *qua* gesture is attached to an image, and, for example, can at times be a laugh to represent the crying baby sister. This game supplants the prior supremacy of pure imitation, but does have the flaw of being contextually dependent. As a matter of fact, the infant is so strongly impressed by his concurrent percepts that the whole symbolization effort remains egocentric, centered, and syncretic. In the first place, he expresses his own perspective which he addresses to himself in a kind of soliloquy about his desires without caring to communicate. Second, he operates in the present and, for instance, does not actually "steal" from another child since the toy, by being here, cannot not be else-where. Lastly, all contiguous events are likely to be part of the symbol irrespective of their real, rather than accidental, relationship: for exam-ple, an umbrella is likely to cause rain.

In spite of his three defects centered around his egocentrism, centering, and syncretism, the child controls the six semiotic functions in a sequential escape from those very defects. He successively masters imitation, game, drawing, image, memory, and language.

To communicate effectively through his representative symbols, the infant has to decenter himself from his desires, views, and situa-tion. That effort has only a limited payoff value throughout the next phase where intuition forces him to cling to properties viewed one at a time (4–7 years old). In line with the preceding phase, the game—consisting of variations around a global situation—leads to an in-creased attention toward selected properties. They acquire a functional role linking one state of an object to another. However, the two conditions where the properties predominate are subjected to percep-tual centration, and instead of being linked with emphasis on the changes, their respective states are compared. For instance, because the two extremities predominate, two rows have the same amount of buttons if their lengths are equal, irrespective of the actual number in the rows. A person is doubly condemned for the dire consequence of his act with no attention paid to the wilfulness involved. The tallest person is automatically older; the fastest object always comes first, irrespective of the relative distance travelled.

The child goes strictly from one state to the next without wider anticipation and so cannot bite far into the future or the past. The result is that he can neither go straight to the end, nor back to the beginning, and so reversibility is not achieved.

The concrete operational stage announces the end of perceptual dominance and the reign of intellectual mobility (7–11 years old).

By varying the percepts that constitute states and positions, the child is ineluctably drawn to view the changes in between. In turn, the transformations due to various activities are compared, allowing classification, seriation, and ordering along all the different dimensions such as size, weight, or length. Able to start from an observed situation, the child can envision qualitative changes among objects in direction of decreasing or increasing amounts.

One can say that he has intellectually mastered decentration, causality, and perspectives. He is thus able to conceive of reversibility, transitivity, symmetry, asymmetry, function, identity, and associativity. Furthermore, the child realizes that through the intension and extension of classes of objects, one can order them by inclusion, and the notion of number can be devised. He can simultaneously transform an object in various ways, keep it identical, bring it back to its original state, create inversely proportional variations among properties. In fact, he can insert that object into the structure formed by the four imagined actions just distinguished, and deduce or intuit the conservation of one of its properties. That conservation would mean that a property stays constant while other features are transformed. For example, bending a wire conserves the length because it can be unbent, has not mysteriously been elongated, has remained the same wire, and finally allows the curvature to compensate for the slight shift in the extremities of the wire. In the same way, he can explain the conservation of quantity (7 years), of weight (8 years), of volume (10 years), and of density (12 years).

Having the ability to observe a change, and to undo it through a virtual action reversing the process, gives the child the use of an "operation." At that level, however, he must think operationally about a real situation, hence the epithet "concrete" that is given to this third stage. Indeed, this level has been hailed as the epitome of Piaget's conservation studies. Whereas the child represents his actions, he must still manipulate and is time dependent in all the operations he thinks of at this level. Even though he knows that $2 \times 7 = 14$, he objects to two cats with seven legs each totalling 14 legs, on the ground that cats only have four legs. The child is operational when he combines, compares, orders, classifies, cuts, and reassembles. But what he operates on cannot be things, they must be, for instance, oranges. Then he is able to uncover their invariant features within his "grouping" structure made up by these very operations.[6]

On the other hand, he represents to himself an ordered sequence of actions which he organizes as a strategy to achieve some ulterior goals. To explain how the result was finally obtained still remains a trifle confused since the idea "because" contains a mixture of psychological, causal, and logical features. To pull out of this confusion with egocentric overtones, a judicious technique would be to oppose his explanations from a social standpoint, and this would make him self-conscious. As with the sensorimotor stage where interacting with objects provoked awareness of one's body as an object in its own right, at this level thinking must interact with other thinkers to induce self-awareness of one's own mind.

The formal stage concludes Piaget's genetic psychology and opens up through five criteria the whole realm of true scientific thinking for the adolescent (11–16 years old).

First, he is at last able to conceive some possible worlds where hypothetico-deductive reasonings operate. The tremendous progress is that the real, being one from among the possible worlds, does not need to be concretely manipulated in order to uncover its invariants. Second, the adolescent wants to test hypotheses and—by holding all variables constant but one—he can induce and generalize about properties, their transformations, and the relations between those transformations. Third, he simplifies the world, and can predict, by removing himself from concrete situations that introduce unwanted variables. To be sure, the adolescent thinks about propositions, instead of manipulating events as in prior stages. Whereas his previous doings made him right or wrong, he now emits assertions that are true or false. Oddly, the adolescent is so inebriated with his newly found intellectual freedom that he lets his imagination run wild; this is the age of idealistic moral, political, and social beliefs. He enters fully into the universe of propositional logic, where a combined procedure of all possible operations is available. Through the fourth criterion, the child masters formal reasoning and thus uses sophisticated structures, such as group, lattice, ratio, permutation, probability, and categories. Finally, the fifth requirement consists in understanding complex equations which represent scientific principles such as the principle of inertia or Newton's laws. Using hypothetical constructs, the adolescent imagines water running upstream or even uphill—something that, at the earlier concrete level, was adjudged to be utter nonsense. Obviously, he could not think in a contrary-to-fact manner before, and water could not rise of its own volition. In another case, his ability to invert relations—and not only classes as before—allows him to foresee that a snail making his way across a table can stay stationary relative to the floor. All that is needed is to move the table in a reciprocal fashion.[7]

To resume Piaget's genetic psychology, one cannot fail to notice that in each of the four stages, the child progresses from egocentrism to objectivity.[8] To do so, he uses a triadic format consisting of an extreme assimilation, followed by a radical accommodation, succeeded by an adaptative organization represented by structured concepts made up of virtual actions.

To be sure, the operational structures must be considered incomplete at any level due to their chronological development. Therefore, short of possessing the necessity of closed structures, they remain subject to influences from the environment and are reduced to explanatory devices within a causal network. This is the orthodox Piagetian interpretation of the accommodative process. Once this process is stabilized enough to avoid conflicts whenever the world is confronted, a synthesis appears in the assimilation-accommodation dichotomy. An adaptation of the intellectual structures to the environment has then been achieved. Hence, intelligence is an adaptation which "is the totality of behavioral coordinations that characterize behavior at a certain stage."[9] It indicates that one has attained coherence, closure, and consistency in a system of intellectual operations whose complexity grows with the number of internalized actions.

In Piaget's early writings, progress is a maturational process, as well as the result of a sequential probabilistic choice function, generated internally on environmental cues. This movement forward is the product of endogenous selectivity and exogenous patterning. Straightforward examples are offered by the construction of invariants. For instance, the conservation of quantity in a block of clay follows sequential probabilistic phases such as reasoning on the length, followed by a survey of width as the most probable property, and then simultaneous viewing of both dimensions. Next, there is a reasoning on transformations with the finding of compensatory aspects of both properties, resulting in the discovery of quantity invariance. Thus, a temporal sequence leads to an atemporal reversible operational structure. Piaget makes numerous remarks on this characteristic shift from the perceptual domain to conceptualization wherein formal hypothetico-deductive thinking translates sequences of events into simultaneous concepts, and vice versa.[10]

To illustrate this evolution, Piaget devised the story of King Alfred of Denmark, whose culinary talents were in doubt when he burnt a cake. The preoperational child is nonplussed and, by centering on one detail, can maintain King Alfred's status as a chef due to his royal lineage. At the concrete level, the story becomes so obsessive to the child that King Alfred loses out to his mistake and is no more the renowned chef. Finally, the adolescent uses his formal reasoning to concoct a solution whereby Danish people are excellent bakers and so their king is one also, despite his human error.

The formal stage allows the adolescent to form alternative hypotheses, and thus to supplant the perceptual and conceptual centration characteristic of the preoperational and concrete levels. A further understanding is provided by the child's own progression viewed in relation to his construction of reality. Starting from an initial symbiosis, the organism carves out its immersion in the world by chiseling multiple attachments to it. Like an umbilical chord, these attachments are behavioral ducts which by defining the world authorize the simultaneous emergence of the self. The whole process constitutes the sensorimotor stage. It is notable that attachments originate endogenously, setting the preeminence of assimilation and, at the same time, controlling the ways in which the environment is met. Progressively, the behaviors coordinate under local pressure to let accommodation preponderate. Thereafter, a remarkable phenomenon shifts the cognitive balance away from the world, and toward the coordination of activities. These are means which, after having espoused the milieu's contours, become representative of it in their own right. Through this cognitive role, one has access to symbolic representation. It is then but a matter of integration between symbols, to obtain a structural construction of an adapted reality which, for Piaget, divides into physical and logico-mathematical knowledge.

Cognitive Psychology

Piaget's shift from age-related stages whose dominant structures reveal temporary equilibria is tied to his abandonment of the probabilistic model.[11]

The new emphasis exhibits a continuous development where strategies espouse the contextual present while being oriented by mental schemas. Thus, instead of structural piecemeal treatments, the world is dominated by a thinking which is functional. Knowledge is paramount, and ultimately results from procedures which process data through a chain of actions.[12] To pursue this matter further and in an anti-Kantian vein, Piaget holds that as the localization of phenomena within space and time progresses, so does the child's decentering from his own body. In turn, so does the object, which becomes pinpointed and inserted in a cause-effect chain. Cognition proceeds from a global object-subject scene to perceptions severed from actions, then to objects fractioned off into their properties, finally to coordination of objects with actions over properties.

The functional evolution of knowledge uncovered by cognitive psychology progresses from sensations to perceptions, and (via an empirical abstraction) reaches object. It ascends to properties by using a pseudoempirical abstraction, and then reflectively abstracts from actions on objects and their properties. Finally, Piaget defines a reflexive abstraction on coordinations of actions to achieve intellectual development.

The cognitive progression just delineated relies mostly on innate functions such as assimilation and accommodation. Hence, adopting a functional approach betrays in Piaget a dependence on his biological background. It contrasts with his use of logical models, which imposes the structured mind and was in favor throughout his genetic psychology period.

One can understand the convergence in his most recent writings between developmental psychology and cognitive processes. Specifically, this means that one does not think through the vision given by logical structures, but by extension or by autoregulated projection beyond the actual. On that account, Piaget is much more on the side of a "structuralist Constructivism" through his cognitive psychology, than the advocate of a "constructivist Structuralism" inspired by his genetic psychology.

The cognitive world described by Piaget forms a homogeneous network of interrelated concepts. It is their analysis that uncovers the tight embedding of self-regulated transformational systems rather than showing an interconnection of independent ideas. Within that world, intelligence is characterized as "the equilibrated form of all cognitive functions."[13]

In other words, intelligence is to know, and thus it is thinking, because thinking is the use of operational structures derived from actions over properties of objects. Operational structures are sets of virtual transformations with logico-mathematical characteristics, of which the main one for Piaget is that the system is closed and autoregulated as all actions are reversible. Piaget sums it up by holding that "to know is to assimilate reality into systems of transformations."[14]

One senses a Kantian flavor in the structures governing knowledge because they organize the real in a predetermined mold. The triad made up of assimilation, accommodation, and organization forces the internal drafting of the environment in a continuous move toward broadening the behavioral field. In fact, it means organizing the pattern of possible actions. All phases of cognition are action-oriented, and in fact stimuli graduate to sensations when they become meaningful in the field of actions. Piaget tells us that sensations are indices for mental assimilation of objects into an action scheme.[15] Thus, on the one hand, sensations are constructs when viewed as members of the cognitive field. On the other hand, a perception gains its meanings within intercoordinations of actions and consists of imaginary ties which complete the actual ones. Accordingly, the latent Kantism that we saw in the preponderance of cognitive structures is enlarged in Piaget to a conceptualistic monism that is not restricted to phenomena, but defines all realities. Thus the child must be considered young since he engenders a viable world, and not naive and distressed in the adult world put forward by Skinner's observationalism.

In order to grasp Piagetian thinking thoroughly, it is crucial to understand the integrative function of assimilation and the differentiation set by accommodation. Let us not forget that the laws of thought, forming successive schemes, mutate under the impact of objects, while being governed by assimilation and accommodation.

The "scheme" is a cognitive tool that is not a structure applied to objects. It is a dynamic process that includes the previously successful system of actions, their actual interplay, and their actual transformations under the pressure of diversified conditions. Objects must be processed by schemes to obtain a cognitive status, prior to their insertion into any reality. On the other hand, and in agreement with Piaget's explicit distinction, "schema" denotes figurative or sensorial configurations produced by a sequence of actions.[16]

In accordance with this view, the assimilative scheme has been described metaphorically by Piaget and his commentators as a digestive process whose gastric juices act on, but at the same time select, the relevant nutriments feeding the body of knowledge.[17] Food is transformed as well as the organism that does the digesting. Assimilation occurs when the food is dealt with by the various gastric juices. Only those elements in the food that can be broken down by the chemicals secreted by the organism will enter the bloodstream. Hence, the food must submit to specific transformations in order to become part of the assimilating body, but the texture, particular composition, and type of cooking impose some constraints on the stomach and its gastric juices.

The organism espouses or accommodates to the condition of the food. If the food is assimilated and the organism accommodates, then digestion can be completed. Similarly, the environment is processed by the intellect only if its schemes handle the elements presented. It requires a *modus vivendi* between the individual and the milieu such that they will interact only if the objects and the cognitive processes modify each other. Properties are extracted from reality by certain logical structures either specified or to be discovered. Their imprints indelibly mark these very properties.[18] They force objects into a molding deductive system, thus justifying the implicative role given to assimilation. Some of those logical structures have been specified by Piaget in his genetic psychology, and include seriation, classification, and numeration.

Accommodation is complementary to assimilation in that it modifies the stock of intellectual devices under the influence of the environment. Given a structure very broadly defined with respect to its possible applications, it is the encounter with the world that will give that structure the characteristics of those applications. That is, a proprioceptive behavior will adopt the contour of its stimulus so as to emerge a full-fledged reflex.

In the first phase of Piaget's cognitive psychology, the infant is restricted to sensorial impressions offered by the quasi-innate assimilatory schemas of sucking, listening, or grasping. The availability of sense-date depends on global activities of the sense organs which offer a succession of sensations without cohesion like a movie running at a reduced speed. There are no organization, no ownership, no awareness, and no observables at this point.

The initial lack of distinction of sensations from the corresponding act stands out when the baby crosses the visual field with his hand, which appears devoid of intention and ownership. Actions and qualities of the subject are glued to objects and oppose any alteration toward permanent and localizable entities.

After the first globalizing phase, perceptions appear as the infant begins to investigate the links between his own movements and those of objects. In some way, it is the variety and looseness of those links that make the object appear and disappear among the various perceptual fields, and that ultimately lead to a break between the subject and his observed objects. But, this progress must occur through a shift to the cognitive domain. That is, loose sensations form into a global perception when the continuity of physical phenomena is transposed into the unity of inferred concepts. To perform this feat, Piaget uses the dialectical scheme of his favorite triad, namely assimilation, accommodation, and equilibrium.

Within Piagetian terminology, the cognitive transposition means that the environment not only imposes its conditions on intelligent acts via a process of accommodation, but must also submit itself to assimilatory mechanisms. The states of equilibrium are achieved through intellectual activities that dominate the perceptual world. At this level, centering is still accentuated and biases the child toward his own perspective. For instance, irrespective of temporal juxtaposition or causal sequence, it is always insults from others which start an argument.

Accommodation predominates as percepts are internalized into specific representations or images. Only when these interact do we have figurative knowledge. In later phases, those representations will in turn be transformed by virtual actions to produce operative knowledge. Instead of representations, we shall then have conceptualization where interiorized forms of objects are general and global.

Piaget locates the intellectual unity in the power to transform perceptions into items which are identified with the very process of thinking.[19] This view is reminiscent of that held by E. Meyerson, who subsumed all cognitions of reality under an identity principle, and was thus able to reduce the cognitive effects to their causes in objects.[20] Pursuing the matter further, we find what looks close to a debt for Piaget when he holds that the whole object is made up of partial objects cut out of the environment by actions of the subject.[21] The resemblance ends when Piaget explains in more detail his conception of the assimilatory process. Specifically, it is an insertion of properties into operational structures, and as such it sets properties into the implicative network of logical reasonings.

Before properties can have a cognitive status, they must belong to some object. Consequently, the next phase of his cognitive psychology will determine the birth of the object. For Piaget, the notion of permanent object not only needs coordinations of different actions, but also simultaneity and/or succession of similar actions. This is due to the dependent and temporary state of perceived objects whose conservation lasts only as long as the action directed toward them is performed.[22] Even the so-called laws of thought are not constant and depend on the activities involved. Indeed, identity principle, the law of the excluded-middle, and the principle of noncontradiction follow an evolution closely dependent on the conceptual apparatus available during any phase of the child's intellectual life. In other words, the semantics of these "immutable" logical principles is in a constant flux and reflects the progressive evolution of the intellect.[23]

The Kantian parallel no longer holds, since formal thinking is in such a constant transition that the final state cannot be foreknown. Likewise, Piaget's doubts about Bertrand Russell's logicism become clearly motivated by the uncertainty coloring the priority of the laws of thought over mathematical axioms. And so, Hamlyn's admonition to Piaget not to clutter both Kant's and Russell's conceptual analyses with genetic argument pays scant attention to these elements.[24]

The object does not sit passive and independent, but is a tributary of multiple activities that nimbly supply properties, including missing ones. Thus, events which can be assimilated predominate. For instance, having heard an object, the child will look for it. Then, having seen it, he reaches out for it, not to grab it, but to prod, swing, or grasp with his hand. Actions pursue objects through their anticipation, and make sure that they are available for subsequent behaviors. Indeed, the felt presence of those objects is proportional to the wealth of action schemes set in motion, and their disappearance will equally be felt relative to that wealth. Accordingly, the object seen must be touched or listened to. If it is touched then it will be sucked, seen, grasped. The sequence of acts determines the group of properties available and considered.

There is a flaw in this fundamentally deterministic constructivism. Indeed, to justify the intercoordinations between ways of doing things such as seeing and touching, which by the way can be considered deportments, Piaget uses associative laws put into play during simultaneous and fortuitous acts. He quickly recovers from this slip by sketching a broad picture of the intellectual evolution that, due to its complexity, entails forgetting a possibly involuntary debt to Humean associationism. Piaget asserts, ardent structuralist that he is, that the whole precedes atomicity when the infant operates in any new domain involving undifferentiated sensations. It is only when interacting with the milieu that some properties are imposed and privileged by being vectorally fastened to actions. The last point illustrates his notion of accommodation. On the other hand, assimilation integrates the intersecting vectors into focused centers which graduate to cognitive structures.

During the next phase of cognitive evolution, the keyboard formed by the basic stock of structures will be played on, leading to a genetic pool-like environmental selectivity of the adequate set of properties of objects. Interrelationships between structures are essentially controlled and filtered by the inputs, producing such fundamental categories as those dealing with objects.

Once the object emerges within cognitive structures, properties can be attached to it through the network of actions. Specifically, acts operate directly on physical attributes, from which they obtain their meanings as sensations, such as looking while shifting one's eyes, listening to visual display, rubbing, shaking, groping. From these actions stem the properties of resistance, hardness, flexibility, weight, sound, and color.

A Piagetian paradox appears when cognition of the object requires a progressive stripping of its affective and purely sensorial attributes. It is recreated, much like a sphinx, within the crucible formed by cognitive structures. The object should, therefore, become impoverished as it loses particular identifying qualities, but it simultaneously gains relational predicates which it shares with other objects. In this case, Piaget, always the coherent rationalist, places permanent benefit for the object always within the structures, while properties other than cognitive are but figments of a temporary, deluding reality. Nevertheless, within the structures' hierarchy, none is to be judged erroneous with respect to subsequent ones, because each one chooses and combines the elements constituting the successive world views. For example, the child, capable of acting out some complex tasks at age eight, will be unable to perceive or conceive them. His ability to use a sling with accuracy is inconsistent with his ignorance of tangential vectors that he only grasps at age twelve. It is as if perceptions are at first cognitively quelled, and appear later under the guidance of schemas. The perceived complies with the known, meaning that assimilation not only integrates in a formal mold, but also suppresses the awareness of sensorial contents. It is via the differentiations of accommodation that properties attached to actions can be assimilated to the schemas, and thus ascend to consciousness.

The preponderance of action shows up forcefully in the next phase of Piaget's cognitive psychology, where a reflective abstraction gives a deeper knowledge which relies on the discovery of features remaining invariant throughout transformations.

A clearer understanding can be provided if we review some conservation studies. For instance, in conservation of substance a clay ball is transformed into a sausage. The child's progress toward realizing the invariance of quantity of matter occurs as follows:

1. The child elongates and surveys only the length.
2. To stretch the clay, he starts at one point and terminates at another. These two terminal points are compared.
3. The child, interested in the stretching, notices a lengthening.
4. Lengthening accompanies stretching and the observed thinning. Children alternate between these two, then coordinate

them, and lastly imagine a relation. The idea of transformation goes together with the possible reversal of a lengthening into shrinkages.

5. Finally, the child conceives that stretching brings on elongation and the compensatory thinning. He is even able to anticipate and thus to conserve the quantity of matter, since he infers from a transformations set which is not observed but imagined.

In short, these results show that the child focuses at first on the stretching and bestows an affective dimension upon the lengthening. It is only through awareness of the thinning that displacement of matter and the correlated compensation ratio leading to conservation come into play. Under these conditions and in spite of a progressive differentiation of various properties, these latter integrate into a system and yield invariance. Curiously, physical properties must make room for operational structures to allow for a more "realistic" world view.

There is a progressive trend in the conceptualization to operate, not on objects or on their properties, but on the transformations of possible actions on the properties of objects. A probabilistic choice function on actions leads to the significant compensatory phase of invariance. To paraphrase Piaget, it is from activity that thought germinates and obtains its reality.

But to achieve the transposition, the mind must become completely functional. This is why the synthesis of assimilation and accommodation falls under the Piagetian heading of equilibrium. This indicates that the organization of sets of actions is adapted to the environment. The properties of equilibrium, such as coherence, totality, and consistency, define the logical structures identified as group, lattice, and a Piagetian favorite named "grouping." A bicephalous process governs both adaptation and the progress from one cognitive scheme to the next. Genetic structuralism is thus simultaneously dynamic and stabilizing.

On the dynamic side, Piaget emphasizes the future-oriented posture of actions rather than their backward attachments. For instance, the infant localizes a moving object relative to its arrival point rather than to the empty space left behind. So action schemes are concretely constructive since they are directed toward the prospects of a gesture.

The second part of the process reflects the stability of constructions arising out of encounters with the environment. There is a conceptualization stemming from observations, and also the creation of relations among perceptions. In an updated point of view, Piaget sets the timing of structural progress right along these constructions that engender one another when contradicted during confrontations with the milieu. To be sure, the conflict between what is conceived and what is presented remains a cognitive phenomenon. It is constituted by a strong bias toward particular properties which are either overestimated or undervalued up to and including disregard. There is thus a readiness to reject some properties in favor of other privileged ones, making it ostensibly a negative act. Notwithstanding Piaget's avowed loathing for Bergson, his position, relative to the role of memory, is partially Bergsonian.[25] Apparently, everything is registered, and then a selection establishes the actual percept. It would have been more coherent for Piaget to locate the conflict at the level of the anticipations attending all particular acts. Still he insists both on a conceptual selection by focusing, and on an active rejection of peripheral aspects. That is why the child chooses the elongation while stretching a clay ball, and discards the thinning parameter.

The final cognitive product appears very much like autonomy from both the external milieu and internal instincts. If that trait can be achieved in a progressive way, then, for Piaget, maturity of the intellect will have been conquered. Of course, this high mark can be obtained only if a deductive system is mastered.

Scientific Epistemology

Piaget uses a common language for the three domains of intelligence, reality, and knowledge. That language is linked to his view that properties of basic mental structures are chosen during the various interactions with the worlds. These properties are put into play within systems whose role is to serve as cognitive tools for the intellect. The use of structures formed into systems confirms what was apparent throughout our previous treatment of Piaget's three approaches to his psychology. Specifically, his genetic psychology dealt with an intelligence that is restricted to the acquisition of scientific concepts; his genetic epistemology uncovered successive realities that evolve toward a structured universe; and his cognitive psychology showed the emergence of a functional knowledge governed by a rational mind. Undeniably, the common language has to be that of science, and his analysis has to be that of a scientific epistemology. The road is thus opened toward using formal descriptions, or on the contrary searching for the underlying rational makeup of the mind.

A pernicious ambivalence that burdens all of Piaget's terminology comes to the fore when one considers that he is not averse to making use in his language and epistemology of all the conditions just mentioned. For instance, some of the key concepts, such as structure or stage, are theoretical terms with an explanatory role and thus preclude differentiating between formal and genetic constructions. Others describe the actual working of the cognitive process, and this description bears on real synthetic a priori structures toward which he has an ontological commitment. Even though Piaget favors the psychologists' empirical search for the origins of various elements shaping thought processes, his preference is tied to the strong belief that those elements are actions whose interrelationships form a natural structure.

To discover the underlying structures, the psychologist has to dissect the child's verbal explanations. Language, however, is a barrier to be surmounted through the careful perusal of the child's answers under the guidance of various guidelines which eliminate randomness, fantasizing, and suggestibility, so as to establish the genuine discourse. For instance, this particular procedure is most apt to uncover the syncretic, nonsystemic, and inconsistent conceptual base in effect around the age of seven. The selected protocol must reflect a trend of thinking from which imitative and playful vocabulary has been eliminated. Hypotheses guide the questions so as to link them in a total configuration proper to the structure in use at any given level. This is a point that, when misunderstood, has led to misdirected efforts among educators. In fact, several theories of instruction were formulated so as to falsify Piaget's hierarchy of concepts and force accelerated training.[26] In their eagerness, the opposition interpret the same facts according to their theoretical prejudices. Faced with a mistaken answer in, let us say, a conservation study, one faction argues for a lack of transfer between independent items that can be compensated by learning tasks. The Piagetian camp differs, and interprets the mistake as a result of the absence of notions that reflects an incomplete set of interrelated concepts.

The language of the child constitutes a barrier that separates the two sides when it is seen as reflecting a logical model into a scientific rather than a verbal intelligence.[27] It is necessary, for Piaget, to be clinical in order to uncover the underlying concepts. When he engages in dialogues with the child, he follows a set of instructions with the deliberate intent of not making "pure" observations, the most important reason being that if such observations were at all realizable, they would give access to singular events, and consequently one could not "listen" to the child's organized thoughts. Accordingly, if one presupposes grouping ability in a child, then three verifications must precede the final judgment.[28]

1. The child can distinguish between parts and wholes, and can separate their compositions into classes (colligation).

2. The child associates elements in a definite order of hierarchical succession (seriation).
3. The child establishes equivalences under a given property (correspondence).

Piaget directs the dialogue so as to allow the child's behavior to betray the operational thinking that takes verbal, figurative, and enactive forms. He imposes a matching between the protocol space and the internal space.[29] The danger presented by such a position is that only traits fitting the hypothesis will be deemed essential in the dialogues, and make up the protocol, forcing the hypothesis to be immune to empirical tests. But Piaget ignores this danger since he believes that the properties of internalized actions, which make up the system, come out in the behavior of the subjects. These subjects betray their inner working by laying open their groupings, groups, and lattices. Metaphorically speaking, psychologists distinguish the structures in the same manner as ethologists sort out the behavior of beetles.

In an early writing,[30] Piaget restricted the intellectual structures to Boole's laws of thought and because of this identification was predisposed to read into the protocols what sometimes looked like a convenient system. In most cases, this logico-mathematical structure embodies for him not only cognitive, but neurophysiological networks.[31]

The protocol is thus made up of characteristic sentences which as a whole exemplify an "observable" conceptual structure. As an intended interpretation, it corresponds to meaning postulates and not to ostensive definitions.[32] The point bears insisting upon because it discloses that the "real" situation, which serves as an interpretation, gets its meaning from the theoretical terms introduced by Piaget, and not from direct observations. This Piagetian trait often takes the form of a predilection for groups that essentially include complementation-like or negation-like operations. The cognitive correlate is inverted action, which is fundamental for equilibrium and thus necessary for the workings of thinking. Piaget also emphasizes lattices, which, in the substitution arguments of relations, allow for permutation, the concept corresponding to reciprocity of actions. Still pursuing logical properties, it is found that inversion and reciprocity are modalities of reversibility, whose role is central to Piaget's psychology. It represents the possibility of coming back to one's starting point and forces closure upon the intellectual structures. It also has the effect of making the system of actions error free, by limiting mobility by stability. To do so, it uses inversion, which cancels out actions on objects, and reciprocity, which reverses the relations between actions on properties so as to establish some relations of equivalence.

For Piaget, a more general structure has to exist in order to repre-sent the dual aspect of reversibility in operational intelligence. Hence, he points out the need for a grouping system, whose mastery comes about in the concrete stage of the child's development, and which partially synthesizes the relational reciprocity and the set inversion properties. Later, a more encompassing Boolean algebra is mastered by the adolescent.

By now we surmise that for Piaget, a scientific epistemology is much more than a convenient and clarifying instrument. It is the very stuff of which intelligence, knowledge, and reality are made. In a catchall phrase, to know truly is to use intellectual functions formally in order to illuminate some precise realities. In that sense, one better understands Piaget's reluctance to attend to factual results, as so many empiricists such as Maria Montessori are prone to do. Instead, he pursues the logic necessary to build these results and their viability, contained mostly in their consistency and coherence.

It follows that intellectual progress toward more stability extends to both knowledge and reality. Accordingly, since the more advanced structures listed above also have a larger field of application, the domain of ignorance will loom larger. It calls to mind the old adage that the more we know, the more we know that we do not know.[33] This is increasingly relevant, in view of the fact that negations so basic for ignorance cannot be observed, but must be conceived within balanced conceptualizations.

It is to establish these conceptualizations that, throughout his studies, Piaget searched for the genetic filiation of structures. His findings were highlighted by a psychologically inspired basic structure that he named "grouping," and that synthesized the mastery of rela-tions and classes by the child. After that he sequenced some sophisti-cated structures going from the group, semilattice with one inverse operation, ring, substractive lattice, Skolem or implicative lattice, mod-ular lattice, and terminated with the complemented distributive lattice or Boolean algebra.[34]

After uncovering each one of these structures Piaget found them inadequate for the complexity of thinking, and so he searched for another one, thus restarting what one could fathom is a never ending sequence. For instance, the simple lattice was found much richer than the group and did satisfy for a while Piaget's genetic ambition. Then, he judged the mathematical properties of that lattice too poor to express all of the child's cognitive complexity. Specifically, it lacks the reversible aspect of negation, which would be better represented by the complementation operation of a complemented lattice. Finally, in Boolean algebras there appear both the set of all included parts which is characteristic of lattices, and reversibility proper to groups. [35] For Piaget, this last structure embodies all the logical operations that are adequate for adolescent cognition. Nevertheless, throughout his publications Piaget remains ambivalent about this final choice, indulging in what looks like playing favorite to the latest mathematical fashion. For instance, if algebra specialists happen to be favoring lattices over groups as a more satisfactory mother-structure, then he will design experiments to show the priority of chain inclusion over reversibility.

As a matter of fact, his very latest writings testify to that sin as they add a new exemplar to the never-ending sequence. The recent discovery is a structure that best represents the child's ability to compare and establish correspondences, namely, "categories". [36]

Piaget's bias toward logical models is translated into what one must judge as only fairly formal results. I apply this restriction on the grounds that, whereas the conceptual skeleton is well delimited owing to its dual Kantian and Hegelian undercurrents, the logical structure is slighted. That is to say its formalization or extrinsic characterization is minimal, and its axiomatization or intrinsic deductive network is absent. [37]

Although logical purity is not present, I question whether it is proper to reformulate Piaget's work in a more orthodox, formal framework as has been attempted by some scholars. [38] These attempts, which at first seem commendable, suffer from the fundamental misconception that Piaget's cracked monument is in need of repairs. In fact, they betray the spirit of his writings, which was to remain closely descriptive of the real child while avoiding the oppressive rigor and austerity of a formalization that he restricted to a normative epistemology. On the contrary, one can even accuse Piaget of a stubborn psychological bias which did curtail the benefits he could have drawn from a philosophical use of formalization. The various advantages that would have served his work well can be summed up in a concise list:

Formal: consistency, adequacy, completeness, independence, provability, decidability

Semantic: linguistic clarity, conceptual unity, interpretability, modeling, meaningfulness

Methodological: depth, simplicity, elegance, testability, synthesis of subtheory

Epistemological: inclusiveness, coherence, Popperian falsifiability, Goodmanian entrenchment [39]

Despite his lack of rigor, Piaget's scientific bent did push him to seek out logico-mathematical structures and this presents a danger.

Indeed, their properties tend to be attributed to their empirical interpretations, and give rise to excessive claims such as the existence of a
parameter to measure cognitive development.[40]

It seems that the impervious universality of the rationalist is
favored over the halting heterogeneity of the empiricist. For one school
of thought, structures and principles govern psychological functioning; for another, physical and biological correlations are viewed as
restrictive laws. Piaget tries to harmonize these options in successively
promoting them along with his explanations of development. Indeed,
at the onset of intelligence he favors the environment viewed as a
contingent centration of percepts. Then, he exalts the formal aspects of
reason, which he endorses as the most likely progenitor of the
homeostatic terminal stage, so reminiscent for him of biophysical
system. Accordingly, Piaget has come full circle.

KNOWLEDGE AND COGNITION

It stands to reason that to reach the complex system that characterizes
knowledge of the world, there must be tools that can uncover it. For
Piaget, those are cognitive tools that evolve progressively and control
the appearance of various actions on that world. To be in control
means deciding on the flow of activities. For instance, all children
begin by repeating their movements, then adopt a rhythm that often is
a mere to-and-fro motion. They progress to a coordinated set of actions
when one of them traces over the preceding one, thus allowing for
anticipation and corrective feedback. *Cognition then takes on the characteristics of a balanced system, encompassing all intellectual operations.* The
reality built by such an intelligence is not a sum total of abstract
properties, but a complex of transformed phenomena tied together by
actions. These are organized into networks containing either their
inverse, reciprocal, or even their associative match. Thus any mental
state is transformed by selected "logical laws" to reflect a structuring
mind. Reals are strongly conceptual in that they contain elements,
states, and transformations of that structuring mind.

In short, to know is to think; to think is to produce several realities
by transforming them successively. To transform is to operate with the
help of imagined actions that, by interrelations, organize into cognitive
structures. The presence of inverses for each action guarantees closure
to the set formed by these actions, and makes it a structure. It is only by
and within these structures that all real events and their properties can

be engendered. Standard opposition by American psychologists centers on this point.[41]

To know emerges as a presentation of various realities via an organized system of related actions that Piaget calls a scheme. One must note that the scheme is more than a single structure applied to objects. It is a dynamic process that includes the previously successful systems of actions, their actual interplay with the milieu and their transformations under the pressure of diversified conditions. The scheme's existence points to the structural treatment of objects prior to their insertion into an adjusted reality. *Objects must be intellectually processed before they obtain an objective status.*

A weakness in this position can be foreseen due to the ambiguous dualism that reasserts itself constantly throughout Piaget's works. Namely, the object influences the subject directly via its reaction to his actions.[42] It is not clear how one is to register, cognize, compare, interpret, and finally adjust to what is fundamentally a foreign body.

Reverting to the distinction between a scheme and a structure, one can metaphorically interpret the latter as a dome so finely equilibrated that every action is a keystone holding a perception. A scheme, on the other hand, resembles a merry-go-round whose sculptures and canopy are structurally functional when activated by the revolving platform, and only then give rise to action-dominated representations. The static nature of a structure gives access to perceptual facts, while the dynamism of schemes produces events. An interesting conclusion stems from this distinction between scheme and structure, which will turn out to be controversial in later Piagetian treatments. From the difference drawn, it can be seen that a reality is not set on an observational basis, but is framed by the knowing person who neither discovers, represents, nor copies.

Understanding borrows the path of a system of active transformations where the object reveals itself only when it is temporally spread out by actions. Fleeting sense-data have to be tied together by actions to become conscious phenomena.

One can exploit Piaget's outline on the genesis of knowledge to contrast and to position him within a sketchy chronology of classical theories about the use of the intellect. For Plato, understanding simply uses experience as an umbilical cord to revive reality out of one's spirit. Aristotle uses the metaphysical faculties of the soul to understand the universal essence of which objects partake. In St. Thomas Aquinas's works, the stepladder of perception, imagination, intellect, and reason brings understanding when it raises the sensations to the level of universals that fit into a deductive network of properties. Cartesian realism sharpens the dual existential modes of St. Thomas Aquinas and separates image or content from judgment or form. Descartes explains understanding as an intuitive grasp of the principles governing those judgments about contents, with experience only a circumstantial catalyst toward that intuition. It follows that reason is all-powerful and controls the production of reality by framing intellectual copies ultimately guaranteed by God. Realism reappears among empiricists like Locke, who tries to reunite what Descartes separated, and identifies understanding with an induction over sensations that are collated around a postulated physical substance. The final product turns out to be representations that contrast with the rational copies introduced by Descartes. Bishop Berkeley elevates understanding and replaces the physical substratum of all objects by a spiritual one. Lastly, David Hume renounces both physical and spiritual anchorages to rely solely on induction over sensations. However, at the end of this intellectual journey, Hume is unable to bridge the representational gap between the intellect and reality, such as the conscious presence of an external world. In this text, I prove that Piaget bridges that gap by justifying exactly that: objects are consciously present and external to a person.

In line with the mixed heritage sketched above, Piaget chooses, as one of his main leitmotifs, not to reject the notion of representation. He interprets it more narrowly than his predecessors by identifying it with an internalization process. One must be aware that tying representation of the real to internalizing the world is Piaget's way of refining and articulating a philosophical problem within his psychology. Nothing is more indicative of the shift away from a metaphysics than Piaget's cognitive psychology that underlines a scientifically minded subject-object distinction. His formal approach centers around a triple dualism where physical knowledge opposes a logico-mathematical understanding, assimilation is contrasted to accommodation, and mental operation is cut off from imagery.

The first one expresses a two-tiered division at the point of impact with the environment. The subject abstracts at least two vastly different ways to yield knowledge on two levels. The lower level is an empirical abstraction that, out of acting on objects, extracts physical properties such as hardness or liquidity. On a higher plane, a deeper level of knowing is provided by a reflexive abstraction whose role consists of attending to the structures formed by groups of actions. Examples of this type of thinking show up when the child discovers the number of buttons remaining constant despite their various rearrangements, or when he realizes whether or not "some or all flowers of a bunch have been set in a vase." Physical knowledge needs a direct contact with the environment, while the logico-mathematical type is pure reasoning. The physical level gives property contents as a direct result of particular actions, while a further reflection on the actions themselves involves various coordinations which introduce a formal framework characterizing the logico-mathematical comprehension.

The second dualism is more orthodox in that it contrasts the knowing subject who evolves, to the various phenomena that he molds. It means that accommodation denotes the changes in structures, while assimilation reflects the increasing wealth of events modelled by the structures.

In the third dualism, cognition is partitioned into a set of imagined actions on one side, and some iconic fragments on the other. While the former evokes network and structure, the latter group corresponds to percepts conjured up without mutual ties or cohesion. As a matter of fact, the loose imagery is reserved by Piaget for the evocative memory that uses it merely to accompany the cognitive schemes. Disconnected images are representations which, being internalized, constitute means for communication. In that respect it is reminiscent of the role Skinner attributes to emotions or all other phenomena with a mentalistic flavor. Cognitive schemes seem to be in this system the sole effective builders of a coherent reality. Still, Piaget is willing to allot to images a more decisive role than the behaviorists, by inserting them as representational content within the grid of action-based interiorizations.

It is worth insisting that actions do uncover physical properties, but only their intercoordinations create the logical structures proper to a relational, thus objective, determination of the world. *Discovery is an integral part of physical knowledge, and invention remains a consequence of logico-mathematical thinking.*[43]

Cognitive processes have representational, functional, and constructive aspects. By insisting on one or the other, it is cognition or knowledge which is emphasized. On the side of cognitive representations lies the psychological subject, while the epistemic subject constructs knowledge.

The split will often attract those commentators whose allegiance to analytical epistemology forces them to sever psychology completely from epistemology. They restrict the former to an investigation of perceptual phenomena insofar as they are presented, retained, and causally linked. In the second case, they are concerned only with an analysis of the logical status of the concepts corresponding to these very same phenomena.[44]

Piaget seems of two minds regarding this split because he ter-giversates between an analysis of knowledge and the status of various knowledges. Analytic writers will be interested in the analysis. On one hand, he accepts close ties between physical knowledge, representa-tion, and imagery, while also linking logico-mathematical thinking, construction, and concept. Furthermore, as a genetic epistemologist, he proposes that figurative and operative aspects are two ways of interpreting one reality, rather than descriptions of two realities. Hence, he abides by the analytic credo of separating the psychological from the logical domains as far as an analysis of knowledge is con-cerned.

On the other hand, the psychologist in him cannot ignore studies that, for instance, show progress in class inclusion bringing uni-directionally similar improvements in conservation. The obvious generalization is to hold physical abstraction dependent on develop-ment of logical thinking. Based on this filiation, where knowledge is concerned Piaget will be reluctant to admit a divorce between its psychological and epistemological status.

While the theory of knowledge developed in this text will mostly be inspired by this second position, I am reluctant to abide by the conclusion of the first. As a matter of fact, Piaget is besieged through-out his writings by the deleterious effects of splitting his logical from his psychological discourse. Of course, the blame has to rest with his pervasive realism, which blocks him from accepting wholeheartedly the conceptual holism resulting from his theory of action. That realism is evident when Piaget attempts to reconcile the interiorized rationality with the internalized imagery, because, in their own way, they both reflect the world. By the same token, he reveals himself to be a nostal-gic empiricist when subjecting the accumulation of sensorial data to structured thinking. There is something paradoxical in Piaget's relying on the same stop-gap procedures as analytical writers. Having emptied empirical data (sensations, sense-data, perceptions) of all rational features, those philosophers reintroduce them through a logical analysis that, at the same time, places those data in an orga-nized fabric.

The ambivalence stemming from Piaget's realism plagues the coherence of his genetic epistemology on two important fronts. First, there is an incompatibility between the genetic demands of an ever-changing reality that parallels the intellectual development, and the realist prerogative that imposes a hidden world unveiling its physical properties as the subjective curtain is raised. This opposition becomes more pronounced with each new stage because the relevant intellectual structure introduces its own properties. Absence of such properties makes the child neither incomplete nor incompetent before or after their usages at the given level. The child is in charge of a particular reality which is appropriate to his body and to his thinking. Hence, to privilege the adult's reality under the pretext that it represents the true world does seem presumptuous unless one adduces a convergence of both, or some maturing faculties. But, under these conditions, Methuselah would have access to the truest world, and—after 900 years—would be the best commonsense philosopher around.

These last few remarks emphasize the prevalence of the stage-centered view inherent in each phase of the intellectual development and the back seat status of the successive tabloids proffered from without by the world. *The instantaneity of representations tied to abstracted properties of objects is superseded by the extended dynamism of the presentations created within the action grids.* As a preliminary to all empirical observations, these grids filter all that is given, and thus obviate any direct reading of indubitable sense data. The given is never pure, because it is always tainted with properties introduced by the actions of the observer, such as the symmetry appearing in objects distributions. Hence, a reality that fluctuates in accordance with an evolving intellect cannot pretend to be unique and is not charted for discoverers. We must conclude that the distinction offered by Piaget between invention and discovery is commonsensical and somewhat artificial.

On the second front of the ambivalence plaguing Piaget's genetic epistemology a dilemma arises out of the fluctuating boundaries separating the realm of experience from the structured domain of the intellect. When there is an increase in one dominion, the other must decrease proportionately. This implies that the role of thinking is relative and dependent on the chosen epistemological option. As a matter of fact, it is this wavering frontier that has allowed associationists as well as idealists, and even Marxists, to pull the Piagetian coverlet toward them. The primacy given to sensorial data determines various alliances. If data remain corpuscular, then we are amidst phenomenalists.[45] If they are observable within a spatio-temporal frame, then the physicalists will force Piagetian readers to be coherent and to refuse any status other than a logico-mathematical one for perceptions. Piaget himself seems to commend particularly this last position as he has often viewed the object to be built with elastic dimensions that in some cases extend to the whole universe. This means that the object partakes of the properties of space, time, and causality, while it travels from one perceptual scene to another.[46] The approach is not new, and as exemplified by Bertrand Russell's relational theory of knowledge,[47] objects are defined only as much as they partake of the full range of innumerable properties. For instance, to conceive of a pink ribbon, one is aware that it is not green, not blue, and so on. Thus, one must be aware of the full range of colors to attribute a particular one. Russell synthesizes this view by the famous motto that the more an object is detailed from within the less can it be known by an outside observer.

Thoroughly relational with respect to knowledge, Piaget warns us against logical empiricism whose atomic sensory data repel him. In fact, he tells us that in any knowledge of the world perceptual activities supplant perceptions. Inert sense data are allotted epistemological roles. The whole weight of his work of more than fifty years of cognitive studies militates against the primacy and the incorrigibility of sense-data, which is the very backbone of the analytic position.

An epistemological analysis is not only a formal study for Piaget, it is an essential way of determining what is real. And this is possible because reality is identified to the conceptualization of objects. With that in mind, philosophical claims have to be intimately related to cognitive capacities. The conflict is, therefore, very sharp between Piagetian thought and analytical epistemologists. An analysis anchored in the conceptual processes is needed because it is independent of performances and specific populations; it articulates the relative roles of the milieu and the thinking subject, and it details the evolution of the formation of our reality. The epistemologist must seek out the conditions underlying the mutual adaptation of the intellect and the real.[48] To develop a theory of knowledge, a Piagetian expert relies on his cognitive psychology and his genetic epistemology with a special emphasis on the central notion of object.

The selection of the notion of "object" as a basic unit of study is motivated by the cornerstone function it plays in the constitution of our knowledge, and particularly by its key role in the historically fundamental idea of mental representation. However, to yield the notion of object, Piaget sometimes relies on discovery and at other times on invention, thereby betraying his ambiguous philosophical bent, which fluctuates from a relational idealism to a punctual realism. When he embeds objects into space, time, and causality, idealism predominates. Instead of an object-subject opposition, the cognitive schemes progressively set up the object to be localized, not straight ahead like a lighthouse, but more like ripples that precede the bow formed by these schemes. Moreover, objects are not preexisting at some limits to be reached. Instead, schemes insert them in a network of actions which allocate numerous properties and proportionally grant a real status. Assimilation, thus interpreted, claims ownership over objects through its own preferential treatment. The environment interacts with hereditary features by submitting the object to clusters of organized acts such as seeing what is heard, sucking what is seen and touched, and hearing what is grasped and seen. For Piaget, that dependence on activities takes three cognitive forms: a description tying the subject to the object; the conceptualization of a system interacting with its subsystems such as classification or ordering; the formation of a conglomerate of differentiated partial systems and inclusive structures, seen in Piaget's grouping notion.

Of course, the genesis of structured forms closely parallels intellectual development. The child, interacting with the environment, builds up the sequence that defines his intelligence stepwise, and induces his knowing words. Understanding only comes for that which can be cognitively articulated and nothing is prescribed from without which does not have a prior meaning within the intellectual framework.[49] This arbitration by the intellect obviates all surprises and thwarts a meaningful appearance of novelties.

Neither knowledge nor intelligence encourages breaking down or summing up the world, because reality remains undivided within the cognitive schemes. This aspect is appropriately revealed by the infant's universe, which is absolute, contextual, and egocentric. Lest we forget, these characteristics are mainly due to their perceptual dependency, which is indicated by the first form above where subject and object are united. Moreover, it was while impressed by these particularities that Piaget decided to distinguish knowledge sharply from representation. The former is dependent on the progressive organization of actions that does not move normatively toward the better or the perfect, but is a sequence of equilibria between scattered activities and object transformations. The relations between actions become formal thinking when they are cast into structures and thus achieve an internal equilibrium. Representation, by contrast, is always controlled by the milieu and, as a result, is parcelled out as images, gestures, and sentences. In its early form, it manifests itself as the unruly and ill-matched aggregate of imitative deportments.

Piaget, anxious to reconcile the divergence between representation and knowledge, attempts throughout his works to establish some parallel evolution between them. That concern reveals a propensity for seeking explanations which are fundamentally psychological. For instance, he has a cognitive and genetic solution for the child who is able, via his imitational representation, to describe, almost professionally, the geographical features of valleys and mountains. That is surprising because his understanding is naive and succumbs to his idiosyncratic notions of space, time, and causality. At first, the representations, even if apparently sophisticated, are unstable and strongly dependent on figural appearances. In other words, they are still contextual, hence heterogeneous without the integrative support of intellectual structures. An egocentric rigidity anchors these representations in the present and does not relate them together. It explains also the lack of dualism that is tied to the absolute status of any actual scene. Hence, knowledge must wait until the object is polarized relative to the subject.

On a generalized level, perceptually and therefore conceptually fixated, the child does not insert properties into inferential discourses; thus he cannot foresee the transformations of objects which would enable him to identify them through time in the typical conservation stages of genetic psychology. Piaget says as much in a characteristic passage: "A world without object is a universe with no systemic differentiation between subjective and external realities, a world that is consequently 'adualistic.' "[50]

This is testimony of Piaget's realism, that is, his belief that there is a world out there, and although one starts from within to reach it, one ultimately constructs it with its actual features. The dilemma is therefore a problem of separation from one's constructed universe. The world is initially glued to our bodies and indeed we cannot be cognizant of it because there is no immediate presentation, least of all a representation. In short, the infant is essentially egocentric, where egocentrism means the world cannot be seen because it is not at arm's length.

As a matter of fact, Piaget's genetic epistemology can be summed up as a constant flight from egocentrism. A study of how we put the world at arm's length indicates an epistemology where we have to show how the real grows and how it emerges as a constituted body. This signifies that we have to give the conditions under which the entities contained in that reality are to be defined and how they interrelate, namely, a search for the interpreted logic underlying knowledge has to be completed. This is an important point because it emphasizes that a genetic study uncovers the framework of our cognitive universe in ways that may contradict the dictates of common sense. Consequently, it is possible to argue against the proponents of the independence of genetic epistemology from epistemology, who appeal to everyday usages as the source of meanings for their terminology.[51]

The next step in Piaget's genetic epistemology is to maintain that cognition originates at the body's periphery and extends into the world through the use of actions. Beyond Piaget, the corresponding epistemology holds that by internalizing those actions in a conceptual network which, as it turns out, is more and more abstract and removed from the immediate sensorial input, one rebuilds the actual world. The procedure is essentially a gradual adjustment between one's representations and the outcome of encounters with the milieu. Out of this progressive match-up emerges that which is repeated, stable, and permanent.

Earlier discussions presented Piaget as being of two minds regarding the role and the links between physical and logico-mathematical knowledge. The presentation is relevant at this juncture because continuity from one knowledge to the other inheres in the view revealed by the last few lines, but an orthodox Piagetian interpretation emphasizes discontinuity. Specifically, the true knowing process results, not from actions but from coordinations of actions. This means that the object is a result of the coordination of actions rather than an element defining the schemas operating on the world.[52] Moreover, the objectivity of the object will increase proportionally to its insertion in the various structures of actions and will not depend on the activity used to reach it.

Back on the trail leading beyond Piaget's genetic epistemology, one must reconcile a continuously growing knowledge and a discontinuous rational mind. The holding patterns of the latter are shifted to broader understandings by a gradual mastery of invariant features. Those are properties remaining constant under the systematic transformations of actions. and this is what Piaget's genetic epistemology's flight from egocentrism means. In short, the assimilation is functionally at the origin of all permanent fixtures, but constitutes, with accommodation, an immutable reaction to the flux of an everchanging environment.[53]

KNOWLEDGE AND AFFECTIVITY

From the previous remarks, one can pinpoint reasons for Piaget's well publicized disregard for affectivity.

The main one hinges on his shifting affectivity to a marginal role in thought processes. Although affects are essential for the flow of energy that gears the body into motion, they do not structure its ways. Actions are initially impelled by a dynamic self-activity that produces tension if unused and translates into a need when applied to the external world.

Obviously, this view is directly linked to various naturalist theories that emphasized internal needs. Examples abound in the positivism of Auguste Comte and Hans Vaihinger, the behaviorism of Clark Hull, the functionalism of John Dewey and Sigmund Freud, and more recently, the humanistic psychology of Abraham Maslow.[54] The Piagetian version wavers between three themes:

1. There is an innate propensity to act.[55]
2. The behavior is stirred by some energizing forces which vary according to interests, affects, and purposes.[56]
3. Obstacles or deficiencies, relative to the use of cognitive schemes,[57] occasion a felt need to compensate or reequilibrate.[58]

A remark is in order on these three options. For all of them, the motivating character of needs begins as the root of all interest toward objects and at some point indicates a temporary inadequacy of the intellect. In fact, this interpretation is so widely acknowledged in contemporary psychological works that it stands as a paradigm.[59]

The first theme insists on an intrinsic motivational force behind our perpetual need to act.[60] Therefore, affectivity would be the incentive behind our urges to seek out perceptions. One could thus say that needs induce the organism into behaviors that modify our experience. This stands contrary to Skinner's brand of radical behaviorism, which promotes experiences as the modifier of behaviors.[61] In the Piagetian sense, continuous activity permits decentralization and then discovery of common features to be added to one's experience.

There is an obvious resemblance to Vaihinger's positivism,[62] wherein the world confronts the individual with a sequence and coexistence of sense-impressions. Out of these raw data, "things-and-attributes" or "whole-and-parts" are constituted in the "sensation-centers" and become the perceptions (objects, ideas).[63] Other "condensation-of-ideas-chambers" are the center for the summation of perceptions into concepts under the rulings of the identity or contradiction principles. The categorization process, which forms sensations-complexes into general ideas, is pleasurable. Hence, man will seek not things, but occurrences of sensations, because out of sensations pleasure arises through the double "condensation" process. Action rather than knowledge shall be the aim of thinking, since it reaps a vast harvest of sense-impressions. Once he is the possessor of some concepts, man finds pleasure in the activity of the various "condensation-rooms" that apply fictional categories to the sensation-complexes, from which he explains, memorizes, and communicates through a never-ending flux of propositions. Reality refuels him with sense-impressions which he consumes as raw materials and renders into finished products in the form of concepts in accordance with some rule of transformation like coherence or minimal expenditure of energy. These fictional constructs have no reality, but they do have "an ultimate practical coincidence with the existent."[64] Finally, Vaihinger is quite akin to Piaget in maintaining that the permanent coexistence of attributes and the sequential order of sense-impressions betray a coherent, consistent, hence reliable reality.[65] The mechanisms adduced are different, but the inspiration is similar. For one, Piaget saw, in the indolence of Caribbean children, their four-year delay to his conservation tests.[66] With less energy, affective need for activity is lessened, and so is cognitive progress.

If we refer to the three options offered by Piaget, we find that the second theme also splits affectivity from intelligence. It keeps the energizing forces attached to affects but distinct from intellectual acts. So sharp is the break that commentators identify the "cold-blooded" variables attached to intellectual development, and the non-Piagetian "warm-blooded" considerations proper to affects.[67] With Piaget's genetic epistemology, affectivity is an epiphenomenon that accompanies, but does not feature in, the structural stem of the adaptive progression. What remains unclear is whether affectivity provokes cognitive activities or, on the contrary, is a consequence of intellectual progress.

In the first case, affectivity is essential to the setting up of encounters with the environment, but stays independent from their results.[68] For example, to master the conservation of quantity of matter, a child seeks out encounters with length, then width, then thickness, and lastly coordinates all three to obtain invariance. He must be drawn to these dimensions by many encounters and that is the function of affects.

The second case in which the intellect dominates affectivity is an admission that there is a gradual valuation of objects. It grades them in terms of emotions or feelings relative to their increased cognitive status.

Some examples come to mind to illustrate this point. Infants are quite callous about grabbing all kinds of objects, and in particular the toys of their little friends. At a certain level of intellectual development, what is in front of them is not conceived of as being absent from some other place. Hence, grabbing is not taking, because the toy is for him "not not" somewhere else. Affective ties and therefore graciousness do not, at this time, resemble the feelings accompanying "more mature" swiping. Other cases tell us that in order to appraise a situation, awareness of what is presented is not sufficient. One must be able to imagine various other aspects. For instance, feeling happy or depressed depends, as the saying goes, on seeing a bottle half-full or half-empty. Only by a fairly advanced intellect will half the nectar be missed.

Pushing this matter further, one entertains the idea that some affective inhibitions are but cognitive blindness. Above the constant emotional feeling for the self, there are the individualization and conservation of one's own qualities. It is the lack of these last aspects which hinders the appearance of the self in certain cultures.

Piaget reduces the traditional intellectual, emotional, and moral three-fold division into a domineering cognitive control. It shows up when preoperational realism (5–7 year-old child) colors all the child's activities and judgments. That is, psychical processes such as painful experiences are projected into the world and inhabit objects.

It is a basic Piagetian premise that valuations are absolute imperatives that form a moral realism through their intimate attachment to actions or objects. The realism consists in a unidirectional projection of ego-centered norms, which thus grants them an external, substantial reality. The advent of operational thought, with its reversible and closed characters, is translated into reciprocal affective conducts, the progressive outcomes of which call forth equality and justice. The various combinations of the formal level guide morality into hierarchical slots of value scales with all their interpersonal and interindividual affects.[69] Intelligence moves toward the rational, the universal, while affectivity yields the random, the singular. In spite of this opposition, the former modulates the latter.

The familiar criticisms against the intellectualization of all affectivity are mostly directed at the lack of heterogeneous and accidental modalities of development which it presupposes. In fact, its grouping structures have such a normative, linear bias that it reduces the emotional traits to a genotypic evolution. No wonder that the latest Piagetian reflections emphasize a cybernetic format with universal biological determinants.

In the same way, motivation was earlier identified as a need for activities. The organism will seek satisfaction of that need through exercises which disclose a disequilibrium. Therefore the need will fade as a result of a homeostatic process that reestablishes a stable state. This means that if motivation is tied to need, then it characterizes not the individual but the species. Something is obviously amiss, because motivated behavior involves desires, aims, and decisions that appeal to conventions, rules, and reasons for acting properly. It is not the needs of a species that should be dealt with, but the activity of human beings. Instead of a psychological study of motivation and comportment, one must build philosophical arguments around intention and action.

A contradictory argument stems from Piaget's choice for an active need. On the one hand the intensity of various motivations is affected by one's liveliness. The greater the motivation, the more industrious and diversified the performances, and the less intent the care for details.

I am touching here on certain details of learning theories which, through the Yerkes-Dodson hypothesis, form a rejoinder to my comments. This hypothesis tells us that a high motivation does not favor the execution of difficult tasks, and is therefore inversely proportional to intellectual achievements. Thus, if motivation is tied to needs, which in the first alternative is a propensity for activities, then it could run counter to intellectual achievements.

On the other hand, if motivation is dependent on cognitive processes, then the consequences are totally inverted. The very presence of intellectual links between the person and objects imparts affective ties which in turn originate needed deportments which are interpreted as motivational.[70] For instance, if one admits that activities and social intercourse are more numerous with friends than with strangers, then one accepts equally increased affective ties. A ball bouncing far away does not disturb us in the least. But, this ball rolling toward us establishes so many cognitive links that it prods us into kicking it with a surprising urgency. Parents are dearer than strangers to the child, because he has established innumerable cognitive links which translate into affective ties. Constant attention of any kind, even punishing ones, are better than none. Mind you, this could mean that total freedom is an affectively dangerous method of education.

The interesting twist given by those views is that need becomes a means to articulate the mental into the physical and even the physiological.[71] Piaget's position on this point once more reflects a fundamentally biological undercurrent.

In spite of apparent efforts to reduce the distance between need and motivation, the gap between the mental and the physical remains basically flawed.[72] Indeed, need is essentially physiological and is used by analogy in psychology. The satisfaction of a need eschews biological disaster and is thus normative for the species which is genetically programmed. By contrast, individual development follows an asymptotic adaptation to a particular milieu. There appears a profound dichotomy between the satisfaction of needs, hereditarily rooted, and the very activities linked to those needs, which are strongly contextual and incipient to individual development. Hence, motivation is specific to individuals, while need is lawlike and governs species. It ensues that cognitive development could be tied through affects to motivation, but not to need.

The third and latest theme adopted by Piaget merges needs and the process of intellectual evolution.[73] Needs stimulate activities during the arrested state of cognitive functions and schemes, which occur at a period of disequilibrium. In that case, cognitive function refers to assimilation and accommodation, while schemes point to generalized and applied structures. Whenever a disequilibrium of our understanding occurs, it takes the form either of a conflict with the functions or a deficiency of the structures. There follows an attempt to correct the former and to reinforce the latter. To realize this, multiple actions cross over the gap that is encountered. Indeed, a correction demanded by a functional conflict means that alternative ways of acting on the world have to be found and exercised. On the other side, a deficient structure has to be made stronger by incorporating another set of actions that will reinforce the first set. Together they should be able to tackle the environment. Accordingly, the cognitive reaction is to differentiate and to integrate various actions so as to submit a recalcitrant milieu.

The evolving intellect appears, after these remarks, not to be a lifelong endeavor to achieve an ultimate state. If we read Piaget correctly, he is not advocating a teleological maturation, urged on by needs toward a final equilibrium. Rather the emotivo-affective quality of experiences colors those that do not fulfill their immediate goals through actions, but this quality intensifies with the number of blocked actions toward an object. Once again, the greater the contacts, the more feeling in case of a loss. Objects are as valuable as they are known. On that account cognitive progress is betrayed by rich affective ties because it reflects a wealthier set of activities, and not merely a more abstract conceptualization.

To summarize Piaget's position, we see that disequilibrium gives rise to new schemes that immediately need to be activated and applied to various situations, where they will most likely lead anew to perturbations. A search due to a need for equilibrium ensues, thus continuing the process of assimilation of reality. As a result, a dual urge for stability and dynamic creation is at the origin of affective ties with the environment.

KNOWLEDGE AND THEORY OF KNOWLEDGE

Piaget, as described so far, restricts knowing to thinking, where "to think" means to reflect on perceived or imagined actions and their interrelations. In turn, actions establish either various correspondences or transform the given data. This process uncovers permanent features that make up one's developing reality. Thus, knowledge consists in sequentially structured sets of invariant properties. A psychology of knowing describes the various structures and their development. On that basis, a Piagetian theory of knowledge should ascertain the conditions under which the constructed properties and their ensemble sustain claims about the world.

We can now understand his bias toward a scientific epistemology. As a matter of fact, sciences aim to predict, and to achieve that goal they must discover invariant properties. It stands to reason that there must be a convergence between Piaget's uncovering of successive invariants in the development of children's thinking and the constitution of a basic stock of scientific concepts. There is then some rationale for Piaget's insistence that a parallel evolution holds between the genetic constructions and science's discovery of the world. In this instance, epistemology backs up the very existence of a science, that is, the necessary and sufficient conditions for the adequacy of our intellectual tools to give us a reality.[74]

Piaget's efforts in favor of a scientific epistemology, while anathema to hard-nosed philosophers, line him up with positivist writers. And this, in spite of his opposition to Positivism on the grounds that their conception of truth is an absolute one, while his own idea of a truth criterion is to obtain the consensus of scientists.

An historical overview is necessary in order to clarify this issue. Auguste Comte, in his positive philosophy of the sciences, rejected the value of explanation and favored instead the role played by prediction. Hence, the search for causes was useless, while laws or constant correlations were found to be of paramount importance.

Ernst Mach followed the same path, and identified explanation with description. Like Vaihinger, he bypassed the notion of substance with a set of functional relations between sensations.[75] In addition, Ernst Mach held that laws are constant connections between sensations which, as a complete serial description, have the predictive power of science and can replace it. It follows that the aim of the physical sciences should be a complete representation of events as given by the senses. One should not ask "why" about any natural phenomena, because to do so is tantamount to questioning the origin of sensations and thus includes them in a chain of reasoning. This would run counter to the positivistic view that the mind passively awaits the assault of sensations which it relates functionally so as to form concepts. These are concentrated sets of activities which give the conditions for ideal experiments on the functions relating the sensations, such as the utilization of a microscope or chemical manipulations.

Analytic epistemologists are indebted to the positivistic views when they maintain that the production of concepts is strictly within the purview of psychology and not of epistemology.[76]

For instance, Hamlyn's dictum firmly separating epistemology from genetic epistemology stands as a revival of the dogmatism of Comte, who condemned the infringement of metaphysics on the sciences. Whereas Comte rejected metaphysics because of its perpetual search for explanations and its ensuing ontological commitments, Hamlyn objects to genetic epistemology on the grounds that it studies the whys and wherefores of concepts. Moreover, the positivist favors science, which seeks certainty in laws and their predictive verifications, and Hamlyn reduces epistemology to a logical search of the formal consequences of its basic set of ideas. Oddly enough, Hamlyn rejects a scientific subject such as Piaget's genetic epistemology for the same reasons adduced by Comte against metaphysics: they both have the defect of positing an ontology. But they look for certainty in reasonings, one through science, the other through formal epistemology.

Analytic writers facilitate their task somewhat by narrowing the role of a theory of knowledge to the elucidation of problems such as: what is it to have a concept? This question is characterized in a manner reminiscent of logical positivism: it is specific, it calls forth a description, and it hints at a representation. Hence, they ensure for themselves sufficient ground rules to arrive at the certitudes of positivists. "Having a concept" reflects an atomistic possession that is a source of specificity. It also reflects the fact that the ownership has to be represented and shown to be believed, so to speak. Therefore, a descriptive display within a linguistic or a behavioral setting is requested. To ensure specificity, complexity, and even understanding, the adult discourse articulating reality is privileged by this group as representing the only source of knowledge.[77]

Unless one admits that Hamlyn is implicitly sustaining a theory wherein consciousness demands verbalization, his position is weakened by the limiting factors inherent in any language. We are alluding to the logical fact that to impose linguistic criteria on models of the meaning postulates of a language, necessarily implies that some structural properties of the real cannot be expressed in that language; this stems from the fact that language contains universal sentences, that is, lawlike statements.[78]

The descriptive and singular aspects emphasized by Hamlyn are antithetical to the prevalent views in the philosophy of science. Succinctly, man's individual progression toward mastery of the scientific concept of object evolves from a descriptive view to an explanatory position. While sensory features are passively attended to in the original and early apprehensions, the achieved product is an object entwined in a nomological network. However, it is true that the qualitative perceptual processes are very sharply differentiated from the conceptual frameworks, as exemplified in conventionalism, where structures are conveniently but still endogenously superimposed on percepts.

One is forced to conclude that positivism has given birth to two clashing lines of thought. On one side analytical writers, when represented by Hamlyn, refuse to mix the business of philosophy and the sciences, but they do grant philosophy rational priorities. By contrast, Piaget places his faith in a scientific epistemology that is a positivist credo, but opposes Hamlyn's appropriation of all valid claims on the side of a totally distinct philosophical epistemology. As a matter of fact, he rejects the ground rules defined by Hamlyn, regarding viable questions, which must be specific about some descriptions of representations.

Indeed, the very support given to his epistemology by his psychology entails, for Piaget, an opposition to specificity, representation, and description. His psychological studies uncover the successive mastery of invariant features (time, space, conservation). His epistemological analyses show how these features characterize an evolving mind that constructs various realities which all qualify as knowledge (animism, realism). Hence, Piaget's theory of knowledge backs up the claims to particular knowledge of an intelligence that progresses in its relation to the world (egocentrism to rationality). In order to establish contacts with the world, however, intelligence relies on activities, and so a theory of action precedes a theory of knowledge. It is not through an emphasis on singular sensations, but via a global analysis of actions that intelligence can be clarified. It follows that knowledge cannot fall back on sensations without involving actions on the real, and this obviates the dualism necessary for representation and description. Moreover, actions as the basis for all thinking preclude the immediate play of specific encounters.

In his particular theory of knowledge, Piaget asserts that *human action is essential among "real" objects, because it is what relates them and ultimately brings about the objectivity of reality.* In other words, the meeting of the subject with objects cannot be an opportunity for a pure sensorial given. Indeed, it must occur through acts which require a when, how, where, whereto, and wherefrom. Intellectual progress, going from perceptual contingencies to logico-mathematical control, is consonant with an improved abeyance to these constraints. Conversely, it implies that there must be a time when the perceptual contact is direct and results in apperception. This constitutes a paradox in Piaget's Theory of Knowledge, which, on the one hand, defines the real within structures and, on the other hand, under the influence of his scientific realism, concedes that the object is discovered, observed, and even found. Of course, a likely source for this ambiguity is found in a psychology that identifies cognition with knowledge. It indicates an overwhelming control by a structured and structuring intellect. The debate is wide open on that score since cognitive experience is arguably part of and not identical to all of knowledge. A main point of contention touches on constraining our knowledgeable world in the straightjacket of structured thinking, leaving aside all other forms of access to it. It is acceptable from a psychologist's vantage point because his specialty could be simply to list cognitive experiences and study their geneses. But that is too confining for an epistemologist, who determines whether these experiences qualify as knowledge.

Piaget, being first and foremost a psychologist, officially opts for cognition with its straightjacket of logico-mathematical structures. His affinity for their closure, perfect reversibility, and equilibrium forces on him a belief in the mind's power to function like mathematical structures, among which he prefers group, lattice, and category. Since mathematics underlies all sciences, knowledge dominated by structured thinking has to be scientific knowledge. For the same reasons, epistemology is essentially scientific epistemology. However, Piaget foresees complete mastery of structured thinking after a gradual intellectual development. The specifics of such an evolution come out in the cognitive equilibrium which improves with every structure and is successively more formal. Initially, thinking uses all the psychical content which is made up of affective, conative, perceptual, and cognitive phenomena. Little by little what is conceived as objective forfeits emotional aspects such as pain or thirst, intentions, and ephemeral contexts, to be finally left with the formalism of classification, ordering, and quantification. The successive invariants which reflect, at every stage, the permanent features of reality, are less and less tied to percepts. They appear in proportion to the decentration of cognition from what is immediately given by the senses. By contrast, the haphazard nature of what is not preserved as permanent comes from encounters with realities which bathe in subjective experiences.

As a matter of fact, intellectual progress emerges from an experiential abduction that is carried out by lifting the intentional and emotional peels hiding the objective real from the subjective one. The decentration occurs by a shift from the self, polarized around specific experiences that make it unidirectional and unidimensional, to a survey of reality using perceptual posts strung together so as to weave the phenomenal world. That is possible only if one compares mentally two or more experiences, and avoids the hypnotic centering on one percept. Hence, the intellect structures by relating what are originally perceptual experiences. The relations are correspondences or transformations where actions are dynamic guides between mental states.

The shift toward a more pronounced structuralization can be neatly characterized by a typical Piagetian study, the progressive mastering of seriation.[79] Originally presented with a staircase made up by unequal sticks, the child reproduces it only after a chronologically lengthy evolution. Before giving a facsimile, he randomly mixes, couples, and places them in roof-like configurations.

For Piaget, the staircase is reproduced on the double base *of a Lockean perceptual representation or internalization and a Cartesian rational copy or interiorization.* The multiple decentrations on the motor, perceptual, and cognitive levels guide the copy which is sketched from the figural representation. Beginning with a lonely stick imbued with every imaginable quality, the child relies on sensorimotor skills to be made aware of the simultaneous presence of two sticks. Only via a motoric decentration will a trio appear in an organized perceptual field instead of being broken down into isolated percepts. The rooftop form that follows accounts for all sticks as long as they can be dimensionally compared forward and backward, in accordance with a relational order. The semiotic function represents the perceptual aspects of the environment through images. But, based on these perceptions, the individual also organizes variations, transformations, and correspondences. He thus reproduces the same game plan that was played out on the concrete field of direct encounters with the milieu. In short, the schemas where actions are tied to the figurative presence of objects, become the schemes operating in the imaginary world of virtual actions and multiple representations. For instance, the variations of a disappearing object become displacements organized like an algebraic group. The constructed permanence of the object constitutes the invariant parameter "e" of the group. The structural rules gradually organize the originally dispersed elements, ending in a coincidence between the rationally built copy and the perceptual representation.

With the previous example in mind, it is difficult to justify a reality that is met and even opposes one's action.[80] There cannot be a world imposing itself piecemeal from without. Instead, the cognitive schemes within which the real is built are in a more or less stable equilibrium and are disturbed from within, so to speak. As a result, one can explain Piaget's change of mind wherein he had to deviate from his earlier probabilistic stance to embrace a conceptual determinism. Specifically, any perturbation that is relative to an equilibrium state jeopardizes the whole scheme, and thus provokes a reorganization toward a stabler equilibrium. On that account, both accommodation and decentration not only originate in internal conflict, but paradoxically are tied to external sources.

The intellect evolves to consolidate its grip on the world by increasing the structural capacity of its cognitive functions. It performs this feat while widening and tightening the interrelations between properties and actions. The widening results form a differentiation which compensates for some perturbations, and the tightening then dictates all integration of subsequent components into a closed scheme. Hence, a stabler equilibrium means that, following some cognitive conflicts, an opening toward various possible outcomes is laced by necessary linkages between these outcomes. Hence, even in his most recent writing,[81] Piaget foresees final victory for cognition over all of knowledge. The epistemic subject, with universal structures, wins over the psychological subject which is embroiled by singular motivations to achieve successive equilibria. In fact, in order to enter the formal stage a child must master strongly structured systems that control the proportion, correlation, and combinatorial parameters. But these conclusions are the result of tests provided by problems in physics. Left aside are thought processes occurring in natural environments. Through a comparison of properties, behaviors, and schemas in various contexts, new horizons are uncovered. They are then intercoordinated within broader frameworks that contain their transformations. Hence, causal relations that embody those transformations reward the steps toward structuralization. Once again, we are faced with Piaget's bias toward scientific knowledge. As a matter of fact, his genetic studies paradoxically uncover reasonings attached to the "why" of corresponding significations, before the "how" of causal structures, showing that one leads to the other.

Piaget's persistent reliance on science makes one wonder whether he reifies the various concepts appearing in his genetic epistemology. Referring to groups, categories, feedback, and other structural features, can either serve to explain knowledge and its development, or be samples of what is, in fact, presented by the mind. In favor of the explanatory model, some commentators blame Piaget for being out of date,[82] but Piaget himself seems to adopt the reification path since he cannot conceive that what psychologists describe is not really there, and this despite the subject's own conscious failings. Cognition for him is an organizer of knowledge within real schemes. They are the categories used by the procedural thinking which compares established correspondences and achieves success by resolving problems. Alternatively, they autoregulate sets of transformations to present objects in the static mold of structures that match any and all logico-mathematical ones. Piaget is squarely for an integrated stability of cognition which is identifiable with the person's developing knowledge.

There is thus a conflation between all structures whether they come from psychological studies or formal sciences. Gyr is therefore quite justified when he argues that in cognitive psychology the distinction between cognition and knowledge is unwarranted. For him, the set of operations used by cognition determines the real. This real is relative to the agent, rather than something out there to be reached by a behavioristically defined subject.[83] While Piaget accepts the constraint on cognition, as a psychologist with a scientific bent, he is a dualist and will oppose Gyr's second assertion; but—as will be shown in Chapter 3—the semiotics of action, which reflects the hermeneutic side of Piaget, also supports Gyr's conclusion. Interpreted epistemologically, the inclusive unity of action reconciles thought-in-the-mind and object-in-the-world. Of course, we must go beyond Piaget's genetic epistemology to transcend his latent dualism, and frame a holistic theory of knowledge. Specifically, this means that the phenomenal correlations proper to his genetic psychology must be transposed into logical relations between concepts which are sorted out in an epistemology. One must not forget that the discovery that mental structures generate cognition is a psychological option. On the other hand, structured thinking, if progressively constituted, circumscribes conceptual constructivism among the various theories of knowledge.

CHAPTER 2

A Semiotics for Action

INSTINCTUAL DRIVES AND REFLEXES

In this chapter I investigate Piaget's transposition of physiological and biological phenomena into psychological events. I aim to uncover the further translation of these events into notions that sustain an epistemological discourse. A literal reading of Piaget shows a bent toward giving psychological phenomena the scientific straightjacket of biological principles. What is less obvious, but philosophically more meaningful, is the Piagetian disposition to suffuse all physical human activities with psychological traits. In the first instance, Piaget furnishes us with a philosophy of psychology. The second aspect betrays an underlying philosophical psychology. Only this last effort explains how behaviors can be the actions of a person.

Through a critical appraisal of Piaget's use of assimilation and accommodation, the notions of reflex, need, and instinctual drives can be redefined, and Pavlov's reflex arc reevaluated.

Various commentaries on Piaget's works dwell at length on his notions of assimilation and accommodation. These are regarded as the innate functional core of man's intelligence. Their predominance is so pervasive that all of nature exhibits them, and even animal species evolve under their phenotypical influence.

The reflex stage, which spans the first month of a baby's existence, must be considered basic, not because it is the most primitive, or owing to its genetic primacy, but because for Piaget it delimits the boundaries separating instincts and physiological reactions from the first glimmerings of intelligence. Most of the fundamental elements of Piaget's genetic epistemology are elaborated at this stage, since the independent organism confronts its environment for the first time and cognition emerges. The baby, propelled on his own, must exploit his inherited behaviors to survive. To do so, he replaces automatic rhythmical activities by systematic ways of behaving.[1]

The primitive reflexes are traditionally interpreted as independent reactions within the fields of vision, prehension, vocalization, suction, and hearing. The first stage includes the embryonic existence which yields gestalt-like "good forms," such as symmetric reception of sensations by the body. Of note also are the orientations and proximal information about the environment, transmitted by the arm. As a first approximation, it can be assumed that in the newborn infant, his reactions to stimuli impinge indiscriminately on the environment. If no sensations result, these reactive movements are expected to diminish in frequency and ultimately to become obsolete. Hence, the performances reverberate back through their sensorial harvest and in some way influence their future enactments. One can assume an ontogenetic determination for all primitive activities.

Based on these common impressions, a tentative hypothesis, which corresponds to the present-day philosophy of pattern recognition, can be delineated as follows: Stimuli that are responsible for the onset of reflexes are weighed and reweighed as cues relative to environmental conditions. Movements terminate in sensations, otherwise the weighing coefficients are modified. Thus, ultimately unproductive stimuli are disregarded. In short, stimuli that do not pay off lose all significance for the organism and do not instigate further reactions.

The continuous use of particular senses initiates a breakdown of the environment into preferred behavioral patterns. These include proprioceptive Babinskian reactions, which relate to touch-related properties, and suction, which incorporates the outside world within its sensorial modalities. A notable feature stemming from the reactive activities is the division it institutes in the world. For instance, suction brings about a differentiation between suckable and nonsuckable aspects of the environment. According to Piaget,

> The infant assimilates a part of his universe to his sucking to the degree that his initial behavior can be described by saying that for him the world is essentially a thing to be sucked. In short order, this same universe will also become a thing to be looked at, to listen to, and, as soon as his own movements allow, to shake.[2]

The egocentric atmosphere surrounding the child at this stage is suggested interestingly by this passage.

At first, specific stimuli initiate generalized forms of activities such as nesting, sexual behavior, and feeding, which Piaget regards as automatic behavior. Correlative to their occurrence, an inherent diffuseness of the sensorial outcome allows the reflexes to be initiated under varied circumstances. Thereupon the successful conclusion of their performance can be interpreted as a generalization phenomenon relative to the various sensations.

The distance schematically laid out between the onset of the reflex and its result is in turn extended by these various conditions, which, as secondary stimuli, can significantly reset the given reflex. This process is traditionally viewed as a search procedure toward a sensory goal standing at the reflex end, which becomes attached to the reflex itself and not to parts of the world. Thus, "the object sucked is to be conceived not as nourishment for the organism in general, but, so to speak, as aliment for the very activity of sucking."[3] Nevertheless, the overriding interests of the organism are kept alive by the unified searching activity of drives, whose goals are effectively and affectively grounded in basic needs.

This dogged persistence of the reflexes to accomplish their task is the source of recognitory assimilation, from which differentiation later originates. Specifically, any reflex reproduces itself automatically and encompasses within its range the various objects that happen to be there. Little by little, the range of objects spreads so much that instead of generalizations, the reflex introduces distinguishing poles both at the sensorial end and at the onset with the introducing cues. Thus, there begins a differentiation among repeated reflex activities which become progressively acknowledged or recognized. The stimuli which at first were neutral with respect to the repetition of reflexes grow psychologically significant. Sensorial phenomena terminating a reflex, and to which the body reacts, dominate the attention of the child and make up his world.[4]

In Piagetian literature, this whole process is viewed as an adaptation. It means that even though an assimilative schema is put into play, the environment enlarges it so as to open multiple access to the goals of reflexes. For example, by studying the sucking reflex, Piaget delimits a threefold division of assimilation: (a) there is an innate propensity for reenacting reflexes, which is considered to be a repetition or functional assimilation; (b) their successful completion is interpreted psychologically as a recognition; and (c) their occurrences, under various favorable environments, are a generalizing process.

Accommodation of the reflex takes place in the actual processing of the environment; that is, the baby's sucking reflex must transform its physical modalities so as to handle the breast. The organism gets acquainted with the world through repeated usage of its reflexes. These are shaped and defined by the varying characteristics of the milieu. Some are selected and others are abolished.

Prohibitive conditions repress the appearance of some reflexes, while successful encounters favor the repetition of others. These repetitions become reproductions as they reappear under various environmental conditions. It is as though the varied phenomena of nature, having been apprehended by means of a specific movement, are then reduced to a repeated uniform manifestation. The repetitive assimilation can then be tagged a learning behavior, which reflects a functionally adapted sequence of movements together with their sensorial payoff. Repetition represents an adapted structuring with a history of anterior environmental guidance which entails that the regular features of the environment are favored over the exclusive ones. Hence, behavior types take precedence over singular instances, which signifies that even *primitive knowledge is of the general rather than of the particular*.

One must keep in mind that at this level knowing is confined to reflex activities, and is thus tied to the organism's needs or instincts. Furthermore, the environment remains essential to the functional manifestation of these needs. Accordingly, epistemological considerations set the assimilatory tools apart from the physical need satisfaction. Piaget accounts for this dichotomy by reinterpreting Claparede's idea of need, which embodies all biological drives and their psychological correlates. This reinterpretation takes the form of substituting goal-seeking reflexes within the framework of a functioning individual. For Piaget, the basic unit is not a specific reflex. It is a process made up of repetition, drive motivation, and interactions between the person and the environment.

In order to show that Piaget does not hold to innate reflexive behavior, one can go to an orthodox interpretation of his views:

> Piaget assumes that the infant is born as a biological organism with a series of reflexes . . . The following three phylogenetically inherited drives (instinctual behavior) are attributed to the newborn:
> 1. A hunger drive plus a capacity to seek and to utilize food.
> 2. A drive towards a sense of balance. . . . Most important, Piaget considers cognitive development to be autonomous from these organismic drives.
> 3. A drive for independence from, and adaptation to, the environment plus a certain hereditary capacity to gain much independence.[5]

If it is strictly instinct that is being referred to, then this interpretation is surely mistaken, since Piaget's three major instincts are those of survival, reproduction, and nutrition.

A serious ambiguity arises from the almost synonymous use of "reflex" and "drive"; this can be partially traced to early Piaget writings, where no sharp distinction was made. But in later works, guided by his desire to delimit the cognitive role of reflexes, Piaget was able to draw on various modern biological theories to bring the difference into focus.

To sum up, behavior is originally governed by innate and spontaneous activities which subsequently separate into particular acts. No associations or summations of separate reflexes can account for the traits of an overall drive. *It is not by coordination but through specialization of a general behavior that reflexes are engendered.*[6] Hence, the reflex has a history created by the confrontations of the organism with its environment. A general area of activities is delimited by its encounters with the milieu, which, in turn, provokes a differentiation of endogenous behavior into specific reflexes. It is much like perfecting a multipronged tuning fork where the particular tones are gradually wrought out by forging the tines.

The repetitive assimilation operates on particular features of the environment, so that the reflex which it embodies is no more under the control of a need or inner force. But, there is still a complex activity where needs set up goals and determine the strength of the recognitory schema. For instance, there is a difference between sucking various objects while having little or no appetite, and thus repeating the activity with no need, and sucking with a resulting swallowing action due to intense hunger. The sensorial reward is, in the second case, a function of the need and its specific epigenesis.

Following these comments, which reflect my interpretation of Piaget's notions of need, reflex, instinctual drives, and their interrelationships, I question the position taken by some of the most cogent Piagetian scholars.

John Flavell states in his timely study of Piaget:

> The organism simply has to "nourish" his cognitive schemas by repeatedly incorporating reality "aliments" to them, incorporating the environmental "nutriments" which sustain them.[7]

To use "nourish," "aliments," and "nutriments" is, at this juncture, quite an unfortunate literal transposition. These terms do not appropriately describe the role played by reality in the assimilatory process. Assimilation demands environmental guidance for its enactment, not absorption. The structuring activities proper to repetition are functionally set into play by stimuli, but remain internally impervious to them. They are definite ongoing processes that originate in response to the stimulation of external events, and terminate with the internally motivated reflex goals representing the needs of the organism.[8]

In his sophisticated study, Hans Furth asserts that

> spontaneous activity of the living organism that reveals itself in rhythmic, global movements is at the source of reflexes; the innate differentiation of a reflex from global activity does not result in a rigid automatic reaction for itself.[9]

This appeal to "spontaneity" and to "innateness" is misguided, as both terms are antithetical to progressive organization, Piaget's main attribute for mental processes.

In the same vein, the basic misunderstanding of the notion of assimilation leads Henry W. Maier to some erroneous paraphrasing: "The very nature of reflexes, the spontaneous repetition by internal or external stimulation, provides the necessary experience for their maturation."[10]

The use of "spontaneous" is misleading with regard to the notion of repetition, because repetitive assimilation is an organized whole with a formative history that leaves no room for spontaneity. In fact, it is not correct for Maier to use the term "repetition" to translate repetitive assimilation. Instead, he should have leaned toward the word "reproduction," which encompasses within its meaning both repetition *simpliciter* and the occurence of similar recombinations of elements.

Relying on my analyses contained in the preceding pages, and on the criticisms levelled at some of Piaget's commentators, some extrapolations are permissible. Piaget admits to the existence of spontaneous nervous activities that are unprovoked and random. But, against the views offered by Furth and Maier, he maintains that these activities have no epistemological status unless they sensitize the organism to some events. In this case, assimilation is defined as a readiness set up by an endogenous activity to react to privileged stimuli.

One must note that Piaget's writings contain certain inconsistencies. On the one hand he appeals to repetition and spontaneity, and on the other he claims a behavior which is epigenetically organized. To introduce the argument, we should be made aware that in psychology the basic properties of an epigenetic process are inspired from biology.

Hence these properties include a causal requirement that ties the successive states of the process. Furthermore, each state emerges with new qualities, but—more relevant to Piaget's design—the epigenetic growth is stepwise and evolves toward greater organization, differentiation, and complexity.

On both counts of spontaneity and repetition of behaviors, the epigenetic approach does not fit in. Indeed, as shown earlier, repetitive assimilation really means reproduction, which is determined by specific external conditions. Spontaneity, on the other hand, shuns foreign stimulants, and is also adverse to causal ties. Hence, spontaneous repetition introduces discreetness and thus precludes systematization, which is central to epigenetic growth. Another difficulty with holding spontaneous repetition of behaviors, is its ties with a groping theory, or trial-and-error reflexology, within which the environment is separated from the internal world. And that approach would not suffice within Piaget's psychogenesis, whose flavor is caught in the following:

> If the child's own crying was intensified through his failure to differentiate between it and the crying he heard, we have an illustration of the point at which the simple reflex will give rise to reproductive assimilation through incorporation of external elements in the reflex schema. After this point, imitation becomes possible.[11]

To further this emphasis on the syncretic totality formed, it is symptomatic that *reflexes do not become eroded out of disuse, but from misuse.* They must function to earn their obsolescence. A confrontation with reality is necessary to determine their modalities. They could remain intact while not being utilized at all, but their existence would in no way define the individual unless they entered dynamically into his interaction with the environment. Spontaneous production could be hypothesized, since it would allow the organism to check, and periodically to readjust, his inventory of reflexes. But, as part of a total organization, the routing would have to be preprogrammed. Thus, it would be inaccurate to call it an emerging spontaneity. Nevertheless, in support of Piaget's position, we should note that in recalling the allusion to continuous yet random nervous activity which occurs independently of sensorial input, one can plausibly talk of spontaneity.

Finally, one can assert that with respect to reactivization under stimuli or as integrative factors within a schema and the presetting of tactilo-kinesthetic terminals, reflexes qualify as an early form of actions. This view contrasts sharply with the classical Pavlovian reflexology, which can be summarized as follows: Through certain innately determined neurophysiological connections, a stimulus or afferent signal provokes a response or efferent impulse. The conditioned reflex is viewed as a reconnection in a unique functional arc of various stimuli and responses. Both reflexes and conditioned reflexes are therefore considered automatic and inflexible, and this differentiates them totally from the notion of action.

Rather than identify all reflexes as actions, which might be considered forceful, I would prefer to introduce a graduated spectrum among reflexes. This spectrum extends from mere biochemical reactions which proceed directly from innocuous stimuli, to those which are integrated within a cognitive framework. Between these two points, there exist conditioned reflexes which require signalization. But, even more crucial there is the specific behavior whose existence is intimately related to external features. We saw earlier that instinctual drives are realized and reproduced only if they become specific by tuning into environmental conditions. These conditions, under the guise of stimulating sensations, are significant to the respective behaviors, and form a progressive meaningful relationship with them. On that ground, the drives originating out of physiological states, enter the cognitive realm by becoming specific activities or reflexes. In that process, they use the repetitive assimilation which tacks sensations onto them. It is a conceptual interpretation of this phenomena that translates the bond between a reflex activity and a feature in the world as the meaningful relationship. That is, the feature is meaningful to the behavior if there is a concurrent stimulating sensation. For instance, Piaget's examples given earlier construed the child crying out of need as the source of external stimuli for a further reproduction of the crying. The sound of crying becomes significant to the activity of crying and transforms it into a specific reflex. The new linkage forms a reflex schema with meanings an essential ingredient. In Piaget's terms, imitation—as a primitive form of language—appears in the process.

The interesting question looming out of the evolution of an instinctual drive to a reflex, and then going on to become an action, is whether it depends on the birth of a semiotics within the realm of activities. Specifically, one must settle whether the stimuli attached to reflexes have meanings, and, if so, whether we should include them among the cognitive elements. That is the point raised by Piaget when he tells us that there is a whole range of transitional reflexes, going from the purely physiological without meanings per se, to the expressive sensorimotor assimilations.[12]

Piaget is anxious to provide a unified picture of the gradual evolution from reflex to action. Accordingly, he advocates that segmented reflexes, through their repetitions, create conditions favorable for functions, sequences, and intersections. In short, the networks thus constituted originate the action schemas which are fundamental for the later conceptual logic. In addition, one must note that any reflex encompasses some sensations, and conversely any stimulus is permeated with motility. This is why one is dealing with schema and not yet with scheme. Motion always chaperones body sensations, as when one places a sound in the direction of one's gaze.

Sensations resulting from movements are more effective and are ontogenetically prior to static images. Hence, proprioception acquires its meaning within the tactilo-kinesthetic realm. This point should not be minimized, and indeed Piaget often insists that it is a cornerstone for the cognitive build-up. In particular, stark motion does not qualify cognitively without being inserted as a functional member in a totality.

The message is unequivocal; *it states that performance requires competence.* Its interpretation is that a know-how entails an understanding and an overall control exceeds reflexive behavior. One can say that to know a thing, one must be able to grab it, feel it, smell it. In short, one must know how to tangle with it, and not simply be "acquainted" with it in the Russellian sense. This means, with respect to earlier remarks, that mere motion of the limbs, such as pushing or shoving, must be supplemented by sensorial components. These provide the various acts and reflexes with the how, when, where, and what, which constitute an observation. Since a multiplicity of acts is involved, together they form an action schema, which defines the thing within a mental representation or a played out sequence of acts with their concurrent anticipated sensations.

It is worth noticing that in moving from instinctual drives to reflexes and finally to actions, Piaget evolves out of biology to reach the kind of remarks that usually appear in psychology. For fear of being judged impatient, one must exercise caution regarding the distinctions, not only between physiological and cognitive functions, but also between biology and epistemology. It is to Piaget's credit that he realized that this delicate operation cannot be dealt with uniquely through various reductionist theses. In this respect, he is heir to E. Mach and W. James, and a contemporary ally of M. Merleau-Ponty and E. Straus.

What makes Piaget's opposition difficult to read out comes with his underlying systemics, which takes on all the appearance of a reductionist approach. Piaget discovered that homeostatic and homeorhesic principles dominate both cognitive processes and biological interactions between the organism and its environment. The analogy between cognition and biology was extended to the physiological domain where those same principles control cellular constructions. To buttress his analogy, Piaget started with a chronological survey of psychological levels which he hoped could be coerced by some causal relations. His numerous writings report them to be the sequence of genetic psychology: the innate sets; habits; three kinds of circular reactions where the first is mere activism, the second is perceptual goal-seeking, and the third is splitting means from goals; sensorimotor acquaintance; semiotics; instrumentalism; perceptual transformations; coordination between properties. By way of contrast, he later adopted a much more integrated series characteristic of his cognitive psychology, which began with reflexes, sensations, percepts, perceptions; moved on to reflections on the object, objects' properties, action on objects, action on properties of objects. It finally closed with reflections on coordinations between actions.

The bent toward a scientific approach is even more pronounced when Piaget submits these two forms of psychological progressions to the systemic mold of epigenetic growth. To ensure the passage from one mental state to the other, he borrows the notion of regulation from studies of physical systems, and makes sure that it respects the prominent epigenetic features. It regulates a gradual originality brought on by emerging and differentiating new qualities. To do that, regulation is defined as obeying two conditions. The first condition is that schemas are readjusted so as to resist perturbations and stabilize structures. The second condition deals with the equilibrium which is always rectified toward increased adaptation.

To be sure, the dangers presented by Piaget's choice derail his search for an unbroken discourse linking physiology to psychology. Scientific rigor dichotomizes the two domains anew. Inherent in a scientific approach lie the consequences that one is promoting the species over the individual, the universal over the specific, the acontextual over the situational. Even more damaging to Piaget's original stance, the observability criteria of operationalism suffuses all investigations with reductionism. The scientific strategy chosen by Piaget is too rigid to refine the wished-for diminishing disparity between the activations of physiological events and psychological phenomena. Specifically, if one wants to have a psychological rendering of a psychological event, then one should be able to conceive that an event may have *a reason* for its occurrence, but not *its reason*. Psychologically, unless one holds a teleological view throughout, an event is tied by a set of norms to results which are not yet goals. On the scientific side, physical events do not intentionally obey procedural rules, and that takes away two crucial aspects of psychological phenomena.

Above and beyond the identification of phenomena, it is becoming evident that what matters is the setting of a given concept in networks which, by tying it to a multiplicity of additional notions, differentiate the various domains (physical, psychological, philosophical).

With reference to a human being, it is not sufficient to reify a body and a mind because one can identify some of their properties. Out of the complex discourses comes an understanding of his various levels, in the same way as spices or other ingredients assume a gastronomical status when mixed in a dish. To start a psychological argument, it is imperative to show that a person's body is no mere physiological or biological ingredient. It cannot be separated from that person: it cannot be bartered away without destroying his identity; it is not pure spatiality divorced from specific situations where it is loaded with the person's intentions and sensations.

Those requirements are certainly not fulfilled via the scientific leanings of Piaget's philosophy of psychology. To uncover a Piagetian philosophical psychology is intended to close that gap. One step in that direction was accomplished in earlier treatment. There, it was argued that instinctual drives become reflexes when they establish a relationship with stimulating sensations representing real features of the world. Pushing the argument one step further, sensations articulate the psychological person into the physiological body, and thereby movement is converted into activity.

To clarify the issue at hand, it is useful to transpose the physiological and psychological terminology into philosophical notions. With that effort in mind, the body, inhabited by needs, tendencies, reactions, and impulses, gains a mental status through beliefs, meanings, and desires. It is only when physical motion secures goals, coordination, constraints, and intentions that it evolves into a human gesture that is fluid, oriented, efficacious, and acceptable with or without social sanction.

To improve on Piaget's cursory treatment of the distinction between the various domains and mainly between epistemology and genetic epistemology, one must add that as the discourse turns from the causal to the conceptual, the motivation and comportment so familiar in psychology undergo a metamorphosis that yields the intention and action dealt with in philosophy. Through this approach, Piaget's critics should realize that in spite of his scientific bias, there remains a path through which he psychologizes the biological phenomenon which becomes more than an event when it is goal-oriented. In order to bring out this feature of a mental act, one will need to pursue further the previous analysis where, through repetitive assim-

ilation, certain sensations were attached to specific activities or reflexes. Moreover, it can then be argued that consciousness is thus
introduced with its concomitant semiotic network. It prevents an eventual reduction of psychology to physiology.[13] Human predicates de-
lineating conscious experience go far beyond observations about brain
processes, and this should be pushed to the point of discontinuity by
two different discourses.

Nonetheless it is true that Piaget's biological bent hampers any
attempts to isolate the psychological traits from the physiological design. For instance, the overall grid of optimal adaptation is a biological
phenomenon, but the particular properties obtained are a mental
contribution through the flexibility which thought processes impose
on the hereditary behavioral program. Specifically, the genotype carries all the hereditary traits whose specific appearance is effected
through phenotypical interplay. The environment can thereby provoke a psychological disequilibrium.

It is described as a phenotypical perturbation that reverberates
into the genotype only if the environment tunes into one of the organism's random variations. For instance, the child indiscriminately sucks
all objects as if under biological constraints. Subsequently, he discriminates between their properties by varying the interplay between the
hereditary instruments he has at his disposal. The particular variation
that succeeds has to adapt to the environment, and it will be those
specific recognitive schemas which are fastened to touching, looking,
and sucking. Piaget is functional throughout. Indeed, the selectivity of
phenotypical organizations, which reflects the mental side, influences
the biological level of genotypic arrangements. Hence, one is unable to
loosen the individual traits studied by the psychologist from the biological attachment to species-dependent characteristics. As far as philosophical conclusions are concerned, it remains an obstacle to finding
the limits of a person's knowledge.

RELATIONS BETWEEN SENSATIONS AND REFLEXES

Out of the previous section comes the claim that reflexes are the
product of a meaningful relationship between instinctual drives and
features of the world. Three further claims will issue out of the present
section. The first one is that reflexes and more cogently *actions have
meanings which serve to present reality to the individual.* The second one
follows from the first and holds that in terms of development, reflexes
are primitive forms of actions, which are pregnant with all their qual-

ities. The third claim asserts that if philosophical mileage is to be gotten out of Piaget's genetic epistemology, then meanings of actions and their roots in sensations are to be considered all important.

So far I have delineated some of the fundamental tenets on cognitive development that are contained, sometimes explicitly, but more often implicitly, in Piaget's analysis of the reflex mode of the sensorimotor phase.

In order to introduce instinctual drives, it was imperative for a correct reading of Piaget to consider them not as needs to be satisfied, but as overall dynamic thrusts incorporated into reflex schemas, and hence a source of specificity for reflexes proper. The total activity from which reflexes spring obviates the possibility of viewing their emergence as spontaneous. Moreover, to account for reflexes fading out from misuse and not disuse, they must function; first, because both obsolescence and reinforcement defined by usage are antithetical to randomness; and second because there are obvious ways by which those reflexes whose appearance would remain unexplained could be abolished at source.

As reflexes become defined in the very activity of the organism, they acquire their modalities in encounters with reality. Hence it is only when in use that they can be specifically distinguished, or rather, that a meaningful adaptation of the body to its environment can be established and guaranteed. The milieu controls both stimuli significance and obsolescence with respect to instinctual behavior. Indeed, it loses its automatism as it responds to the specifics of the various situations. These modifications are aimed at adjusting the organism more closely to the contours of reality, providing a source of systematization and, ultimately, of adaptation. Thereafter, reality is grasped by means of a set of loosely connected elements, which are remnants of the rigid hereditary drives.

Next, the fluidity resulting from the multiple accommodations has to be consolidated, and this is achieved by a reiteration of newly formed sequences of motions, which Piaget calls repetitive assimilation. Its main effect is to bring regularity and order to the occurrences of phenomena. What is provided therefore is a source of permanency, relative both to sensations and reflexes. Metaphorically, this resembles the orthopedic procedure of rebreaking bones to cement them in the appropriate functional mold.

To recapitulate, the important acquisition is the consolidation of adapted reflexes which stemmed from a reproduction of partial elements of original processes recombined in newly directed ways, and repeatable henceforth.

The various needs that Piaget sees as having the role of some primeval effective mover "sensibilize" the sensorial apparatus so as to prepare a reaction to the required environmental events. These events, in turn, become stimuli whose status as cues varies with the consolidation or obsolescence of the respective reflexes.[14]

As noted, these last two characteristics of reflexes are acquired at the response end. That is to say, the ways in which consolidation or obsolescence may be analyzed depend on the processes occurring at the intersection of the organism and the outside world. This aspect is important to the notion of regulation which is so central in Piaget.

Stimuli, while fulfilling their role as cues, participate in the formation of sensations which are properly the significant indices for the reflexes, and are thus instrumental in shaping their ontogenetic history. Accordingly, movement of the body is dependent on all the senses and is itself reflected in the sensorial domain by the proprioceptive and kinesthetic messages. Asking for the cognitive status of a movement should not be interpreted as a demand for a possible reductionism, but rather as a request for the corresponding sensations which delineate human qualities. In short, the lift is from a mere kinematic event to the realm of psychological acts. To give a cognitive status was also Bruner's aim when he characterized activity as movement that requires the attainment of a goal. As the sequel will show, this is a salient aspect because it claims that action intends through representations by sensations and that intended percepts are modulated by encounters with the milieu. In other words, one senses only what one aims at via one's representations. The endogenous preponderance is obvious in a blind man whose sense of touch overwhelms all sight impressions, even after an operation has restored his sight.

The foregoing details indicate Piaget's understanding of the development of knowledge. It is obvious that he rejects a knowledge that relies uniquely on sensations. Similarly, immediate acquaintance through images or perceptions cannot be retained. The opposite tack is also discarded since mere behavior has no direct representational status, and therefore no cognitive meaning. Piaget's choice is to study how knowledge arises out of the interaction between the behavioral and sensorial fields. Hence, the usual interpretation of Piaget's approach as interactionistic, where the individual interrogates the world, must be transposed into the more specific epistemological view above.

One must carefully delineate the interactions between behavioral and sensorial components to uncover a Piagetian theory of knowledge.

The relation between sensations and reflexes appears complex and is essentially subdivided into three main categories. Firstly, a stimulating sensation is a factor contingently necessary to the onset of the reflex. Secondly, another sensation terminates the motoric end of that reflex where its occurrence determines the next segment of the overall behavior characteristic of the need: suction terminating in wetness will be followed by swallowing. Thirdly, the modalities of an ending sensation refer back to the onset of the reflex, and influence the future of that reflex in the life of the individual concerned. For instance, Piaget states that "in case of hunger, success alone gives meaning to the series of gropings."[15]

We see that sensations are strategically located within a total behavior. As will be shown later, the three possible links between sensations and reflexes are essential to equilibration when they play the same role among actions, but for the time being these very same links have a role to play in the particular existence of individuals. On the comportmental level, any environment carves out the philogenic strain of a human being to produce an adapted ontogenic behavior. It performs such a function by affecting the onset of reflexes. This corresponds, on the biological level, to the genes, which contain the hereditary traits, and which in a given milieu interact with it to result in phenotypical characters.[16]

It is appropriate at this time to introduce a particular terminology to designate the three links tying sensations to reflexes and/or actions. The three terms are the semantics, the pragmatics, and the meaning of an action. Together they define a general semiotics wherein a system of actions can present the constructed reality of a knowledgeable person.

To sum up, the semantics of a language refers to the relations between signs and the denoted universe of objects and connoted properties. The pragmatics describe the relations between a language and its user in terms of the rules governing the applications of that language. Meaning relates the symbol to the cognitive elements such as purpose, intention, or thoughts. These three linguistic features will be utilized to describe the threefold link tying reflexes and/or actions to sensations.

In dividing the relations into the threefold distinctions of semantics, pragmatics, and meaning, I exploit the pioneering labors of C. S. Peirce and C. Morris.[17] For my immediate concern, this framework can unite the dispersed psychological elements.[18]

In building a semiotics, my purpose is fivefold. First and foremost, I am of the opinion that in accordance with the Piagetian message, actions form a semiotics that constitutes a constructive and dynamic conceptual presentation of the world. This function can only be exhibited through a careful articulation of the relations holding between the sensorial and motional segments of behavior. My second aim is to develop the difference of degree rather than of kind between reflex and action, and I conclude that there is a continuous development from one to the other. Thirdly, by elucidating the links tying action to sensation, and by borrowing from the various interpretations of traditional semiotics, more and more facets of Piagetian epigenesis can be expressed. My fourth resolve is to frame Piaget partially within the Peirce–James–Dewey tradition, so as to utilize their linguistic slant for a neo-Piagetian philosophical discourse. My fifth goal is to forge an appropriate framework to bring out Piaget's perpetual shifts between the biological and the psychological domains which, despite his denial, are so Bergsonian in their orientation. These shifts become most prominent when a distinction has to be drawn between figurative and operative thinking.

Having expressed above the orthodox view of semantics, pragmatics, and meaning, it remains to adapt it to a semiotics for the Piagetian concept of action.

In the first instance, a sensation occurring at the onset of a reflex correlates the various stimulating factors and directly determines the existential conditions under which the reflex is to be used. It means that movement and sensations are causally and temporally related. This is properly intended to delimit the action *semantics*.

Secondly, when the reflex actually results in various sensorial occurrences which lead to the resumption of a drive, under normal conditions it fixes the action *pragmatics*.

Lastly, the sensorial confrontations of the organism with the environment are reflected into the modal components of the reflex, in such a manner as to reinforce, diminish, or otherwise modify the aims, sequences, and expectations of future uses. *The meaning* of action is properly characterized under these conditions.

The semantics, pragmatics, and meaning of reflexes are determined by the modifications imposed by nature. These can only be accomplished through the specific exercise of the original instinctual drives that lead the individual out of the accompanying automatism. To my mind, this "environmental fielding" points to a source of cognitive enrichment that is a *generalizing assimilation,* and from its role we can tentatively tag it as a *carrier of meanings*. Pragmatics, on the other hand, can be assimilated to the *recognitory* scheme, which drafts the instrumental features by which reflexes are realized. I will further extrapolate and associate semantics with Piaget's third assimilatory format: the *repetitive scheme*. I will argue later that these tentative identifications are meritoriously gained through the particular role these schemes play toward the construction of the notion of object. For the time being, suffice it to point to their influences over stabilization and permanency, which are primary ingredients of the external world. In some sense, the semiotics related to the schemes represents the child's capacities. It means that the child is able to mentally present regular events which, in a less than accidental way, accompany similar happenings of the world. According to the distinctive schemes identified above, the development of knowledge through the child's capacities is quite systematic and passes by periods of variations, coordinations, and repetitions. It is a role for the generalizing, recogritory, and repetitive assimilations to ensure such progressive stabilization.

One is far removed from a maturationist's point of view. The commentators who view Piaget in that light have not adequately analyzed his interactionism. The functional invariance of assimilation and accommodation is divorced from the permanency of real features constructed out of interactions with the world.

If one is able to intimately link assimilation, under all its forms, to the world's regular features, then one is able to break the absolute idealistic hold of the mind. For Piaget, this means that he is neither a monist, nor a dualist. His theory of knowledge has to take into account the dual but unifying role of the assimilatory schemes and their semiotic capacity. The mind has no choice, by its very function, but to produce a permanent reality.

Those epistemological aspects explain my insistence on finding the ties between Piaget's psychological processes and the role played by the semantics, pragmatics, and meaning of actions.

It should now be clear that the interaction of the environment with the reflexes yields a world that is not aimed at or reached for, but becomes known in a constructive and dualistic fashion. Knowledge of reality is constructive, because the pattern inherited from the instinctual drives provides a frame whose segments remain in disarray within the generalizing assimilation, but which are soon assembled under the recogritory scheme, to be finally consolidated by repetitive assimilation. Also, knowledge of reality is dualistic. On the one hand, nature being the original architect of the hereditary stock, it retains the same role in the breaking and rearranging of these segments; on the other hand, thought processes provide the structural functions and the dynamism that consolidate what we ultimately call our knowledge of the world. For all that, the traditional body-mind dualism appears irrelevant, and Piaget cannot support a representational theory of knowledge. He has to adopt a holistic view. However, to uncover the particulars of this position, it will have to be ascertained whether his biological bias demands a reduction of mind to body, or conversely whether the cognitive interpretation adduced above forces a definition of the body by the mind's attributes.

ADAPTATION AND HABIT

My earlier analyses differentiated instinctual drives from reflexes. They showed that a particular existential status was needed for every reflex. Its inception, repetition, and subsequent modalities demanded orientations which were sensorially grounded in a specific milieu. In other words, in terms of hereditary "montages," preeminence was given to general activities which were reactions to, and only later were directed at, the world through singular reflexes. We also saw that for Piaget, the first transactions of the organism with its environment delimit the functional tools of man's intelligence. These tools consist of the various forms of assimilation that change the instinctual drives into performing reflexes. The choice of the particular performance is interactive and must be possible, not only due to environmental conditions, but more importantly, due to the organism's potential.

The inherent flexibility thus uncovered defines the range of accommodations and, after consolidation of the various behavior patterns, the hereditarily determined adaptations.

The notion of acquired adaptations is very particular, and reflects the gradual coordination of reflexes into an overall scheme of actions. Piaget, the biologist, maintains that there is a gradual neurophysiological transformation that chaperones each and every reflex performance. Piaget, the psychologist, considers that every new form of interaction with the environment is a move toward cognition of the world. Hence, to every new cognitive aspect, there corresponds a physiological element. The biologist remains satisfied by this endogenous construction which he calls a phenocopy. For Piaget, the evolution from hereditary to acquired adaptation is made possible by a dissociation of assimilation from accommodation which at first form one functional unit. The process begins with the various steps described in the previous sections, and is basically the unit formed by an unidirectional access to the real provided by reflexes. These reflexes are cognitively realized within the assimilatory processes, which means that their separate targets have to be sensorial. For example, a tactilo-kinesthetic sensation leads to hardness or softness, while a gustatory one independently proffers sweetness or acidity. At this stage, they do not combine, and hence the various activated senses are completely divided.

Extrapolating Piaget's thought, we realize that the unidirectional access results in undifferentiation which means that a sequential union of assimilation and accommodation achieves a common cognitive end constituted by a specific sensation. All the various components cannot be distinguished because they possess no independent signification relative to the consolidation of reflexes out of the instinctual drives. In Piaget's terms, signifiers and significants are not yet differentiated.

It must be emphasized that the baby's universe is fundamentally dependent on the reflexes at his disposal. The world is subjected to precisely delimited gazes, and, in a general way, that is what assimilation means. On the other hand, the sensorial molds within which that world must be shaped are specified by environmental conditions. The range and characteristics of sensations are selected from among all possible forms by the specific encounters with nature. This can only be obtained through regulatory processes, otherwise called accommodation. The resultant interplay between the organism's range and exogenous selections ultimately achieves an equilibrium which is an adapted organization. In the latter, adaptation points to the permanent recurrence of appropriate sensations, while organization represents the mental, stable totality formed by the union of movements with sensations.

Metaphorically, the development toward stable levels can be viewed as a chess game, where boards and pieces correspond to the basic features in physical and physiological domains. Rules are added, so that strict limits of conduct may be adopted, and the modalities of reflexes are defined on the basis of existing alternatives. Together both aspects result in a regulated and organized game on the board and on the environment. A message transpires out of this metaphor. Even though the physical and regulatory constraints determine the overall activities, the particular conditions surrounding various interactions with the environment provoke individualized behaviors. *Hence, even at the level of reflexes, the organism does not unfold, and the milieu does not impose.*

So far we have not perceived any polarity stemming out of the confrontation of the organism with the world. This absence follows from the intrinsic unity of the reflex whose very functioning calls forth the results. Existence of reflexes comes about because some particular result circumscribes them within an inherited drive. Acquisition at this stage is a consolidation of firmly cemented sensorial experiences that coalesce with the reflex. For Piaget, further progress obtains only because the outside world shapes reflexive activities. It should be noted that interactions are essential to these new developments, and the milieu is just a medium within which the instinctual activities assume specific reflex formats. For example,

> When the child systematically sucks his thumb, no longer due to chance contacts but through coordination between hand and mouth, this may be called acquired accommodation . . . (there is no instinct to suck the thumb), and experience alone explains its formation.[19]

Piaget's operational view of intelligence is surfacing at this level. There has been a shift from mere encounter to directed activity, which is accounted for in Piaget's earlier writings by probabilistic models, but in the more contemporary ones, by deterministic regulatory mechanisms.[20]

On the side of probabilistic treatment, Piaget places the origin of new coordinations with haphazard behaviors. Some of them are sterile and others pay off in interesting sensations. Repetitive assimilation, giving birth to a newly acquired behavior, reproduces only those interesting effects. In subsequent works, Piaget adopts a deterministic approach where coordinations result from regulations. Only compensations for lacunae or conflicts direct the choice for a particular behavior, and the new element has to fit within a systematic activity.

At the level of instinctual drives and to pursue the matter further, Piaget introduces various goals for reflexes so as to explain acquired adaptation. At first the repetitive assimilation consolidates reflexes cast out of drives. Then, the coordinated reflexes are repeated under the guidance of the new sensorial retributions.

The shift has a cognitive meaning because sensations, which had no status to begin with, are slowly separated from the reflexive behavior and this gives them their independence. Tightly cemented to a movement, a sensorial modality belongs and even determines the appropriate reflex, in the same way as the lead enclosed within the wood defines a pencil. The various sensorial modalities introduced via the coordination of reflexes are distinguishable from there. The fact that a reflex can use other reflexes to have access to several sensations is the source of their separation and so of their cognitive status. Again, the pencil is a handy analogy. If it is mechanical and if various colored leads can be inserted, then the lead stands out as a determining feature of the coloring pencil above and beyond the pencil simpliciter. The coloring variety increases the independent importance of the lead relative to its structural support, and in proportion alters the role of the latter one to make it more of a means.

It is worthwhile to notice that the actual exercise of an instinctual drive sets off the adapted reflex. The possibility of combining various reflexes appears thereafter, and this aspect is concurrent with the cognitive birth of sensations. It is in this sense that practice precedes representational intelligence.

The point is important because it foreshadows Piaget's interesting conclusion that explanation trails prediction, which in turn requires practical results. Indeed, he emphasizes this aspect in the later period of his life where success is distinguished from understanding. Later developments will show that the conceptual network or intercoordination of actions, which embodies explanation, brings at its sensorial tail-end the goal-oriented prediction. But, in order to ensure an epistemological expression for the cognitive breakdown between explaining and predicting, *the classical notion of a representation of the world has to be replaced by the idea of a presentation of reality.* This correction is self-evident in the Piagetian system since praxis is closely tied to the intellectual domain. To clarify the matter, let us reconsider the ontogenesis of reflexive behavior. The reflex issued out of an instinctual drive does not include a separate role for sensations since they have no cognitive status. Later, coordinated reflexes multiply access to sensations, and make them, at the same time, cognitively accessible. Their newly found role is to direct behavior and their status is to be anticipated. Those terms are crucial because they indicate a constructed knowledge which in fact means a presented reality. A further message is that knowledge is proportional to the functional configuration of acts with their sensorial aspects. Hence, knowledge is relative to some cognitive level, meaning that it is not something absolute which remains a target to be aimed at by the individual. One can construe that the cognitive schemas anticipate and thus tune in a sensitivity to the surroundings. It will be the role of regulations to ensure a terminal adaptation linked to this sensitivity. On that account, I interpret Piaget to mean that knowledge follows an ontogenic progress toward a heightened "sensibility" to the world. On that score, present day children turn out to be not only more primitive than adults, but cognitively less sophisticated than the original primitive man from paleolithic times. The gist of that remark is to oppose the opinion that ties genetic evolution to thought processes. The individualized process does not accommodate the view that ontogeny recapitulates philogeny. At this stage, one cannot even adduce that this could be done through the processing of an informational legacy.

Indeed, there is no need to appeal to Brunerian representations such as iconic, enactive, and symbolic languages. Instead, one must concede an individualized presentation of reality which anticipates the real. Progress is personalized and dependent on the multifaced interactions between the individual and his milieu. These qualities become obvious in Piagetian type experiments where marginal children swiftly move to a higher cognitive level from the pretest to the posttest. They evolve due to their own experiences and history.

For later reference, let us recapitulate the significant steps alluded to in this section. First, acquisition can be dependent either on the sense organs or on the proprioceptive domain which controls specific activities. Secondly, behavior leads to goals which are those very sensorial attributes that in turn "direct" future actions.

The second developmental phase provides the occasion for the child to recombine or to associate elements of his reflex schemas under environmental pressures. The novelty consists in the fact that the choice is imposed from the outside, and it differs from the automatic variations of the first phase which were but exercises of the hereditary stock. These new schemas tend to be repeated under what Baldwin called "primary circular reaction," and which Piaget associates with the formation of habits. Further particulars of the notion of habit center around its links with some need that must be satisfied. The habit imposes some unity on a sequence of movements because as a whole it tends toward a goal that satisfies the need. In other words, the newly formed associations must integrate within an ongoing schema and cannot simply be a passive copy of reality. The integration is still endogeneous.

There is a genuine construction in the very assimilation of new elements, and this particularity altogether bypasses the notion of a reproduction of reality. Habit, as an early form of intelligence, is identified with full-fledged gestures with their concomitant ends. It cannot be simply a conglomerate of independent movements linking various landmarks imposed from the outside. Actions have to be part of the presentation of reality as carriers of significations relative to that real.

This position is pregnant with momentous consequences, because it leads to epistemological claims. The structural unity, embodied in the presentation of reality, is imposed from within the cognitive process. However, the particular contents which obtain its meaning within acts, originate in the outside world. Thus, it stands to reason that Piaget rejects any trial-and-error theory governing habitual and intelligent behaviors. As we saw above, he borrows the main line of thought from one of his teachers, E. Claparede, who argued that trials are always directed either physically by a need, or psychologically by an "awareness of relations" dependent on some hypothesis.

Raising the issue on the epistemological level means that sensations, on the road to becoming properties, are not simply associated, but are "logically" tied. There is no question of contingent reinforcement; rather there is an imposition of necessity. The structural constraints imposed on coordinated activities establish the relationships between sensations, and thus define their significance. For example, the sight of green grass will be the occasion, not of a collation of "green" with "grass," but of "grass implying green!" More typically, "Pavlov's dog salivates at the sound of a bell, after having heard it at the same time as he saw food, because then the bell 'implies' food." In brief, causation between physical events is replaced by logical relations between concepts when habits are formed.

Piaget resorts to a semantic implication rather than the material implication of propositional logic.[21] In dealing with the claims concerning a child's knowledge, Piaget is not concerned with the satisfaction of a formula in first-order logic. In other words, he will not seek the real world that makes an assertion true in it. The necessity of greenness stems from the activity which, by giving access to grass and to green, conceptually gives birth to both notions and thereby justifies a meaningful entailment between grass and greenness. Coexistence between properties is not yet acceptable. Rather, at this level a constructed real appears with no alternative available. The absence of other possibilities introduces the feeling of a necessity.

The importance of these remarks (which appeared to me in 1975) cannot be minimized because they reflect Piaget's deeply entrenched antiempiricism. He cannot fathom that sensations, originating in sense-data, can abruptly land in the middle of the mind. To belong to thinking, they must be inserted in thought processes and thus gain their credentials. And these credentials mean belonging to cognitive organizations. In Piagetian terms, it means entering via the only door available, that is, via actions. Indeed the only bridge linking the world to cognition is the one formed by those all-domineering actions. This even holds at the earliest level of reflexive activities where instinctual drives become that bridge through their particularization into reflexes. Only then can one hint at the inception of personal control over what were inherited traits. Hence, Piaget in saying that actions or reflexes bestow a cognitive rank to sensations means, for me, that they obtain an epistemological status as properties. Only then can we say that the person is conquering the universal nature that befalls him as a member of the human species. Earlier I had stated that reflexes, on a continuum with actions, were the agency through which the biological being was psychologized. Now, at last the person as a knowledgeable subject can be argued for.

Indeed, not only are needs activating instinctual drives being talked of as psychological motivation, but in turn activities are viewed as governed by the epistemological intention. Going back to our previous discussion on semantical ties between concepts, I am struck that in his latest writings, Piaget reconsiders the development of the notion of necessity. He transfers it from empirical abstraction in his earlier views to reflective abstraction.[22]

What matters for my epistemological interests is his seeming dichotomy between empirical abstraction where contents are extracted directly from experience, and reflective abstraction based on the structural features of actions. From the remarks above, the necessity of semantical implication colors the conceptual level of properties only if there is a cognitive process where sensations are inserted within some activity. Hence, during the early stage of reflexive behavior, meaningfulness requires both reflective and empirical abstractions; but, in a stronger claim, a theory of knowledge where reality must be defined cannot separate these two intellectual functions. To frame a scientific universe is another matter altogether, and for Piaget this means mastering "purified structures."

To be part of an organized process is the way for sensations to be related, and so to be knowledgeable properties. On that ground, Piaget rejects the trial-and-error model because it entails ignorance either of the means to be used or the end to be reached, and prediction is minimal. By contrast, habits, through reliance on needs, must be organized to probe for a goal in order to satisfy them. There is, then, prior to the actual confrontation with the milieu, a systematic sequence that is designed to sift out the results of any activity. The sensations uncovered are necessarily tied together by that very sequence. This is another justification for the earlier argument that the repetitive assimilation represents the reflex semantics constituted by initiating stimulations. Piaget is very explicit on this issue. "Each trial operates on the next, not as channel opening the way to new responses, but as a schema enabling *meanings* to be attributed to subsequent trials."[23] This aspect is crucial, and warrants the further developments given in later sections.

"Grass" or "food," denoting objects, are the end product of a complex action schema. The properties "green" or "sound of a bell" correspond to sensations which are the result of an action. As a consequence, properties are integrated through existential encounters with the world, and their predication is the upshot of a reproduction. With the second part comes the repetitive assimilation whose essential role is to direct the pattern of action schemas. In other words, it is only as part of a preestablished directed activity that the property can be cognitively relevant. We are far from an automatic but nevertheless random concatenation of passive associations.

It is now understandable that any particular sensation has a significant place in an action schema whose semantics converge toward a global concept for objects. Moreover, two crucial roles have been uncovered and both hinge on the all-important assimilation. The first leads to the logical necessity that holds between properties and is essential to the notion of object. The second touches on the orientation of activities toward the world. Piaget has the last word on these two aspects when he asserts that "implication is the internal product of the assimilation that ensures the repetition of the external act."[24]

The assimilatory process is crucial because it intellectualizes the products resulting from encounters with the world. What this means, as we saw above, is that assimilation organizes sensations to give birth to properties. The effect is a construction which is an intellectual product. Conceptualization, which for Piaget is synonymous with interiorization, henceforth limits the object within an organized set of acts together with their sensorial correlates. The restriction applies also to sensations when they are related to one another in the context of these sets. From these, assimilation introduces the conceptualization that establishes logical bonds between sensations *qua* properties and replaces the causal ties of physical events. The gist of such remarks is that whereas sensations belong to the corporeal and the psychological domains, objects and properties are subject to conceptual jurisdiction. Another worthwhile comment is that physiologically as well as psychologically, the notion of object has no status. Only the epistemic subject has access to it.

ASSIMILATION AND ACCOMMODATION

A definite trend appears across the previous sections, and it centers around the crucial importance to be given the relations between movements and sensations. Within the Piagetian system, to determine these relations means to understand the links between the figurative and operative aspects of knowledge, the form and the content of cognition, and also the world and the known reality. However, in an epistemology, the last filiation is the dominant one.

To advance the cause of this understanding, a semiotic dimension is superimposed on reflexive activities so as to pave the way for talking about them in action terms. A strict expression in Piagetian terms only mentions the interplay between signifiers and significants. Being able to differentiate between them is correlative with cognitive development; but, inversely, not to distinguish them is characteristic of primitive thinking. At this early stage, according to some commentators, the signifier, which is causally related or sometimes coincidentally linked to the significant, plays the role of an index attached to it.[25] Later, on, the signifier graduates to the symbolic function of a sign standing for other things.

I have serious misgivings about this interpretation of the semiotic function. In the first place, to posit a signifier standing for a significant is tantamount to admitting a representation of the world. It also introduces a discontinuity between the thing signified and the sign for it. Both consequences are not consistent with Piaget's theory of knowledge. Second, an index which is part of, or causally linked to, an object so as to meaningfully replace that object, presupposes a logical maturity unwarranted at this stage. Thirdly, to account for behavior toward objects by using the simple signifier-significant dichotomy, lacks the necessary semiotic complexity.

A partial treatment of these misgivings is offered by our account of reflexive activities. If it is respectful of Piagetian thinking, then his theory of knowledge might well be at odds with his genetic psychology. So far, in answer to the misgivings above, we may say that Piaget's epistemology supports a notion of reflexive activity where sensation and movement are indissolubly tied.

In turn, the world is only given when presented via this activity as a knowledgeable reality. The index is easily interpreted as any sensation which is the end term of a movement, and part of a behavior. Finally, the trilogy of pragmatics, semantics, and meaning of an act confers enough semiotic complexity to explain its relation to an object. Of course, it is our job to confirm these views by a further analysis of the relations holding between a movement and a sensation.

The main role ascribed by Piaget to the second phase of a child's development is the dissociation of assimilation from accommodation, opening the way to a polarity between the world and the self. The division thus created originates in a new form of repetitive assimilation identified as a "circular reaction," whose main role is to consolidate the infant's own new fruitful activities. That is, the motor segment of drives—meaning the protrusion of the tongue in sucking, or thumb-sucking—is spontaneously activated and, due to its relatively wide range of operations, pays off in new sensations. These become interesting in their own right and are thus superimposed to form regular reflexes. A reproduction of the phenomenon results in a gain via the functional integration of the new product in the overall activity.

Concurrently with the "circular" form of assimilation, Piaget discerns a special type of accommodation that is constrained by the instruments used in reflexive behavior. To begin with, the "circular reactions" consolidate the new sensorial correlates within the semantics or the onset of the motoric side of hereditary drives. Moreover, they settle more firmly the assimilative role of the reflex schemas. By contrast, the new accommodation just mentioned introduces a semantics stemming out of the proprioceptive segments. For example, the sucking baby adopts a favorite posture that later will initiate, on its own, the sucking behavior. Indeed, the kinesthetic sensations concomitant with the posture will belong to the reflex schema and, whenever present, will inaugurate the appropriate deportment.

These acquired and significant relations are not drawn from the environment, nor do they combine the reflexes' schemas; they utilize the sensorial data contained in the assimilatory scheme itself. This development must be regarded seriously, because it will become important in a subsequent analysis of the bases for our cognition of reality. In short, the important lesson to be drawn here is that there are sets of interoceptive attributes which by informing on one's inner sensations are concomitant with the purely mechanical side of a physical motion. Their status as means toward tactile sensations can change drastically, and can replace the latter in the onset or semantics of reflexes and/or actions.

This indicates that relative to knowledge, the body has a similar standing to the environment, and must gradually gain its cognitive status. The body's insertion in the semantics of reflexive activity gives its various conditions (states, tension, etc.) a semiotic role. Hence, such behavioristic favorites as need, satisfaction, and motivation enter the cognitive universe delimited by Piaget when they have interoceptive attributes. Furthermore, and in a stronger form to be seen shortly, they can direct, not only the body's activities, but a person's actions, as part of his semiotics. This point would be my counterargument to J. J. Gibson's claim that "the perceiver does not contribute anything to the act of perception, he simply performs the act."[26] The very condition of the body becoming part of the semiotics of an act, has a direct influence on the kind of activity that is used to interact with the milieu.

To illustrate the details propounded so far, Piaget studied the sucking reflex which struck him as slightly anachronistic. It seemed, relative to its external coordinations, so much more sophisticated than the assimilation and accommodation discussed above. It consists of the mutual integration of the visual and sucking schemata, as exemplified by the suction reaction of the infant on seeing a bottle. On the surface, we have two independent assimilatory modes interacting in such a way that one is meaningful to the other, that is, the visual to the sucking mode. The following two factors will become useful ingredients in our explanatory framework to be developed later on:

1. Intercoordinations of schemata are a source of objectivization because they involve independent behaviors demanding adaptations and interactions.
2. The recognitory assimilation depends in some important sense on the ties linking schemata, and refers to the coordination or interplay of various behaviors, such as touching and grasping.

I shall now describe a paradigm of human activities wherein one can pinpoint the assimilation, accommodation, and organization that constitute acquired adaptation. This will replace the hereditary schemata.

Visual impressions primarily serve the role of sensations for visual reflexes and stand as their own meanings within that particular assimilatory mechanism. Therefore, any object is immersed in the visual act of seeing and is important only insofar as the object is attached to that act.

A dilemma arises out of the autistic atmosphere created by such an interpretation whereby the objective real is not yet defined. Visual schemata have to confront the world *qua* world at some point, and this is brought about when Piaget argues for the cooperation of the generalizing and recognitory assimilations, plus the intercoordination of various schemata. Generalization surges directly out of spontaneous visual scanning which sweeps an extended field of visual impressions. Later, this field breaks down into several tabloids requiring different visual assimilatory schemata: static for permanent objects, slightly oscillatory for slowly moving ones, dynamic for quickly moving or even disappearing things. Above and beyond these oculomotor differentiations we also have qualitative fields such as intensities of light or the color spectrum.

Particular eye movements are directed toward a specific category of visual impressions to be gleaned from the environment, and so characterize "looking" as a purposeful behavior. Thus, the use of schemata encompasses visual impressions within a recognitory assimilation which yields a looking act.

The generalizing behavior is the original source of a subdivision of the visual field, which in turn defines a recognitory assimilation and presages possible coordination among the various visual schemata.

At this point there is still no objectification accompanying visual images, because cooperation between the various behavioral modes, such as grasping or tasting, is nonexistent. A configuration of sensorimotor schemata is a prerequisite for objects and objectives.

The infant coordinates the various schemata in a chronological sequence and thus extends their meaningfulness. That is, the longer the chain of acts, the more sensations are intertwined with movements and the richer the semiotics of that particular behavior. For the looking act, first there is vision and hearing, followed by vision and sucking, then vision, prehension, touch, and kinesthetic impressions.

An explanation is required for the sudden occurrence of these coordinations, since it is obviously an important step in Piaget's genetic epistemology. The shaping of our cognitive universe into a coherent whole depends on these coordinations. Moreover, the links thus established among various schemata clarify the "implication" alluded to earlier, namely, the notion which replaced simple association in conditioned reflexes. Besides, the predictability factor in cognition is touched upon for the first time in the constructive side of the acquisition of semantics by reflexes and/or actions. Specifically, given a property, its ties with other properties must refer to the actions which comprise its coordinated schemata. On the psychological front, this means that one does not visually scan the environment merely to see or to look, but to catch, to push, or to hear.

Reiterating this important step, let me stress that the semantics of an object-word not only brings into play a variety of properties associated with the entity denoted by that word, but also the actions directed at or productive of such properties.

In recapitulating the cognitive elements brought forth by the visual sense, it is found that accommodation, assimilation, adaptation, and organization are prominent throughout. Accommodation schemes are traced to the ability of the visual reflexes to specialize in accordance with the color spectrum, rate of motion, and intensity range proffered by nature. The reinforced attachment of the visual reflexes to any sensations from these fields illustrates some acquired adaptations. Moreover, the specialization is a function of consolidation by repetition, of extension by generalization, and of differentiation by recognition. All in all, these activities represent the three modalities of assimilation.

On the psychological front, it is of note that after their independent stabilization the various visual fields are coordinated and later combined with other schemata such as prehension. This typifies an ever-present cognitive organization that originated in the all-encompassing trend to subordinate nature to the functional needs at play in the instinctual drives. For example, if the infant looks at and hears the same object, thus coordinating the visual, auditory, and postural schemata, it is because he originally tends to look at everything. Thus, he is visually stimulated not only by a noise but equally by auditory gestures of the neck and ears. The cognitive function at play is the generalizing assimilation.

This contiguity of sensations does not result in simple associations, for it is directed by the respectively independent schemata; it leads instead to reciprocal assimilation. Piaget claims that "the child tries, in a sense, to listen to the face, and to look at the voice."[27] Even more to the point, and to counter a proassociation bias where relations are symmetrical, is the fact that the assimilation between various schemata can be unidirectional. For instance, hand movements are closely watched by the child, while the converse is not always true since he can look at moving things without having the hand follow through.

Unfortunately, these reciprocal assimilations are a matter of psychological findings. Piaget does not present us with any satisfactory explanations. Thus, at this significant juncture, where the object begins to exist in its own right and not as a mere appendix to the schemata, we are only presented with psychological reports. His advocacy of a genetic development in the cognitive construction of reality therefore becomes slightly gratuitous. To strengthen the underlying epistemology I propose an analysis based on the semantic, pragmatic, and meaning aspects of action, which I shall pursue in the following sections after having resumed Piaget's psychological findings.

In his survey of prehension, Piaget observed that at one stage of development (1–2 months old), the infant behaves in such a manner that seeing objects does not lead to grasping them, nor does groping bring about sucking. At a later stage (3–4 months old), babies suck objects that are grasped, and grip those held in the mouth.

The child at first exercises his reflexes without special motives: he looks for the sake of seeing, and sucks while rejoicing in the sucking only. Progressive steps are marked by reinforcement of repetition, extension by generalization and its concurrent accommodation, and, lastly, by differentiation through recognitory assimilation.

The evolution to the next phase is dominated by interest in the object itself rather than the activity used to handle it. In order to achieve this shift, the infant coordinates several schemata which at first are simply conjoined singly, and then suddenly synthesized in an overall and total organization reflecting adapted relationships between the various behaviors.

From the analyses presented thus far, it can be summarized that Piaget rejects associationism on the grounds that above and beyond the simple signalling role of one sensation in relation to another, the two sensations are part of a total activity that does not discriminate between them. In fact, his observations indicate that sensations do play this role alternately, and that during the fifth stage of prehension and vision coordination, they act simultaneously as signals to each other.

A stronger argument can be made against associationism by looking at the very functioning of the patterned reflex where the purported "association" fails. Indeed, no association accounts for the directedness of the activity in which the sensation is integrated as a means of fulfilling an end rather than as a signal. Piaget exemplifies this point by denying a simple association between the image of an object and any grasping behavior. Instead, he views the object as the goal to be reached by the grasping reflex, which is to be satisfied by gripping that object. Let us not forget that interoceptive sensations are part of the semiotics and thus tied to other aspects of the object by the concurrent movement. It is in the total assimilative act that an object becomes meaningful, because every property depends ultimately on the act producing it, which in turn relates it to other properties. Or, "the associative transfer presupposes a relation *sui generis* between the act and its result instead of constituting it."[28]

In order to clarify the process by which meaningfulness molds sets of sensations like a cocoon, Piaget introduces some very astute distinctions. From there, one can build a neo-Piagetian position. The continuity inherent in the cognitive growth of all individuals requires integration of new experiences within existing schemata instead of random associations. This is achieved by the various assimilatory tools and their correlative accommodation, as discussed previously. Specifically, actions are directed by their sensorial results, but conversely serve as media for their linkages. According to Piaget the goal-directedness stems initially from need-satisfaction of instinctual drives, which in turn polarize all reflexes toward the organism, thus forcing them to be assimilatory.

The most interesting part is the overt claim that sensations which terminate an act also give it goal-directedness. This becomes even more significant when one considers the prospect that these sensations verify and confirm the new behaviors. This particular aspect will be elaborated later. Yet to be answered is whether or not one can identify the processes responsible for the power by which new sensations are attached to old reflexes, and new reflexive segments tied to established sensations. The first process is an assimilation of the milieu into an activity, and can be exemplified by a child who sucks not just the nipple but knuckles or pacifiers as well. The second process is an accommodation, in that typically the grasp presenting the pacifier varies under environmental constraints so as to merge with the sucking behaviors and their sensorial attributes. This pattern of cognitive activity shows that at the level of sensorimotor activities, assimilation concentrates on the sensorial aspects of an action, while accommodation is based on the motor phase.

So far Piaget has emphasized that since encountering the world is an ongoing activity, then no individual action lends itself to an associationist description, and this on three grounds. First, such a description would have to assume an association between elements extracted from that activity, out of context, so to speak. Secondly, it would not account for repeated stimulus-response sequences, since the observer would have to re-enact identical conditions and thus restrict the field of these activities unduly. Thirdly, the enormous independent variability of both the organism and the environment requires the use of functional relations to be described at all. That role is played by constant behaviors that compartmentalize certain features of the first together with a selection of the second. In turn, the functional relations are controlled, and thus steadied, by the cognitive functions—assimilation and accommodation.

The mutual adaptation, thus proffered, obviates the need for the notion of "affordance" propounded by J. J. Gibson. Eager to reduce knowing to perceiving so as to have an objective knowledge, Gibson uses "affordance" as the ability for objects to offer properties which the organism can afford to perceive.[29]

Piaget opposes Gibson since he cannot accept a direct and immediate access to manageable properties offered by the environment. Instead, Piaget proposes that meaningfulness of sensations obtains via their subjective destiny where they acquire the quality of a property only if they are reached through an action.

The only concession made by Piaget to associationism is to identify the associative transfer with the motor phase of the reflex. This reflects the pressure of the environment to accommodate the organism; learning prompted by external conditions would result from a transfer of known sensations from an old behavior to a new one, such as grasping with one hand or the other. Adverse to associationism for the reasons just listed, Piaget also rejects gestaltism, but for exactly the opposite reasons. We note that nowhere in his system is there room for a gestalt "structure" emerging as a ready-made synthesis of the various sensations. It finally makes sense instead to hold that the world is a tributary of one's activities, while these activities are essentially structured by reality. The objective real is made up of objects whose cognitive status depends on the actions directed at them in assimilation and whose imprints register on these very actions in accommodations.

Piaget goes along with the "total" character of experience and posits a history for it which accounts for the active mutual assimilation of the multiple schemata: the child grips an object and sees it, then all at once looks at the object, the hand, and the grasping of the object by the hand. The whole sequence forms an undifferentiated picture. The visually perceived hand belongs both to the oculomotor effort of the eye and the sensorimotor part of the hand motion. The child is genuinely "looking at grasping."

Assimilation consists of the simultaneous activities of several schemata, each one engrossed in all of its processes and prolonging them for the very satisfaction they give. Ultimately, they merge into each other and form complex configurations.

Here I must part company with Piaget, as he adopts a neurophysiological reductionism, and the terminology he uses—such as total experience or complex configuration—simply denotes the phenomena observed without placing them in a wider explanatory frame. I suspect that under gestalt influence, he is satisfied with an appeal to organization, to totality. These are basic concepts which allow one to grasp the senses of limits, closure, or symmetry, and which may represent for Piaget the very structure of the nervous system. But, unlike gestalt psychology, the mutual assimilation of schemata is neither innate, nor purely in the perceptual domain.

Nevertheless, this reductionism permeates Piaget's cognitive psychology, and weighs on the stable organization of operational thinking. On the other hand, it does not sit well with Piaget's equally crucial dynamic evolution of thought processes. His conviction is so strong that in later works he welcomes any model of the nervous system which can be represented by closed mathematical structures. For instance, McCulloch-Pitts's neural net shown to be isomorphic to a Boolean algebra is, for Piaget, a "momentous discovery."[30] His underlying biological bias makes him more optimistic than is warranted by the still wide-open reductionist theses in psychology.[31]

SEMANTICS AND PRAGMATICS: COGNITIVE INVARIANCE

At the end of the previous section, we noted that Piaget has a propensity to use the language of gestalt psychology. He constantly appeals to a developing totality. It is an unhappy phraseology and does not translate the Piagetian spirit correctly. Hence, I show that the rationale for coordinations of schemata lies in the actions themselves. When one performs a visual act, it is misleading to say that it terminates in visual sense-data, and leave it at that. To begin with, much more than simple visual sense-data exists in an adequate semiotics. Another reason is that it is somewhat hasty to insist that a visual sensation originates the visual act, as other sources can be found.

It is plausible to admit that the stimuli constitutive of a visual sensation proper stem from various sources—ocular, tactile, auditory, need, with their interoceptive correlates—and these constitute the onset or semantics of the visual act, as explained in an earlier development of the subject. With this particular notion in mind, we can say then that the infant not only sees, but looks with his eyes. In other words, the stimuli at the body's periphery are not so discriminatory as to belong exclusively to one sense, or that their ulterior cognitive allegiance remains unique. In that sense, while one sees with his eyes, it becomes reasonable to look with one's hands or ears. I would also hold that this is what is meant when we say that the blind can see. On the empirical front, ordinary textbooks in neurophysiology show my point not to be excessively venturesome!

> Projection to the sensori-cortex is both by pathways concerned with one modality only and by pathways common to a number of different sensations.[32]

As developed in former sections, stimuli become cues toward the formation of sensations that, being the onset of reflexes and/or action, constitute their semantics. The exercise of the behavior is the occasion for the occurrence of another set of stimuli. At this point Piaget introduces the vital requirement that the resultant sensations be matched to the expectant and expected set.

Thereupon, the subsequent segments of the reflexes and/or actions are exercised, using as their onset the stimuli resulting from the previous element. That is, the end result or pragmatics of the original segment becomes the semantics of the following element. One must note that these elements are different acts and that they must interlock to form a chain. The condition is obviously the setting of a comparison between the end of one act and the beginning of the next one. Hence, to have a complex activity, the sensation resulting from one act must match the onset stimulating another act. An interlock can then be well established, indicating that various acts are in the habit of succeeding one another, and thereby form a behavior. In that case, the resulting sensation of an act must match both the habitual result and the onset of some other act. We have then a favorable comparison with an expectant and expected set as required above by Piaget.

I am now able to pursue the matter on a conceptual level and assert that what is recognized can also be viewed as what is repeatable. The assignment of the semantics, which was automatically preestablished in hereditary drives, is now open to acquired adaptation, under environmental influences or, more likely, under the various assimilatory schemata in use at that particular period.

This semantics can be the onset defining exteroceptor or distance receptor modalities, such as the cutaneous, auditory, or ocular. For example, Piaget uses coordination of schemata to explain the mouth sucking all grasped objects and, at a later stage, the hand gripping all sucked things. Furthermore, he relates vision to prehension by accepting that all gestures are prolonged or repeated concurrently with their visual stimulations, and that, vice versa, any movement provokes a steady gaze. Hence, the various sensorial domains are related via some activities. In being repeated, they subsume the multiple spectra, but at the same time use them for their own expansion.

A further cognitive progression shows that for the tactile sensation to be responsible for sucking, it is part of the pragmatics and the semantics of that reflex. Moreover it can, in turn, start a grasping motion by belonging to its semantics. Conversely, a cutaneous stimulus located anywhere on the body will originate sucking following the mechanoreceptor sense-data associated with hand movements.

We may recall that the generalizing assimilation, as the source of cognitive enrichment, extends the conditions under which a reflex and/or action is exercised, and so allows the baby to grasp all seen objects. Moreover, stimuli can participate in several action schemata and, conversely, can combine to promote a unique behavior. Increasing the various attachments between sensations and motor segments, together with their proprioceptive bonds, permits the objects sensed to be perceived. Indeed, instead of a unique sensorial determination, the object gains in objectification by standing at the crossroads of several sensorial pathways.

Piaget considers the coordination of schemata to be a momentous gain toward intellectual development. They represent the source of objectification. In contrast to earlier stages, where an object appeared only as a simple sensation attained by a reflex, the simultaneous sucking, seeing, and grasping provoke the birth of an existential status for it.

A translation of this important point into my semiotic terminology will clarify what still remains ambiguous in Piaget's work. Take for example the visual tracking of hand movements. As a first approximation, one can say that the eye focuses on the hand, whose various movements are successively accompanied by corresponding eye motions. The elements coming into play belong to the visual, tactile, and interoceptive fields of sensation. Their influences at the beginning or at the end of a movement determine their meaningful roles in the realm of actions. In a deeper sense, it is only via these meaningful roles that successive acts interlock and become a "total" behavior.

Visual sensations, which are part of the pragmatics of hand actions, are also associated semantically with the mechanoreceptor aspect of such actions. Conversely, the tactile sensations responsible for hand performances become part of the semantics of oculomotor reactions and engage the eye into following the hand. At first, sensations are elements of recognitory assimilation, then they play a role in repetitive assimilation.

Intersecting assimilative activities are specifically the recognitory and repetitive schemes. The question to be asked at this juncture is: What are the conditions obtaining in the sensations concurrent with some actions which make them recognizable and then repeatable? Answering this question will reflect on our ability to tie together the multiple loose ends exposed in Piaget's explanations, and to build up a neo-Piagetian epistemology. For instance, the brunt of his attacks on the connectionist brand of behaviorism centers around the lack of mental ingredients tying the response to its stimulation. However, the presence of a need which must be satisfied means that any connection between a perception and the ensuing behavior must contain a meaningful relationship with that need.

The loose ends referred to pertain to the exact manner in which meanings penetrate the imposed association of stimulus with a particular response, and that problem will presently be considered.

It is valid to assume that coordinations occur between well-established schemata. Recognition prevails when a cognitive presentation is matched by the actual occurrence of an event. This signals success for a prediction. It follows that in the intellectual realm, recognitory assimilation consists in the fulfilment of sensory expectations. Thus, actions can be adequate instruments to confront reality, because they test and confirm anticipations relative to existing sensations. The matching notion will be analyzed further in later chapters.

If expected sensations are realized through a matching process, then a behavior can resume. In fact, one active segment interlocks with another, and its pragmatics is truly in control. Under these conditions, a common feature braces two acts and is a source of *permanence*. To be sure, the predictive power of recognitory assimilation is an essential ingredient of that permanence. On the other hand, the pragmatics adequacy in relation to reality establishes the set of stimuli as a valid semantics for various reflexes and/or actions. Another effect is that as reflexes expand their realm of activities, they are bound to acquire permanent features as soon as they enter the cognitive world.

These reflexes and/or actions are schemata—hence already successfully repeated—which must necessarily share their semantics in the sense that some *invariances* are delimited. Accordingly, for actions to have a common stimulating onset reflects the person's propensity to uncover the regular attributes of the world. I must insist on the semantic function of the semiotics of action regarding the critical notion of invariance. This means that quasi-logical properties obtain outside of the purely structural schemes of the operative level. Furthermore, stimuli incorporated within recognitory assimilation denote adaptation of the organism to the environment. Equally important, these stimuli single out the relevant and constant features of reality. They then constitute the experiential stock that will guide general activity into specific actions. What stands out at this point are the multiple roles that sensations play once they are enrolled in cognition. They can be part of the semantics of an act, but also belong to the pragmatics of an activity. In the first instance, they restrict a goal-directed movement, while in the second case, they reorient an overall behavior. By partaking in both tasks, the sensations give a definite trend to an activity. It is this transfer from an instrumental role as a means linked with ulterior goals, to the semantics of a directed and repeated action, that defines *cognitive invariance*.

For example, the objects that the hand is able to grasp can also be sucked, with the tactile sensations used as a cognitive invariant in the pragmatics of the grasping reflex and the semantics of sucking. The unspecified and almost accidental occurrence of the first, becomes the pointedly satisfying nature of the second. In like manner, sucked objects are grasped, but curiously enough this occurs much later for the infant. To be consistent, I have to hold the later grasping more situational and goal-oriented than the earlier activity of the same type. As a matter of fact, some of the tactile properties uncovered in sucking liquid, for instance, cannot be carried over into the semantics of grasping motions. These remarks can be extended to the various intercoordinations of schemas, and reasonably justify their appearance on the genetic scale, thus providing Flavell with the explanation he could not come up with when he remarked that "the eye-hand relation lags behind the mouth-hand relation. Although there is no ready logical explanation for this *decalage*."[33]

The significant results stemming from the coordination of actions are that in transposing sets of stimuli from the conclusion to the outset of movements there are cognitive and epistemological consequences. That is, a sensation acknowledged by the recognitory assimilation and resulting from an activity brings into play the repetitive assimilation. The corresponding property is valuable both for the pragmatics and semantics of the actions concerned. It is via the epistemological framework of this last remark that pragmatics underlies the appearance of permanence and semantics that of invariance. Those two notions are vital to the concept of an object and to the conceptual formation of our reality.

It is clear that to express these points, three levels of discourse are needed. In the first, one deals with biological and psychophysical entities like movement, stimuli, and milieu. The second treats such psychological notions as behavior, sensation, and cognitive functions. Lastly, I introduce a semiotics within an epistemological format where action, property, and reality are prominent. The first two domains represent the orthodox Piaget, while the third one is Piagetian in spirit and neo-Piagetian in scope.

Going back to Piaget's writings, we find a curious mixture of cognitive psychology and genetic epistemology. For instance, he asserts that the first stage of children's development lacks intelligent behaviors, because there are as yet no purposeful actions which can be broken down into auxiliary movements reaching for perceptual results. By contrast, this stage views single reflexes as susceptible to radical transformations under the influence of specific agents in the sensorial field. These transformations can generate various cognitive elements which are either the motor means used by the reflex, or the end as constituted by the sensations.

These original forms of activity, reenacted under the impact of appropriate sensations from which they derive their semantics, acquire a habitual character from repetitive assimilation. Therefore, acquisitions at this stage are new sensations, assimilated by the old reflexive schemata, and consolidated by a rearrangement of the motor schemes which reenforce them by repeated behavior. The kinesthetic or proprioceptive information thus obtained can become significant in its own right for more complex sets of actions.

What was at first undifferentiated repetitive play of reflexes attached to discriminated sensations, becomes directed usages, not only to seek, but also to find certain sensations. Only then can we talk of accommodation to the body's structures. For example, the Babinskian reflex is transformed into a grasping motion.

Once the organism ascertains what the world has to offer, it takes an active and self-guided role in manipulating it to its advantage.

Aside from these mental reorganizations of hereditary behaviors, Piaget emphasizes the coordinations between schemata. They assimilate one another, in the sense that the motor phase of one reflex schema takes the sensorial phase of the other as its semantics, and, conversely, the sensation of the second becomes the pragmatics of the first segment.

The child ties the visual and grasping reflexes into a single activity which repetitively handles all seen "objects." He then forms a sequential chain using grasping, seeing, and sucking to bring back toward his mouth all things grasped when seen. The multiple combinations between the tactual, visual, and sensorimotor fields are at the disposal of the infant. As a result of the mutual assimilation of these various domains, the real emerges into an objective entity. On the cognitive level, recognition, which determines the rise of invariance, becomes a polarizing source between the self and the world.

The repetitive, recognitory, and generalizing assimilations are utilized to achieve major progress in the intellectual domain. They extend the realm of sensations via the use of general forms of activity such as moving one's arm, or gazing; but those sensations have a cognitive status only when repeated exercises yield similar results, and are thus established to be an integral part of an action. In particular, it is only after multiple attempts and a proper stabilization in sucking his thumb that the child will have adjusted his facial muscles to yield adequate sucking sensations. New arrangements must be created from the disparate elements supplied by the hereditary drives which in this case is a systematic sucking behavior.[34]

What strikes me regarding the sensorial domain is the sharp distinctions that must be progressively established not only between the various means utilized, but also among the resultants of actions. One cannot assume natural and preexisting schemata, and that is what those experiential distinctions ensure.

In the example above, visual sensations are as messages, part of grasping and also of oculomotor activities; vice versa, to hold an object leads to tactile as well as visual stimulations. The privileges traditionally granted to physiology by virtue of the bonds between the respective sense organs and their sensations do not carry over to cognition. There, the personal touch of new schemata reveals strings of acts and sensations blending various sense modalities. The causal theory of perception is obviously rejected in the Piagetian system.

On that account, an overall picture of cognitive progress emerges. Starting with global instinctual drives, various reflexes are specified through encounters with the environment. Thereafter, activities become more global again. This occurs by generalizing both via the means interchanged and in the results accepted. Prior to a cognition that spreads into distinctive actions, assimilation reigns supreme because no firm schemata can be subjected to environmental pressure and hence accommodation is as yet uncalled for. Consequently (unlike Piaget) I acknowledge no legitimate grounds at this level for a cognitive difference between accommodation and assimilation: both are subordinate to adapted behavior. This is a re-enactment of Piaget's earlier misunderstanding where, in the first stage, global reflexes were not distinctly subject to assimilation and accommodation. The point has been faithfully taken over by commentators who explain that

> a reflex schema is always activated en bloc as a rigid totality. If it can, without alteration, assimilate and accommodate to an object, it does so. But if the properties of the object necessitate some new accommodatory adjustments . . . no adaptation is possible.[35]

To counter such a view, it is sufficient to recall that each reflex has a history, which originates in an instinctual drive. Moreover, to justify that reflexes become obsolete from misuse and not from disuse, there must be an adaptive mechanism.

Piaget's position leads to these misunderstandings because it can be subdivided into opposing assertions. On the one hand, he holds that it is possible, at this early stage, to effect numerous sensations through one sensorimotor act, while conversely attaining a unique sensation via several motor segments. To adopt such a view is to render the sensorial end independent of the mechanical means. On the other hand, he also propounds that reflexes are generated by a need activated at the point of encounter with the world. Adoption of this alternative means that each sensation defines its related reflex, and thus eliminates the independence of the means from the end. It follows that the accommodated motoric segment relative to any specific act must be solidly fastened to its assimilated sensation.

The second conjecture describes acquired reflexive behavior and precedes the first one, which occurs much later on the genetic scale and involves coordinations of actions. Hence, since in the latter case, there is no split of the means from the end, no differentiation between accommodation and assimilation is warranted.

A further ambiguity ensues from Piaget's view that reflexes are sometimes phylogenetically inbred and at other times are subject to ontogenetic development. Obviously the first opinion permits the immediate use of accommodation, but at the same time it allows sudden shifts in schemas occasioned by the replacement of linkages. This viewpoint is associationistic, and thus anathema to Piaget's spirit. Furthermore, this opinion is weakened by the misguided notion that accommodation of motor segments can be "not intended." In fact, they are part of a schema only after consolidation by repetitive assimilation, and the acquisition of sensory goals. *At this stage, therefore, there are no ways for an action to depart suddenly from its original schema without, by the same token, becoming cognitively irrelevant.*

Significantly, these sensory goals direct and thus also, by their occurrence, confirm the adequacy of their respective behaviors. The coordination of various schemata makes it plausible to link various meaningful units by appealing to the appropriate pragmatics. That is, properties belonging to one sensorial area are assimilated to another by becoming the goal of a sensorimotor behavior defined in the latter domain. For example, hardness is looked at or greenness felt. These aspects render conglomerates of sensations impervious to partitioning and are therefore not amenable to an empiricist position based on congruent associations. Since they admit to an ontogenetic development, they also contradict the assumptions of orthodox gestalt theory which maintains that these conglomerates are a priori, homogeneous, perceptual structures and the origin of any cognition. Piaget shifts their formation to the terminal point of cognitive growth, but along the road to that development he admits to the existence of levels where equilibrium denotes a relatively stable schema.

The notion of equilibrium must be further elucidated. For, in appealing to a temporary emerging totality, Piaget, the genetic psychologist, is only labelling a phenomenon, whereas there exist potent arguments to explain it by the mutual assimilations of various schemata. Firstly, specific sense-data qualify as stimuli for various sensorial domains, and can thus be integrated within the respective sensations. Secondly, a sensation that was instrumental in judging the effect of an action can then be used as the onset of another one. Essentially *this means that in order to repeat complex behavior, one must first recognize part of it.* Recognition was found to be the fulfilment of a sensorial expectation, thus providing a source of permanency which, in turn, is the root for predicitons. This latter remark testifies to the adequacy of directed actions onto the world, and justifies their sharing the invariant features uncovered, where invariance is a cognitive property reflecting repeatability of actions.

I am thus inevitably led to posit that, whereas the primary circular reactions are the source of "objectivization," the coordination of actions is the base for "objectification" which is circumscribed unequivocally by permanence and invariance.

CHAPTER 3

The Object:
An Epistemological Study

The object is a focal point in Piaget's psychology. One can wonder whether this privileged status owes anything to the fact that it epitomizes the upshot of his numerous psychogenetic studies, or rather to the fact that it constitutes a traditional cornerstone in all epistemological analyses. In this chapter, I assign responsibilities and, by the same token, cast an introductory light on Piaget's dissent from the empiricist position. His dissent traces a road that leads to knowledge of objects through their presence to one's body. Naturally, I acknowledge by this contention the exclusive role of actions whose nature is, as shown previously, to fasten the sensorial mode to the motor domain. With this in mind, *the body is paramount as long as it can be shown to be that of a person.* Piaget has done just that by identifying a person with his body. The leading point is that a person's consciousness, rather than being restricted to a Cartesian intellect, is shackled to his body through his acts. However, the identification is not complete because Piaget, by shortchanging its intentionality, can be accused of not "psychologizing" biological behavior sufficiently.[1] Of course, if guilt has to be assumed then Piaget is guilty of this omission, because instead of processing the world through the body he relies on a scientific mind whose gestation is ever present. We should fault him for his eagerness to free an abstract world from a person's body. This translates itself by a sorely lacking analysis of one's encounter with the world.

EPISTEMOLOGY AND GENETIC EPISTEMOLOGY

For Piaget, first and foremost, the object is interwoven in the intellectual schemas that attribute to it an enduring substance and its essential steadfast properties.[2] Thus, it depends neither on the indubitable molecular sense-data of phenomenalists, nor on the incorrigible percepts of physicalists. To talk of an object, one can either peel off its prerequisites along developmental lines, or reason out necessary ingredients accordingly, one should sharply differentiate between the logical analyses of various psychological fragments, and the genetic psychology of logical phases. If for Piaget objects are controlled by an epigenetic intelligence, then they must be subject to developments, and not immutable, prior to observations, as the logical empiricists would have us believe. In fact, for him, cognitive frames vary with every level while their functioning remains constant. Opponents of this point of view, including Bruner, cherish fixed mental structures whose uses fluctuate, but in either case one must allocate responsibility for the object's features. The traditional solution is to divide them into form and content, where apodictic and empirical origins are apportioned. In support of Piaget, it is fair to mention that neither environmental control nor innatism is acceptable for him, since the adult is at a loss both to preserve and to promote among others the quaint objects so characteristic of childhood. Quaint objects they are, due to their odd admixtures of space, time and causal makeup. There is no question that a commonsensical adult withdraws his rational support from under the farfetched concoctions of the child. This is where Piaget's acumen is at its best against the commonsense appeal of logical empiricists. They will only consider those features of the world to be worthwhile that appear so to the adult mind, but spoilsport Piaget is ready to envision as worthy toward a theory of knowledge those quaint and even idiosyncratic things done or said by infants.

Using his genetic psychology, Piaget describes the chronology of objects-properties. Within his cognitive psychology, he introduces and uses the functional constancy with which any object is handled so as to unveil its metamorphoses. Finally, through his genetic epistemology, he discovers the successive intellectual structures which change progressively the crucial components of the object. Therefore, presentation of his epistemology, if one can be devised, consists in making claims regarding knowledge of an object, claims that do not necessarily coincide with common sense. To rely on an adult's report about his perception and conception of an object is to grant special privilege to one alternative among many. There are other renderings with their own coherence, and Piaget believes that ontogenetic aspects are relevant to choosing among those alternatives. For instance, common sense dictates that to account for a sighting, visual sensations, causally linked to stimuli in the eye, are the natural and even more strongly the logical claimants. But, earlier analyses offer the alternative claim that whereas physical explanations follow the route just shown, cognitive relevance, which translates into an epistemological claim about properties of objects, suggests that the eye does not have the exclusivity of visual sensations and sensibility.

Still, the following ambiguity remains, which will only be resolved in Chapter Five, when I shall be able to elaborate on the details of intellectual progress. To sum up, the relative equilibrium which stabilizes cognitive structures at each level, settles intelligence into a relatively static mold. This could make it seem that the intellect is autonomous relative to both the milieu and the genetic makeup, particularly for the adult mind and its productions. A dangerous precedent is set if, in a subjective mood, the reality presented by the adult mind is taken as criteria for the world and makes claims about it. Knowledge is then reduced to the view of a "grown up." Indeed, that is the view accepted by empiricists because it embodies "the standard" to which a child is expected to compare his naive perceptions. On the other hand, for Piaget, adult thinking is rational, so perception and memory, which lack reversibility, the trait par excellence of reason, do not define objects. As a result, direct observations lose out to logical constructs. If our reality is constructed, then the world presented by the adult has a history and claims about it have to abide by proposals congruent with the construction. To privilege adults' viewpoints foregoes reference to their ontogenesis and admits all competing plausible claims to knowledge. None is selected, except those profferred by common sense. Thus, the enormous proliferation of "realist" theories of perception. Herein lies an obstinacy which ties all legitimate epistemic notions to grown ups, and refuses dynamic shifts according to age, situation, or person. By contrast, Piaget abundantly illustrates his relativism by using his genetic studies to unfold the semantics of basic concepts. For example, an infant is unable to hold a dialogue until he properly conceives others, and he destroys his sand castles to rebuild them from scratch for lack of proaction and retroaction. Piaget also states that the nearsightedness resulting from the child's egocentrism evolves into the intellectual farsightedness of later years. Claims to knowledge by an adult overseeing the basic notions covered by these examples should be inspired by their heuristic contents: knowing a language and communicating with it entail knowing something about others; to modify something, one must know the past and somewhat the future of that something. Thus, any new knowledge is multidimensional and undifferentiated before gaining "deep" structures. I took some of Piaget's genetic results to pursue epistemological interests. The point is not whether it is momentous or trivial, but rather in what manner examining a sucking baby can help me understand the knowledge that I, as an adult, claim about bottles. Before a scientific mind, engrossed in category or group theories, operates on a conceptualized universe, there are down-to-earth basic constituents to be faced.

On a more substantive level, Piaget maintains that to obtain a legitimate concept of object, the child must progressively master various prerequisite notions such as substance, permanence, externality, independence, and invariance. This terminology reflects his cognitive interests, whereas authors with an analytical bent define material objects in a somewhat different language. For example, Joske gives us the following definitions:

> "Material object(s)" . . . are three dimensional entities, which are composed of matter, bounded by surfaces, exist in public space, perdure through time, behave as manipulable units and possess qualitative complexity.[3]

Garnett, in the typical language of commonsense realism,[4] says of the physical object:

> It can be devoid of any or all of the qualities we find in our sense experience. But it cannot be devoid of the notion of *something*, some characteristic property or quality, that endures and is extended. This "something" must also interact in some ways with other physical things, and these interactions and any other observable characteristics it has must be *publicly* observable, and the enduring extended "something" must exist *independently* of anyone observing it.[5]

Returning to Piaget, it should be noted that the reflex and the primary schemata stages covered in the previous chapter yield results which support the genetic acquisition of the properties mentioned in these quotations. But the analogy stops there, once we discover that these writers postulate a true world that subtends all those properties. Indeed it is not objective reality which dominates any epistemological inquiry, but rather the road toward its determination.

The world gains its trusted status through a relational network that steadies properties within its intercoordinations of actions. The genetic process leading to this world uncovers a specific role for sensations. They are not items in a static conglomerate that stands neutral and independent relative to a perceiver. Rather, they interact with movements to form the dynamic components of both perceptions and the semiotics of action.

This opinion stems from Piaget's refusal to grant to sensation alone an original cognitive relevance which would reduce it to a mere stimulus. It is only as part of an action that it has significance, and enters into the world of real objects. Possible confusion, from a purist point of view, commences when the psychological talk around sensations, perceptions, and environment evolves imperceptibly into a philosophical discourse around properties, objects, and knowledge. Thus, Piaget's position, being rooted in a genetic psychology, has to be translated into an epistemological analysis. This means that an interpretative effort has to be made to justify why objects are mediately defined within the intercoordinations of actions with all the concomitant properties, such as invariance or permanence.

The discussion cannot legitimately be judged irrelevant on the grounds that the modalities of the given are to be resolved in psychology and that epistemology starts from there. In a classical vein, the first domain establishes causal links between phenomena and the second analyzes the conceptual relations tying the corresponding ideas. For example, on the empirical level, looking for an object does not cause it to be found, while, conceptually, to seek implies to find.

For all that, one can argue that even though epistemology does not utilize the roads to the given, it analyzes the status of that given as evidence toward our knowledge of some facts or others. A likely analogy is to be found in propositional logic, which does not determine the truth of its premises by investigating their observational credibility, but only guarantees truth preservation throughout the formal manipulations.

It is crucial to define, not the particulars of that given, but rather which entities are to count as a given. The basic phenomena most accessible to genetic epistemology should guide epistemological analyses and not simply limit various domains given in adult awareness.[6]

Throughout this text, I often echo the basic premise that genetic epistemology has a fundamental role to play in epistemology. It centers around the choice of crucial concepts to be made regarding a contemporary theory of knowledge, around the relativism and pluralism which rightfully mark knowledge, and around the operational meanings which bind all essential notions into a coherent philosophical position. The gist of this last point is that with no profound divisions existing among behaving, thinking, and seeing the world as it is, one cannot assert that the mind inhabits the body. The point is momentous, because if we can justifiably claim that the person, as an agent, unifies his body with his mind, then the behavior described by the biologist and the thought processes studied by the psychologist can be integrated into a knowledge of the world, analysed by the epistemologist. This is the particular sense I give to Piaget's admission that he is a realist in all his three roles as a biologist, a psychologist, and an epistemologist.

Many philosophers of the analytical school oppose such a view, and insist on a complete breach between genetic psychology and epistemology:

> There is no reason in principle, then, why the two subjects, Epistemology and Psychology should have anything to do with one another since the first, when so conceived deals with the logical or a priori problems raised by perception while the latter deals with the empirical facts.[7]

They also emphasize that the traditional role of epistemology has been to allay skeptical doubts by justifying our ordinary claims to knowledge.

This position is acceptable only on the grounds that psychology and, more particularly, genetic epistemology, is a description of the acquisition of the concepts underlying our commonsense beliefs. The way in which these basic notions are acquired is irrelevant to a logical study of their relationships, since it is assumed that the semantics of these concepts is directly accessible to the philosopher through an armchair-type analysis; that is, a careful perusal of ordinary language[8] or of the modes of thinking of common sense[9] will produce the a priori conditions for certain claims. Piaget in a cynical tone opposes such inroads into the cognitive realms, by accusing the analytical philosophers of gratuitous reconstructions. He also argues that, by granting common sense profound insight into thought processes, philosophers extend expertise to almost everybody, and this is presumptuous.[10]

One can argue that a genetic epistemology does not guarantee that common sense is the right reference level, but may offer alternative conceptual networks. Those networks in turn can only uncover their logic through a redistribution of the respective semantic roles that the concepts play toward one another. The epistemology then cannot be dissociated in fact, but can be separated in principle, from the genetic epistemology which offers alternative positions.

Piaget offers such an alternative. His genetic epistemology does not result in an epistemology based on common sense. By contrast, Ayer presents the view that epistemology begins where psychology ends because epistemology treats only our claims to knowledge.[11] He offers two logical paths to these claims: the hypothetico-deductive and the inductive. Starting with some premises, one asserts knowledge of some conclusions obtained from them; that is, sensations, as given, form the foundation for our knowledge of objects. Along the second path, objects have properties above and beyond what is obtained from sensations. Hence, it is not through a deduction that we have knowledge of them; but the jump from sensations to the existence of objects is not a qualified inductive step. It follows, says Ayer, that owing to our inability to anchor our claim to knowledge either inductively or deductively, there cannot be any such claim. Hence, there is a gap between knowledge and a theory of knowledge.

The logical gap delineated is bridged by three other epistemological schools. Intuitionism asserts that human beings have the power to reach objects directly. Logical constructivism argues that objects can be reduced through definitions or reduction sentences to sense-data sentences. Finally, representationalism finds lawlike links between sensations and their objective causes in the external world. The induction process is accepted as reasonable by these three schools. Indeed, they confer on all claims to knowledge the privilege of initiating their evidence with incorrigible mental events.

In his genetic epistemology, Piaget does establish the status of such evidence. Yet in the process he finds that the claims to knowledge are directly based on the cognitive relevance granted to these so-called givens, hence partially vindicating G. E. Moore's direct-access-to-the-world argument.[12]

Searching for that elusive given, Piaget seems to locate it in the conflation between the motoric and sensorial elements of actions. From earlier analysis we have seen that a completely different interpretation must be given, which is Piagetian in spirit, but not literally expressed in his writings. In fact, while one must pry in his cognitive psychology to identify the various functions operating within thought processes, it is imperative to transcend his genetic epistemology to establish how the given becomes a viable reality. A semiotics of action, not explicitly found in Piaget, is essential to any understanding of how a theory of knowledge can be based on his work. For instance, if one wishes to include sensations as part of knowledge, one has to realize their role in cognition and the part they play in actions on the world. Specifically, the cognitive relevance of a sensation is not to be found at the end of an action. For it to enter cognition, it has to be either within the meanings of one single act, or belong to the pragmatics and semantics of a complex activity. In terms of knowledge, the world only appears as presented within the expectation of an action or as articulated in the intercoordination of actions. The latter condition is a source of stability and permanence. In short, intercoordination of actions is the proper locus for objects. Hence, a Piagetian epistemology rejects any immediate given. Cognitive relevance, giving birth to consciousness, obtains only within a conceptualization.

The position is comprehensible within the broader scheme of

Piaget's view of the world and of man in it. It should not be forgotten that a historical setting for genetic epistemology is presupposed. Man had to develop in order to survive. His intellectual tools are subservient to that goal. At present, the man we are dealing with is the final product of a successful mutational branching, as opposed to one of the arrested stems which were not adapted to their environment. This aspect explains Piaget's insistence that intelligence is an adaptation. It follows then, that survival demands action on the environment, and hence correct prediction must ensue, which in turn entails a permanent world. Thus, intelligence has to look for and discover the *invariants* in the world that are instrumental in man's survival. Short of that, it is totally gratuitous for Piaget to elaborate a theory of knowledge.

Against this background, the proponents of the world as merely given are contrastingly "ahistorical." They seem to plump man into the world, where he attends to mirroring his environment. Notwithstanding their empirical allegiance, one senses a remnant of theological determinism.

The evolutional conceptualism presented in the previous paragraph explains Piaget's accusations against the proponents of empiricism, realism, and a priorism. His main objection decries their persistence to posit thought as anterior to acting.[13] This brings to mind Furth's conclusion to the effect that Piaget's position is a reaction against the traditional mediation to knowledge of the world by internal representations.[14] Knowing, by contrast, is defined, in a Piagetian conceptualism, within the encounters with the environment. This view about knowledge opposes totally a copy of the world presented within a Cartesian dualism.[15] The radical criticism levelled by Piaget may be likened to G. E. Moore's brutal reaction against both idealism and sense-data constructivism; but Piaget relies on an elaborate genetic epistemology, while Moore is quick to pledge blind allegiance to common sense. Piaget organizes the coherence and stability of the world within the conceptual process, thus obviating altogether the Berkeleyan's refuge in God;[16] but, in an important contemporary about-face, he rejuvenates the mental predicates prohibited since Hume shrank the class of indubitable entities to mere sensations.[17]

PIAGET'S CONCEPTUALISM

Piaget's view is that the role of recognition stands foremost in the acquisition of the notion of permanence, and that it stabilizes the environment into partitioned sets of sensations which are pictures for the occasion. Specifying the nature of that recognition becomes a problem, since Piaget rejects as genetically premature, and experimentally unsupported, the associationistic hypothesis of a mental image evoked whenever the corresponding sensation occurs. He turns for help to action schemas when he asserts that "for recognition to begin, it is enough that the attitude previously adopted with regard to the thing be again set in motion and that nothing in the new perception thwart that process."[18]

To fulfill the promises contained in this quotation, it is appropriate to recall my interpretation of recognitory assimilation. It incorporates sensations within the pragmatics of actions whenever these latter match the expected ones, and henceforth lead the behavior to resume. This aspect is aptly exemplified by the hungry baby setting himself up in a posture encompassing certain sensorial expectations. The lips sensing milk and the gratified stomach constitute the recognition that leads to the resumption of the sucking behavior. I must insist on this interpretation of Piaget's recognition because it surprisingly indicates an inside track to behaviorism. Indeed, attitude can be defined as a predisposition to behave in certain ways. Of course, mental correlation would require, behind the predisposition, a system of values underlying various beliefs about some situation. Notwithstanding the fact that the mental aspect is not called for here, the disposition to behave means a posture accompanying the presence of objects provoking the given attitude. In turn, the posture puts into play various interoceptive stimuli that enter into the semantics and pragmatics of various acts. Thereafter, recognitory assimilation can play its main role.[19] If conditions are ripe, anticipations are matched with predisposed attitudes and the appropriate behavior resumes.

This framework points to Piaget's notion of recognition which is especially tied to the fulfilment of actions. Of course, the realization is possible only as long as action's anticipations are not impeded, thereby not requiring accommodation which would operate within a generalizing schema. He openly advances these points in the remark that

> assimilation becomes "recognitory"; that is to say, perception of objects . . . as a function of the multiple activities delineated by the generalizing assimilation. Therein resides a first principle of exteriorization. . . .[20]

The possibility that actions be impeded imposes a thwarting potential on the sensory part of actions rather than on movements per se. It has to be so on the cognitive level since signification comes with sensations, and Piaget locates "attitude" in their interoceptive counter-parts. Indeed, the use of the notion of attitude points to the endoge-nous origin of sensations, and more importantly introduces continuity and even acquaintance with things to come. Once again, we notice that the child's action extends in his personal history. In point of fact, recognition is first established in the activity itself, thus transcending the level of a random reaction to the world.

I consider Piaget's appeal to "attitude" to be significative if directly attached to behavior, but its use is vacuous if attitude refers to a set of beliefs which engage the individual in evaluations. As a matter of fact, no infant's action could be due to the ideology that such meaning would require since he would be unable to master one. Nevertheless, a Piagetian advocate would argue that the ambiguity introduced by that term is well-nigh intentional, the reason being that, for Piaget, evolu-tion of cultural attitude is paralleled by the structured progress of the individualistic intellect. In our present case, it means that the child evolves from directed behavior to evaluative thoughts. To the early ways belong the first or more behaviorist sense of attitude, while the second sense is more appropriate to the later form of thinking. Hence, "attitude" changes from an absolute (because strongly behavioral) notion to a pluralistic notion. By way of illustration, a child's view would, in a gross way, copy the Judeo-Christian attitudes toward homosexuality that followed a sociocultural path. In the beginning, homosexuality was seen as an absolute violation of divine laws. Its advocates were thus condemned to the tortures amicably inflicted on heretics, as portrayed in Dante's *Divine Comedy*. Later, it was viewed as a monstrous mutation. More recently, homosexuality has come to be regarded pluralistically and merely a variation whereby a woman's psyche inhabits a man's body, or vice versa. A further illustration is provided by the child whose irony, humor, and metaphors evolve with his hypothetico-deductive reasonings where several possible worlds can be interchanged.

From the above, Piaget's behaviorist coloring, which arose out of one's sense of attitude, is cut short as soon as his notion of behavior is examined. The requirement for a semiotics interjects a new dimension: that is, behavior is part of an action, and, as such, demands a past and a future within the personal history of the child. Directed action encom-passes some expected properties and recognition becomes, at the same time, the fulfilment of that specified prospect and the resumption of a latent activity. In short, there is no such thing as a reaction of the organism to the environment, and so behaviorism is unwarranted.

Unhappily there is an underlying vagueness among Piaget's treat-ments of the relation between action and recognition, and this provokes some seriously misguided theorizing. The main reason is to be found in his antagonistic approval of conceptualism and realism. We will deal with this problem next. Succinctly, for Piaget the world is seen as primordial and even present to one's gaze. It is acknowledged only when it resists our actions. Otherwise, it is ignored either if presented as an awesomely strange obstacle, or if it offers no resistance whatever by being unobtrusively and routinely apprehended.

Here, the influence of the nineteenth-century French ideologists is noticeable, particularly that of Maine de Biran and Destutt de Tracy. They related consciousness to the feeling of effort which is everpresent in muscular exertions.[21] Maine de Biran went one step further by bringing into play an active faculty pervading all knowledge and thus influencing percepts. Piaget interpreted that point to mean that the perception of seeing graduates into the act of looking. Maine de Biran pursues this thought further by arguing that the muscular activities drafted along any actions bring in the self as being a willful power:

> It is in this change in the muscles, surely, that effort shows itself internally. Effort is simply the soul's particular power in action. . . . Let us say, then . . . that the same internal feeling which reveals to the soul its own particular effort identical with this act of will, reveals at the same time the organic modification produced by the effort. . . .[22]

It is historically interesting to find that introspective psychologists argue that the will impacted in motor behavior yields awareness of the world. Meanwhile Locke, an empiricist, proposes voluntary perceptions as the source of awareness:

> I cannot avoid the ideas which the light or sun then produces in me. So that there is a manifest difference between the ideas laid up in my memory . . . and those which force themselves upon me and I cannot avoid having. And therefore it must needs be some exterior cause and the brisk acting of some objects without me, whose efficacy I cannot resist, that produces those ideas in my mind, whether I will or not.[23]

To accommodate both points of view, it is sufficient to consider Locke as being on the side of Destutt de Tracy, and to admit synonymy between "resistance" and "involuntariness." So, while the introspectionists emphasize the intimacy of acting with its correlative holistic and intentional subjective ingredients, the representationalists presuppose the sensorial atomicity of ideas.

The contrast between a reality founded on willful actions and one based on involuntary imposition pervades Piaget's thought. Whereas he faces the first position on the cognitive level, he admits the second through the back door of a quasi-vitalistic cybernetic point of view. Curiously, this ambivalence shows up most forcefully throughout his relatively recent writings, *Biology and Knowledge* and *Memory and Intelligence.*

Maine de Biran claims that the efficacy in motor activity is modified by habits. He asserts that habits will erase any distinction to be made between involuntary and voluntary acts.[24] The corroding process is due to the normalization of behaviors and associated sensations, which decreases proportionally the effort required, and thereby the willful activity source of knowledge of the self and the nonself. Indeed, for Maine de Biran, the conscious self springs forth at the intersection of the body with the environment whenever the latter offers some resistance to the former. One is conscious of oneself only as a perpetrating agent kept in check by a counteracting world. The polarity created by the antagonism of the real toward the self is a prerequisite to knowledge.[25]

It follows, according to the historian Brehier, that Maine de Biran is a pioneer in forwarding the idea that voluntary motions are the source of all sensorial knowledge. This conclusion is admirably consistent with Piaget's leitmotif that the inception of all understanding is the person as an agent interacting with its milieu.[26] Specifically, to know x is not just to be acquainted with x, but to be aware of the very process which frames the world. In a peculiarly Marxist phraseology, one must not only own objects, one must control the means used to produce them.[27] And again, to know is first and foremost to act so as never to be detached from our sensorimotor roots.[28]

To complete the analogy with the nineteenth century ideologists, we need from Piaget the confirmation that actions are grounded in sensations. He willingly provides this when he defines an action as an intentional behavior which modifies the properties of objects and has as its goal to do so.[29]

The following quotations exemplify and clarify both Piaget's debt to Maine de Biran and the subsequent sharp limitations he sets on it:

> The fact that the idea of force owes its existence to inner experience seems to be beyond dispute. To Maine de Biran belongs the merit of having stressed this origin.[30]

Also,

> Maine de Biran had the great merit, on the other hand, of looking for the origin of the idea of causality, not in an external succession of any kind whatsoever, but in action itself where we can order the succession of acts by means of our intentions . . . justifying the notion of causality as a productive act.[31]

As we can see, there is a long tradition which persistently forages for the details of the central and complex notion of Action. While it is true that for Piaget actions are at the origin of all knowledge and intelligence, it is also true that without a proper dissection of the notion of action the cognitive universe cannot be epistemologically set and understood. This explains why, lacking such an analysis to guide him, Michotte, the Belgian epistemologist, misunderstood Piaget and openly asserted that

> it is probable that an extreme "syncretism" (via an undifferentiated blending) holds sway at this time, and it is no doubt correct to conclude that the impression of immanent motor activity provides the first datum of experience . . . and this fits exactly with the views of Piaget.[32]

The meaning of Michotte's interpretation is dubious, if one listens attentively to what Piaget says:

> It does not mean at all that the impressions of effort, expectation, satisfaction, etc., which may intervene in the course of the actions, should be attributed to an internal substantial subject located in the consciousness.[33]

William James offers another option in his argument that awareness does not stem from the efferent control of muscles, but that it originates in afferent impulses to the central nervous system. On the strength of this alternative Piaget has misgivings of establishing the self and its volitions in an immanent consciousness of efforts. Clearly, in maintaining that the world must submit to a framing by action schemes, Piaget rejects this subjective monism. *Consciousness is therefore to be found neither in a direct apprehension of objects, nor in an intimate acquaintance with the action itself, but stems from the interaction between the act and the object.*[34] In other words, the meeting of cognitive processes with the world generates awareness and thus foregoes altogether the need for a ghostly self, watching and participating in the body-machine action. For Piaget, to know is to achieve through the interiorization of our actions, a set of transformations within which the invariants determining objects are uncovered. The act is thus the source both of the abstract concept and of reality. Herein lies Piaget's rejection of the ghostly self, which is the perennial judge and absentee landlord of representationalists.

This homunculus's main duty is to generate perceptions actively out of sense data, so as to internalize all real events causally. By opposing both the empiricists and ideologues on this particular theme,

Piaget is philosophically committed to a knowing act that relates events to concepts without any mediation. The knowing act yields knowledge and awareness directly, and by presenting the real, foregoes the need for representations in the conceptual domain. But Piaget still retains representations for figural internalizations.

I find the above interpretation particularly apt for Piaget's views on causality. He describes it as a blending of a "feeling of efficacy" with sense-data from which radiates a sense of alertness. Michotte, in his research on causality which reports Piaget's views, was misled by this confusing appeal to a "feeling of efficacy." As a consequence, he emphasized affectivity, which is certainly not an essential ingredient in the Piagetian cognitive system.

The emphasis so far has been on the knowing act. It becomes more and more evident that we must have a thorough sifting of events occurring at the organism's junction with the environment so as to ascertain their status. Unhappily, Piaget weakens his position by bestowing a role to sense-data, and in doing so he bows to the dictates of the realism subtending his scientific humanism. I shall argue in later developments that this position is not consistent with his basic constructivism.

Meanwhile, in his later works, Piaget renounces some of his early dualism, couched in an affective language, and espouses a holistic view. He characterizes it by a cooperation of various psychological modalities inhabiting consciousness, such as meaning or purpose, which represent the individual and reflect the underpinning system of actions. It still remains for us to see how the semiotics of actions contributes to consciousness.

The lengthy digression on Piaget's debt to some of the originators of introspective psychology was to help us understand what awareness of the world means in his genetic epistemology. At the same time it sharpens our comprehension of his deep-seated contradictory allegiance to a faith in a subtending reality, on the one hand, and a monistic conceptual definition of it on the other.

Piaget's apparent dualism is rooted in the fundamental inability of the ever-present motor activity to yield, by and of itself, conscious knowledge, while at the same time being able to fasten a unified cognitive universe within the active sensorial field. In line with this second aspect, the successful completion of activities encompasses segmented and successive actions which make up recognitory assimilation and push forth a stable reality; but regarding the first aspect, the medium for actions is made up of movements. It runs the risk of resulting in an arid conation if such actions become blocked. Of course, any blocking will occur at the sensorial end of the action. Herein lies the difference between "thwarted" and "maladjusted," alluded to by Piaget in many of his writings.

To thwart knowledge of the world, it is enough for the individual to have sense-data that does not lock in with the sensations of an action schema. Maladjustment, on the contrary, causes shunting of ongoing behavior via a readjustment of the motor means. The specific details relative to this issue, which are so central to Piaget's epistemological position, have so far been presented only tentatively, and will be further clarified in subsequent sections.

To pursue the matter, let us recall that all conscious fragments, no matter how atomistic, are conceptually specified by the semiotics of actions:

> Consciousness is certainly not an epiphenomenon, since it consists in a system of meanings interconnected together by implicatory relationships, which excludes any reduction of consciousness to physical causality.[35]

This means that instead of mediating the classical controversy between the nominalists and the realists, Piaget's conceptualism offers a reality that is functionally dependent on the ways the intellect organizes actions. This points to his rejection of ostensive definitions in terms of face-to-face encounters with public observables. Therefore, at no time is there an objective world that is perceived and thus merely discovered. John W. Yolton deftly supports my analysis by asserting that

> the common meaning to the term "encounter" on all levels is something like (as Piaget suggests) "assimilation of and adjustment to the environment". . . . The environment of the organism is twofold: The *preenvironment*, the world within which the organism develops to consciousness, and the *significant environment*, the world we finally come to know consciously. . . . But, in the life of the growing infant, the pre-environment plays a silent role. It is the significant environment which this organism first comes to know. . . .[36]

Yolton ultimately proposes that the content of one's awareness makes up that significant environment. I, of course, take exception to a reference to Piaget's interpretation of the notion of encounter which leaves one with a feeling that something substantial and purified is readily available on the other side of the encounter. My particular objective has been to show that this aspect remains ambiguous and in need of considerable elucidation. As to Yolton's other points regarding a significant environment, they relate directly to my analysis of the semiotics of actions. The silent partnership of the preenvironment is Yolton's rather diffuse way of marking an intermediate stage in the development of consciousness. This could be the internal process standing between instinctual responses and the semiotic level. For example, fantasy-content, which gives preeminence to recognition and thus to a preliminary assimilation, shows that a meaningful real is cognitive first of all.

Yolton, like Piaget, flirts with idealism. He holds that no matching between perceptual contents and some reals is possible, since no given datum is available for the purpose of comparison. Accordingly, in all endeavors, one remains locked in the conceptual ramifications of one's cognitive universe. To postulate an ontology would remain exactly that, mere points dulling the edges of Occam's razor: "I can mean or understand objects to be nothing other than they have been constituted by me in my significant environment as being."[37]

RECOGNITION: THE PERMANENCE OF THE WORLD

All the elements adduced in previous developments are included pell-mell as essential features of the world, but still remain loosely appended to actions and action schemas. My aim in the present section is to disentangle this knotty problem by working out the epistemological role played by those elements that can be identified as invariance, stability, and permanence.

As was brought out in previous sections, Piaget describes recognition as a "readjustment" that compensates some minor "maladjustment" of an object to the assimilative process. He also asserts that recognition "is only the realization of mutual conformity between a given object and a schema all ready to assimilate it."[38] Thus, on the surface he seems to appeal in the first case to an elaborate differentiation procedure with subsequent corrective devices, while in the second, a simple matching test is called forth. A reconciliation of what appear to be contradictory theses is in order.

When, at the beginning of this chapter, I established a link between Piaget and the nineteenth-century French ideologues, I discovered two contentious points. Firstly, Piaget rejects the dualism proposed by Maine de Biran to explain the mind's awareness of the body via the resistance offered by the environment. Secondly, he also spurns the spiritualists' postulate of a will that controls muscular efforts from within, and does so via efferent innervations that send the message of resistance by the world from without. Through those means, the ideologues were able to place the person in his body and psychologize his physical movements. Even though Piaget has exactly the same ambitions, he realizes them by different psychological explanations. It is left to us to build an epistemological discourse that fits in with Piaget's explanatory framework.

To that effect, I agree that recognition consists in the resumption of a behavior correlatively with the fulfilment of expected sensations obtained through directed movements. The first aspect implies coordination of schemata, as delineated earlier, while the second refers to a matching process occurring at the sensorial terminus of an action.

Coordination of schemata involves transference of sensory elements from the pragmatics of one action to the semantics of another. Thereafter springs cognitive invariance; but interestingly it doubles as a coherence factor in the cognitive world via the cohesiveness it introduces between significations.

These prominent features can be illustrated by the intercoordination occurring between the schemata of hearing and seeing. There, heard objects are stared at. Psychologically, this means that listening to a particular noise arouses various expectations which are then anticipated. In that case, vision is expected and precedes the oculomotor act. We have here a primitive form of predisposition which stems from intersensory linkages.

An even more general statement by Piaget corroborates this view:

> A sensorial image which is at the point of intersection of several currents of assimilation is, through that very fact, solidified and projected into a universe where coherence makes its first appearance.[39]

Sensorial congruence, through actions, determines stability within the belief universe, and constancy in the environmental conditions. The first parameter denotes both a sequential convergence toward specific cognitive selections and a relatively manageable range of variations among stimuli, while the second refers to the multiple recurrences of sense-data. Merged together, stability and constancy characterize permanence, and thus reinforce the grounds for repeatability of actions.

Preponderance of constancy during the first two stages of a child's development gives rise to a subjective permanence. It precedes the objective or logical permanence that characterizes adulthood. This subjective permanence stems from the affectivity inherent in needed sensorial elements concurrent with repeated actions. Once again, we see how useful interoceptive stimuli are for action schemata. They set the attitudinal posture necessary for the disposition to act again.

On that account, Piaget's twofold descriptions of recognition can be reconciled. The "mutual conformity" factor in assimilative processes relates the anticipation inherent in actions to their sensorial reward and satisfaction. "Maladjustment" followed by "adjustment" is part and parcel of the sequential process leading to the stability mentioned above. A possible neurophysiological illustration of the interpretation offered is outlined in the current literature:

> The "Bowery el" effect, the "Furst effect" . . . suggest that we tune out the recurrences of the world by making a "model" of the external world within our nervous system, and testing input against it. We somehow can program, and continuously revise or reprogram, our models of the external world.[40]

More importantly, the predictive nature of action brought forth by the recognitory assimilation introduces a model and tests it. There is thus a constructivity inherent in the performance of an act. Significantly, it forces consistency in cognition by making sure that the "right" property is constructed. Seeing an object sets the stage for expecting, testing, adjusting, matching a further grasping behavior. The constancy and stability of both the visual and tactile properties corresponding to the original sensations ensure the permanence of an already acknowledged reality.

The crucial attributes that characterize the objectivization process mature slowly. This is due to the contingent relation between the sensorial field and particular acts of the individual. Those relations integrate sensations and thus implicate properties within the subjective realm of intentions, imagery, and idiosyncratic experiences. This particular trait is exemplified by the baby's strenuous efforts to see what is heard. Out of listening he expects and even anticipates certain visual sensations. When finally uncovered, the object listened to assumes the magical power of something wished for and which could, if need be, reappear at the infant's whim. The very fact that something akin to his anticipation did appear, puts this conation into play.

Granted that invariance originates in the coordination of schemata, we have the direction taken by cognition to compensate for its latent subjectivity. One feature of invariance is its independence from the immediate surroundings, and thus its ability to nullify contingency which is the source of subjectivity and of the singularity of simple action.

The ontogenesis of the various notions leading to the permanence and invariance of reality reminds us that a basic Piagetian tenet holds for the gradual emergence of objectivity. For instance, if an infant does not pursue in the least a disappearing object, then we must conclude that it is not yet an object. In the psychological realm, "objectification" is to be mastered at this stage, and this means mastery of an object's independence from one's own action. Piaget theorizes that the infant is still dealing with images appearing and disappearing into nothingness, with only the oculomotor act to cause their rebirth.

Thus, with respect to specific sensations, objects are given an image status lacking spatio-temporal continuity. The genetic solution is to be found in the intercoordination of various schemata such as grasping, viewing, or smelling. It is only when a visual sensation belongs to several schemas that it gains a permanence which is the source of its objectivity. The isolation of its appearances attests to its subjectivity and is compensated for within an organized system of actions. Piaget's solution to the problem posed by subjectivity is to construct an objective reality within "total" mental structures. It could be interpreted as a nod toward the gestaltists. Knowing his distrust of the perceptual bias shown by gestalt psychology, I have to differentiate his organized schemata from their global "good forms." To achieve this goal, I find an appropriate instrument in semiotic analysis, and particularly in the semantics of intercoordinated schemata; but we must note that using a semiotics of actions reflects Piaget's appeal to schemata where sensations as figurative elements loom prominently. This approach is closer to the perceptual demands of gestaltists than the strict field organization which their "good forms" innately impose. However, this second aspect is closer to Piaget's notion of scheme where structure dominates.

A hint at the kind of explanation expected from Piaget's study is offered by his analysis of the child's propensity to coordinate the various factors entering into the grasping ability. The child is gradually able to uncover various notions such as the depth, length, and hardness of an object. They control its localization and his image. An even more explicit example is furnished by the curious observation that the baby chooses the mother over the bottle as the earliest objective entity to be distinguished in his world. Gouin-Decarie points in the right direction through her conception of the origin of the solidification of the cognitive universe; she notes that "the first to be solidified and cut out as an object will be the mother. Why? Because she is at the intersection of the largest number of schemas."[41] I disagree on a moot but crucial point relative to Gouin-Decarie's more general interpretation of Piaget. Her chosen mode of expression unwittingly reflects a "category" mistake when she states that "the visual pictures . . . are capable of mutual coordination" and "cut out as an object will be the mother." The sensations adhering to visual pictures are treated on a par with the properties defining an object. This levelling is to be avoided if Piaget's psychology is to be differentiated from his role as an epistemologist.

In short Gouin-Decarie integrates the descriptive aspects of psychology and the conceptual domain of epistemology into a common language, thus creating implicatory relations between elements belonging to different levels.

Oddly enough, this misunderstanding can be traced to Piaget's own loose, and therefore misleading, concept of action. It is to be remembered that permanence, cognitive invariance, etc., characterize the object scheme, whereas object *simpliciter* is described as:

> What I call an object is a polysensory complex, i.e., something one can at the same time see, hear, touch, etc., but a polysensory complex which in the eyes of the subject continues to have a durable existence beyond all perceptual contact.[42]

The distinction drawn between object scheme and object proper, either as a token or as a type, is tantamount to differentiating the legitimacy of the possibility of object from its existential status. The object scheme is closely associated to logical features, while the object proper is dominated by sensorial attributes. The first is an epistemological notion, while the second refers to a psychological description.

As a consequence, one can foresee that a logic of action evolves parallel to a descriptive behavior, and that explanation can thus become understanding. Herein lies Piaget's contribution to a theory of knowledge, yet it is also a source of confusion. On the one hand, he sharply separates the logical or implicative framework from that of the sensorial, and therefore contingent or explicative one. Ultimately he opts for the former to define operational intelligence. On the other hand, he intimates that together the logical and the sensorial frameworks make up the action-oriented cognitive realm. This knot, holding tightly motoric segments and sensations, gives rise to properties such as permanence or invariance, but he sometimes forgets this ontogenetic ruse to attribute the instantaneous presence of affective elements to metalogical predicates. For example, he drafts for himself the notion of "totality" which, as a gestalt category, is subject to immediate apprehension, and simultaneously counts it as one of the operational abstractions, mediately obtained, within the object scheme.

Piaget's interpretation of Maine de Biran suffers from the same defects. At the beginning of this chapter I critically appraised the flaw centered in Maine de Biran's introspective approach. He claims that the affective sensitivity inherent in efforts establishes the logical status of the world. Frightened, it might be suggested, by the incorrigibility of feelings, Piaget concurs with my criticism by rejecting affectivity as grounds for the object or even the subject. Indeed, if feelings are incorrigible, then they are to be accepted without question, and so will be the objects they subtend. A constructive theory of reality cannot abide by such a stringent criterion. Any knowledge must be subject to revision. Nevertheless, Piaget admits to an immediate access to externality and a permanent world through the resistance of objects. He even goes as far as accepting a direct access through encounters with the world. In a previous discussion I brought into play the role of "maladjustment" and "adjustment" as a source of recognition. We can now use both these genetic notions to vouch for the conceptual failure that would accompany an imposed choice between a world from within and a reality from without.

Gouin-Decarie's peculiar admixtures, exemplified by a coordination of schemata which originates the seeing of a phenomenally objectified mother, can now be justified as a legitimate intuition of Piaget's sweeping combination of structural elements and sensorial attributes. An illustration is provided by Piaget when he identifies recognitory assimilation with the perception of objects. As a further step, he modifies this identification and accepts "sensorial images" in schemes. Finally, he functionally relates a perception to actions.[43] I can thus claim that the letter of Piaget's "pure" form, as something devoid of content, is not always Piagetian in spirit.

However, the further claim that perceptions are linked to actions is certainly not warranted under his constructivist psychology. In a cognitive sense act, sensation and perception are not separate entities. Thus it is not coherent for him to link sensation to acts, because they are part of them, and only in a loose way can it be said that at the psychological level movements are tied to sensations. As for perceptions, they are constructed out of actions, and thus include sensations as constitutive elements. Any attempt to link perceptions to actions is colored by an associationistic bias, such that through a many-one function the one action is grabbing at a multicollated group of sensations passing as a perception. Meanwhile, the cognitive percept is constructed out of interlocking actions, but in a one-to-one mapping of each sensation attached to a movement. Moreover, the perceptual quasi-puzzle thus shaped out has emerging properties like goal-directedness, which transcends the additive sum of sense data hypothesized by empiricists. The reality built is not the scientific one, but the everyday one subjected to epistemological inquiry and viewed by a theory of knowledge.

Through the semiotics of action, Piaget's distinction between scheme and schema becomes fuzzy. This ambiguity is not supposed to happen since schemes reflect the operative and structural nature of intelligence, while schemas embody the figurative and symbolic role of the intellect. I hold the fuzziness to be inevitable because Piaget has not clarified sufficiently the epistemology of a person's direct encounter with his milieu. He has not insisted as other authors have done that "action is primary and concrete, thought is secondary, abstract, and derivative."[44]

At the intersection with the environment there are, under the various descriptions, psycho-physical stimuli, psychological sensations, and epistemological properties. No matter the level at which they enter into the forum of our discussions, these sensory elements have to be obtained. That is, they attain an existential status by and within an act. Herein lies Piaget's ambiguity. For an act to reach something, it does not have, in a psychological sense, to change that something. *Piaget's fundamental postulate has been that actions transform objects and their properties.* Hence, any set of actions has to be a scheme whose function is to operate on the world and change structure into structures. (For Piaget, structure is a set of transformations). Of course, this exclusive function can be traced to Piaget's debt toward the pragmatists, mainly William James and John Dewey. As we saw in an earlier analysis, this meant for Piaget a restriction of the meaning of actions to their results. Those were strictly reduced to the function that objects could fulfill and thus actions were but means to use and transform the world. The same reduction governs other authors who identify acting with doing. They presuppose that to act is to modify the world. Normally, this viewpoint entails for them an opposition of the self to the world. As we will argue later, even though the agent as a doer could oppose the subject as a thinker, better claims can be made for a consciousness emerging out of acting without provoking a dualism polarizing material and spiritual entities.[45]

By accepting the idea that actions reach without transforming, and have a role within cognition, one keeps track of the sensory elements. In fact, any significative role includes these elements as part of the semiotics of action. My present obsession ensures that on the way to Piaget's sophisticated entities such as reflected and reflective abstraction or structure and scheme, there are genetically anterior elements such as activities and sensations. Epistemologically, the request is for primitive notions that later on justify claiming knowledge by transformations, correspondence, or substitution. In order to be cognizant of an object, Piaget always asserted that one must transform it. In his latest theorizing, the object requires awareness of changes through establishing correspondences by various coordinators such as ordering, enclosing, or identifying.[46]

Surely, the account is not terminated, as the claim that two objects are there to be compared is wanting. One can ask as to their status, location, makeup, "reachability," etc. To my mind, the semiotics of actions fulfills this role, and accounts for the various acts, connections, and sensations which are put into play. It thus explains the kind of matching processes to be expected. The epistemological requirement that properties and objects be tranformed or compared in a conceptualized reality, while still closely tied to the world, is fulfilled by the semantics, pragmatics, and meaning of actions.

CHAPTER 4

The Emergence of the External World

INTENTIONALITY: PIAGET'S COMMITMENT TO MENTAL EVENTS

In this chapter, I pursue further the contention that Piaget's genetic epistemology is relevant to epistemology. I do so by articulating in accord with his psychology such basic notions for any claim to knowledge as sensation, perception, action, and object. Their meanings, set in a theory of knowledge, authorize further claims about what it is to observe, to perform, to be competent, and—most importantly—to have access to an external world.

Let us not forget that Kant considered it a "scandal" that no adequate analysis of the concept of *externality* had ever been presented. I show in the conclusion that post-Kantian efforts have also been in vain, and that neither William James[1] nor G. E. Moore[2] has successfully provided a solution. My attempt at such a solution is very much germane to Merleau-Ponty's approach[3] where the conceptual framework is delineated out of psychological studies. I will leave to the richly documented work of Kohen-Raz[4] a parallel neurological and neurophysiological interpretation. As for a theological version, J. MacMurray[5] takes care of that. One more remark, destined for the reader, concerns the particularly meaningful alliances the issues raised in this chapter form with the contemporary works of M. Moroz,[6] J. W. Gyr,[7] A. Gurwitsch,[8] M. A. Boden,[9] and J. J. Gibson.[10]

In the first two chapters, I introduced action as an epistemological concept whose cognitive equivalent is a movement always accompanied by sensations. The modalities of these associations point to a wealthy realm of notions that include intention and conceptualization. An orthodox view of Piaget presents action schemes as giving access to the structural features proper to a notion of object, and tentatively to the behavioral "whys and wherefores" characterizing a coherent cognitive universe.

To further an epistemological understanding of action, Piaget's psychological studies should be reinterpreted. From four to eight months old, the baby gradually evolves from a performer to an agent. His movement results at first in a single sensation which, because of its uniqueness, is indissolubly united to the original motion. One cannot then talk of intention since a separate sensorial goal is not distinguishable from the performance. Later, the coordination of various exercises and their mutual interdependence as means and goals introduces the possibility of intentional acts. It is thus not at all feasible to talk of the infant as an agent until he has reached that cognitive level. Herein lies an interesting ploy whereby some epistemological conclusions can only be reached and enlivened if prior psychological distinctions have been made. Indeed, the causally related phenomena of movements and sensations determine the conditions under which intentional acts are articulated. If we accept such mutual assistance, then it stands as a direct rebuttal of analytic writers who refuse any infringement of the empirical into the conceptual domains.[11]

The opposition is even more specific between the empiricist theses which hold that sensations are directly given, and Piaget's view, inspired by cognitive findings, that sensations are mediated by some activity. Previous developments proposed that sensations must be cognitively significant in relation to a specific action, lest they remain unacknowledgeable stimuli.

To inspire oneself from cognitive studies has serious repercussions on the epistemological status of awareness, consciousness, and intention. Piaget makes a distinction between directed behavior and intentional acts on the basis of one's awareness of the presence of a goal, and because as a biologist he considers purposefulness to be within the teleological drive of the species instead of in the individual. If the result is tied unconditionally to the movement, there is no awareness and consequently no intention.

A recall and exploration of these fundamental ideas are in order at this point. Piaget considers directed behavior to be part and parcel of the set of reflexes that emerge out of hereditary drives. Yet, he pushes a wedge between reflexes and intentional acts. Earlier considerations led us to believe that hereditary drives are diffuse tendencies which have starting blocks but no points of arrival. For example, the bird may have a nesting instinct, but no particular nest in mind. On the issue of the existence of goals, Piaget is closer to Aristotle than to Plato, because Aristotle chose an inner potentiality that orients the individual, rather than the particular end that Plato's man is predestined to achieve.

The hereditary drive can be oriented, but not directed, since no precise sensorial goal is yet established. Only when exercised does a drive result in a sensation and qualify as a reflex. Thus, the species that bestow various impelling forces, via the set of genes, cannot be the locus for purposeful behavior. It is the individual exercising in a particular milieu who will construct reflexes aimed at sense-data. Hence, reflexes span the gap between the phylogenetically determined drive and the ontogenetic act. They gain their sensorial specificity in a developmental rather than a maturational mode, which permits us to make the perhaps trite claim that *awareness, as defined above, evolves through an epigenetic process.* Yet the triviality is only apparent, because many philosophical schools rely on a natural sort of awareness. To reject instinctual consciousness is to point to a weakness in, for example, the Intuitionist School of which Bergson is the most prominent member, and this is no mean task.

To return to the main thrust of the argument, one can say that Piaget distinguishes between directed behavior with fixed sensorial retribution which is not accompanied by awareness, and action schemata resulting in vicarious percepts which induce intention. It follows that the variety in sensations which is tantamount to a presentation of one's goal introduces intention or awareness, while purposeful behavior can be automatic and still be representational. Piaget thus separates intentionality from representation.

To identify directedness with representation, and intention with awareness, should be open to further scrutiny due to the paradoxes it fosters. If, for instance, directedness includes instinctual drives, then automatic behavior demands an intellectual involvement with its psychological and neurophysiological correlates. Another case dealing with intention and awareness would mean that conscious states imply having reasons for their happenings, but paradoxically a remembered dream can hardly be intentional. On the other hand, to attach intentions to representation conveys the belief that, in view of the respective identifications with awareness and directedness, all mental events are purposeful. By rejecting that position, Piaget declines to view all thinking as having a purpose. Once more, he repudiates a basic tenet of the strong brand of pragmatism held by Dewey and known as instrumentalism.

Earlier analyses showed a breakdown of the signification of actions into a semantics, a pragmatics, and a meaning. This semiotics introduces mediating factors, thus blocking any fusion effect between the goal and the onset of an action. In addition, the dependence of intention on segmented schemata reflects a desire to view awareness as the underlying tie between the notions of reaction, purpose, and mediated perception. I prefer to disclaim the interference of the awareness factor, which is more aptly used in introspective enquiries than in a genetic epistemological study. In fact, to accept awareness as the criterion for intentionality would make fright reactions a purposeful behavior since one is very conscious of them. On the other hand, walking is a reflexive behavior within the purview of Piagetian psychology. Piaget confirms our fears when he writes that

> we see only one method of distinguishing intentional adaptation from the simple circular reactions peculiar to sensorimotor habit: that is to invoke the number of intermediaries coming between the stimulus of the act and its result. . . . Intention is thus determined by consciousness of desire, or of the direction of the act, this awareness being itself a function of the number of intermediary actions necessitated by the principal act.[12]

To admit the complexity of an act to be the determining factor for awareness, which in turn defines intentionality, is very much to hint at behavioristic criteria for mental predicates, and forces one to agree with Tolman's attribution of desires, wants, goals, and intentions to animals (rats and dogs).[13] Furthermore, the form chosen by Piaget to render "intention" makes it a secondary process that contradicts his own assertion that consciousness is not an epiphenomenon.[14] The spuriousness thus introduced gives support to J. Watson's total rejection of this notion:

> Consciousness—oh, yes, everybody must know what this "consciousness" is. When we have a sensation of red, a perception, a thought, when we will to do something, or when we desire to do something, we are being conscious. . . . He (the behaviorist) dropped from his scientific vocabulary all subjective terms such as sensation, perception, image, desire, purpose, and even thinking and emotion as they were subjectively defined.[15]

Forewarned of Piaget's cavalier treatment of behavioral reductionism, we should find it expedient not to take him at his word, but to interpret his opinion quoted above to be a supportive argument for mental events. He is quite explicit in that respect when he assigns to actions various psychological attributes such as mobility and searchability, purposefulness and directedness. Moreover, by segmenting acts, he allows for a refined way of differentiating or even equating them. (These traits, particular to mental events, have been judiciously analyzed by F. A. Hayek.[16]) The progressive conceptualization, proportional to the complexity of actions, is strikingly supported by the influence of stimuli on the realm of significants. As the intermediaries increase, so does the multiplication of intercoordinations, which in turn corresponds to an increased extension of the sensorial spectrum. It follows that the conclusion of an action becomes more and more remote from its onset as the number of linkages increases.

The generalizing assimilation plays first fiddle in the event of a segmentation of schemata. It then integrates the pool of new sensations that is available at each link and is rendered accessible through the various encounters with the environment. In a broad sense, these sensations reverberate toward the interpretative basis of the action, and modify that basis so as to influence future exercises. In short, they influence the conditions, the aims, the purposes of these actions. The role they thus play is within the meanings of action as against the pragmatics and semantics which are, so to speak, more achievement-oriented. Hence, instead of goal-directed behavior, multiple actions favor purposefulness. Now I have pinpointed the gist of Piaget's analysis, which was to find a *functional dependence between the complexity of action and intentionality.* And I have done so through reinforcing the role of the conceptual network of meanings attached to actions while pushing further afield the possibility of immediate responses to given stimuli. The more meanings one can introduce into an act, the stronger the intentionality. Concomitant with this, the appeal to consciousness has been rendered parasitic. In a psychological sense, this means that motivation is strongly tied to interacting behaviors, and awareness is a secondary effect.

One must bear in mind that the complexity of actions also refers to the "zooming" effect of successive assimilatory acts which are appropriate for precise qualitative determination of objects. Here, I refer to the previous analysis where it was held that general activities "reach" or touch down the world when specific sensations are attached to singular movements. Hence, the constructed reality is a specialized form of the world. Approaching the world cognitively is similar to a lunar landing where details appear as more and more appropriate scannings produce filtered resolutions. When we referred to the "zooming" effect of assimilation, we meant, in a similar vein, that assimilatory acts produce a wealth of meanings. *This sequential specifica-*

tion is responsible for the directedness of intentionality often alluded to by Piaget, and also the ongoing activity constitutive of the encounters with the world. The latter factor feeds back the results of actions which sharpen the "model" of reality, and ultimately identifies the objective "thing" by an adequate sensorial matching.

The notion of model utilized here is an important issue and it will be the subject of a later section: it will be only remotely connected to phenomenist-inspired designs[17] and more in line with phenomenological patterns.[18] Another facet, revealed by the previous analysis, shows that Piaget does not place consciousness at the point of encounter of the self with the world, as did the French ideologists who saw it as a kind of mirror-image of the self bouncing on the environment. Rather, Piaget inserts it within the meanings of actions, establishing differentiation as the determining element because "consciousness arises from dis-adaptation and thus proceeds from the periphery to the center."[19]

Stimuli, at this point, are the primitive ingredients toward representationally setting up expectations, which only become specific within the zooming activity. *By tying intentionality to the generalizing assimilation, we render explicit the open-endedness of intentional behavior, and thus obviate the use of achievement as a criterion. Hence, intention is not goal-directed.*

Purposefulness and goal-directedness, which are achievement-oriented, associate with the recognitory and the repetitive assimilations, and therefore belong to the performance level. Intentionality, which is open-ended, depends on the generalizing assimilation and is thus part of the competence domain. Based on these alliances, we must judge Chomsky to be misguided when he criticizes Piaget for his appeal to repetition in the genesis of concepts. From the above, Piaget is essentially staying at a performance level. Hence, it is a completely different argument from the one Chomsky opposes to the empiricists' use of repetition in the learning process. For them, some kind of competence is called into play since learning concepts call for the use of an induction over events, but these events can only be appraised at the performance level. This objection does not apply to Piaget's repetitive schema, since it originates endogenously and functions in anticipation of some selected sensorial phenomena, and so no induction is called for.

The importance of the generalizing assimilation, relative to the repetitive and recognitory assimilations on the segmentation of actions, confirms the notion that the acquisition of meanings occurs within ongoing and established structures. Conceptualization is, therefore, not a peripheral addition, as Quine's cobweb model of synthetic reasonings tends to suggest.[20] Accordingly, intentionality meshes with conceptualization and, as is customary with Piaget, by-passes altogether the affective domain. It structures the world in a future-oriented perspective; that is, it emerges from an unadapted application and, via the meanings of specific actions, modifies the representational onset of future behavior toward a converging equilibrium.

This is a distinctive variation from the analytic tradition. Indeed, *ordinary language* philosophers line up events and infer their mutual independence from the dictates imposed by their analyses of linguistic utterances. The logical features of concepts are revealed by everyday conversations. For instance, one discovers that intentions are conjoined to events by temporal links. In other words, human acts are aimed at and temporally situated relative to an intention. This means that intentionality is characterized by its essential time reference.[21] It stands to reason, so it is argued, that the performance corresponding to these envisioned doings cannot occur in the past or even in the present, but must be aimed at in the future. One cannot intend to walk yesterday or to look now. One intends to walk at a later time.

Essentially these philosophers hold that while one can look at and describe the performances, the intentions can also be viewed. It remains, then, to tie the strings relating doings and intentions, and seemingly they are of a causal nature. By contrast, and in keeping with the incisive epistemic analyses of Donald Davidson, I opt for the intrinsic opacity of intentional expressions toward real events. If I intend to pay my fare, then the particular coin composition is irrelevant. The real coins with their distinctive characters are ignored and so are opaque relative to my intention. In short, the truthfulness of my intentions cannot be ascertained by an objective scrutiny. The events are generically tied to the intention that intends them only through their meaningful status relative to the action that reaches for them. There is no objective temporal reference frame onto which one could first tack the intention, and then the particular act. Having an intention, is not like having a handkerchief in one's left breast pocket, but like having a talk, or having a pain. There is no such thing as intending to have a sensation. An intention is not the resultant of an act. It exists within acting and so it is atemporal. Relative to intentionality, the search for a causal relation between events is quite unenlightening. Rather, matters are clarified by the introduction of a directed agent that relates, atemporally, the intention to the act within a conceptual field of meanings.[22]

Let us recapitulate the position attained so far: *a neo-Piagetian interpretation introduces intentionality as a function of the segmentation of acts.* Unless one bypasses a Biranian interpretation of action which introduces consciousness in the act itself, one must conclude that Piaget is forced to adopt complexity as a behavioristic criterion for intentionality, the mental event trait *par excellence.*

An interpretation of the concept of action reveals that this multiplicity favors the occurrence of new sensations, and gives increasing play to generalizing assimilation. In the process, meanings predominate and, as such, tie intentionality to the complexity of actions, but they also make it dependent on a sequence of adjustments to reality which ultimately define it within a correct presentation of the world. Moreover, one should recognize that under this analysis consciousness is attached to the generalizing assimilation and meanings of actions, forcing the intuitively coherent view that consciousness is of the real, but is once removed from acting through its conceptual dependency.

There is an alliance between these conclusions and the findings of Merleau-Ponty, who argues for a consciousness dependent on the power of acting rather than thinking.[23] His analysis is even closer to mine as he incorporates the meaning of sensations into the motoric domain only if they can be clasped by an adapted system of actions which magnifies that meaning.[24] Nevertheless, on the strength of my analysis in Chapter 2 of the continuity between instinctual drives, reflexes, and actions, I disagree with Merleau-Ponty regarding his clear-cut distinction between reflex and sensorimotor behavior. He sees reflexes as elementary reactions to individual events where built-in mechanisms prevail. While strongly questioning Pavlov's reflexology, which reduces action to reflex by stripping it of all nonphysical and nonphysiological attributes, Merleau-Ponty does not use the reflex as a genetic step toward the full-fledged "human act."

Merleau-Ponty's analysis supports the thesis that genetic psychology and genetic epistemology are relevant to philosophy. This is vehemently opposed by various analytical writers, chiefly D. Hamlyn and H. Siegel.[25] They argue that psychological hard facts are separated from and irrelevant to philosophical analysis. It is but thirty years since Merleau-Ponty, in defense of his *Phénoménologie de la perception* and *La structure du comportement,*[26] had to fend off similar attacks, which questioned his elucidation of philosophical puzzles via the use of psychological findings. On this issue, one must read the lively debate in his *Primacy of Perception.*[27] This same fight is still raging in the Anglo-Saxon world.[28] I would claim that the argument hinges not on whether or not empirical data should be dissociated from philosophy, but rather on its relevancy to the philosophy of _____ (the blank being filled in with a particular discipline).

Returning to the discussion about intentionality, it follows from previous analyses covering the relations tying intentions to generalizing assimilation and complexity of actions, that a person is able to give an account of his own behavior; that he can relate various sensations to his action and so give unity to the event; and that he relies on his past experiences to justify his present behavior. To sum up the literature on the subject, all these aspects essentially characterize the classical notion of a person's consciousness.[29]

The segmentation introduced within complex actions, and which operates in the developmental stages of iterated behaviors, increases continuously, emphasizing the compartmentalization of activities into *means and ends*. On the one hand, to be a means reflects an intermediary position, and is thus associated with a pragmatics denoting resumption by transfer of sensations from the resultant of an act to the onset of another. On the other hand, the role of "end" matures into that of a "goal" via the "zooming" demands of specification, and thus gives *directionality* to intentions. The important added notion is that this direction is shown to be *open-ended* because intentionality is determined by generalizing activity, and this is a never-ending process of gradual adjustment, otherwise known as accommodation. Hence, genetic growth tracks the new by adaptation, and is kept in check by the past. This last quality is brought about by the pragmatics of action, interpretable as recognitory assimilation. Piaget aptly differentiates between these two types (meaning recognitory and generalizing assimilations) in viewing certain acts as controlled by the transactions within the milieu, and others as dependent on the intercoordinations between various segments in a complex behavior. This opinion foreshadows later developments where Piaget sees the source of physical knowledge in action itself, while coordination of actions yields logico-mathematical reasoning. It is worthwhile to point out that, contrary to the dictates of intuition, generalizing assimilation relates to the second conception, whereas recognitory assimilation is tied to the first.

Generalization refers to the process of incorporating new elements (defined in the sensorial domain) into the experiential stock, by taking into account the differences separating the unfamiliar from the expected. In short, *intentionality represents assimilation within conceptual representations by going through the meanings of actions.* Furthermore, intentional acts are also defined within the pragmatics of actions or recognitory schemas, and are consequently also inserted in a conceptual frame. Hence, on both counts, intentions must refer to, and be mediated by conceptualization. These conclusions set Piaget squarely against a Bacon-Mill empiricist's tradition on the subject of induction over sense-data, and explain why, in his later published writings,[30] he sides with a quasi-Popperian approach to scientific knowledge; namely, the non-inductive procedure of testing hypotheses.

The predominant role played by the mind as a mediating agent between sensation and performance is the result of the increased complexity of behavior through the intercoordination of actions. The mind becomes less and less subject to direct environmental control, and more dependent on its own accumulated experience. This self-reliance was defined previously as the result of the meanings of actions embodied by the generalizing assimilation.

This evolution was first noticed in the transformations of instinctual drives into systematic reflex sequences. That is, under environmental pressures the linkages constituting the reflexes were loosened and new arrangements were admitted. Repetition of the selected few consolidated them and brought forth regularity and order in the phenomenal universe. The same process is reenacted for complex actions.

Whereas any stage begins with the creations and solidifications of coordinated actions, the next phase evolves under the progressive reorganization of the chains thus formed.

In a loose manner Piaget describes the latter phenomenon as experimentation that provokes, under the impact of unforeseen events, the breaking up and recomposition of schemata. This in turn leads to a distinction between the intermediary links or means and the terminal acts or ends, which bears momentous consequences. Let us recall the consolidating role of repetitive assimilation, which reflects a reliance on the uniformity of past experiences. This is sustained by the amalgamation of act and sensation prevalent in the early stages. By contrast, severing the means from the ends introduces a combinatorial freedom among actions and in so doing initiates inventive behaviors. Directedness can transcend the past to add the new dimension of choosing among goals, and this brings it one step closer to intentionality. We are corroborating the findings of the preceding section that any mismatch forces the use of generalizing assimilation, the open-endedness of which is to be interpreted as the resetting of the semantics of actions into new combinations. Repetition, as a valid cognitive tool, follows upon successful completion of an act. This paradoxical view is advocated by Piaget in the explicit and often repeated assertion that *no completely new idea can be understood*! To buttress this point, we need but recall the conclusion of the first section where it was established that *only that which is recognized is repeatable*. In fact, any new phenomena must be integrated within existing schemata by a recombination of various behavioral fragments, and this means modifying the motoric element before integrating it into the sensorial domain. These comments obviate altogether any possibility of acknowledgment at first sight; besides, they support Herbart's apperceptive mass, which loomed so large in the preparatory lessons and pedagogy popular among the teachers of yesteryear.[31]

Talking about the pragmatics of actions means bringing into play the inherent power they have to anticipate and also to expect. Specifically, some sensation is supposed to follow from some movement, and this synthesizes past experiences. Having seen a red and round thing stimulates my reaching out to meet hardness (anticipate), and makes me almost feel coldness (expect). The schema formed by these acts including various sensations, leads to a host of other actions which cohere with the recognized apple (predict). It is understood here that there exists a link between a representation and predicted outcomes. One expects sensations, while predicting properties attached to an object. Of note, the gradual evolution from expectation to anticipation, and then on to prediction as coordinated schemata becomes more complex. *There appears a strong contention for intentionality to be related more to prediction than to expectation, which is achievement-oriented.* Another interesting aside accompanies expected sensations when they have to be mere intermediaries within the pragmatics of actions: they gain the role of means in the gap created on the way to a prediction. In other words, an expected sensation can be the actual result of a movement, but by anticipation it also belongs to another movement. Hence, it becomes the link toward the resumption of an action. By belonging to the pragmatics of one act, the sensation is joined to the next one via its newly found semantic role. The hardness resulting from reaching out toward an apple sets the stage for bringing it toward the mouth.

The breakdown of a complex act occasioned by mismatch disrupts the conative interpretation brought about by expectation and anticipation. Indeed, it forces the expected sensation out of the pragmatics and into the semantics of future occurrences by an appropriate adjustment within the meanings of the respective actions. Thus, in Piaget's terminology, the lack of recognition "sets intention free," and eliminates the immediate use of repetitive assimilation. It makes sense since repetition is experientially dependent or "turned toward the past." The grounds are set for a search of fertile rearrangements or "actual invention."[32] A round and red thing which cannot be bitten like an apple will let loose many unexpected behaviors.

A moot point stemming from these considerations is that when

the reverberation via the generalizing assimilation encounters insur-
mountable resistance because of the semantical network's inability to
accommodate the differential between the expected sensation and the
actual occurrence, a complete break in the cognitive dynamics occurs.
The permanence of the world, due to either recognitory or repetitive
assimilation, is suddenly lacking. There is a break not only in the
continuity introduced by the pragmatics of action, but also in the
conceptual realm governed by various meanings of action which normally introduce other sequences of acts. Herein lies, I suggest, a
sketchy explanation of the halted behavior of children faced with
disappearing objects, construed in the affective domain as a lack of
interest. A stimulated movement will lead to other movements only if
some expected sensations enter into the pragmatics of the one and the
semantics of the other. Hence, in the absence of a payoff, the resumption of a behavior is halted due to "sensory deprivation." Thereafter,
any activity can come into play which, for the observer, looks like
incoherent behaviors.

With respect to the "zooming" sequence of acts leading to specificity of objects, the earlier the inability to adapt to a pragmatics of actions
occurs, the wider the spectrum of potential reconnections in various
directions within the field of meanings. Hence, the less chance for
incoherent behaviors. Turning this around, the more specific the percept proffered, the less likely it will be that a chain of acts is reestab-
lished following an unforeseen phenomenon, and the more probable
that a search for the object is discontinued. For instance, a cube will be
pursued with more assiduity than a lifelike model of a truck.

At this juncture, additional primitive concepts which are useful
for our epistemological claims have to be uncovered. It is propitious to
reestablish close contact with Piaget's genetic psychology. In it he
discovers that the secondary schema of the sensorimotor level is a
determinant factor for the development of the notion of invariance. I
concur with this opinion because, as we have already been made
aware, this stage is characterized by a complete reorganization of the
cognitive stock of actions. The various encounters with the environment are the occasions for differentiating between applicability and
non-applicability of schemata. This provokes a sectioning of the chains
of reflexes utilized in the first and second stages: object-to-suck or
not-to-suck enables the emergence of *grasping*. This could not happen
earlier because sucking had only one outcome and that uniqueness
was the source of indivisibility. Indeed the presence of a grip appears
only when its use as a means is questioned via a doubtful suckability.

For Piaget, the pool of freed segments can be drawn upon to form new sequences that are then randomly used repetitively. Any accidental connections, which allow for some reflex schemata to be put into play, are automatically reproduced, and result in a new stable chain.

Instinctual drives are primarily exercised freely. The fact that they are not always gratified by some precise sensory outcome results in aimless activity. From time to time these aimless activities succeed and then connections occur which provoke new behaviors. For example, a dangling string, haphazardly struck so that bells attached to it ring, will be swung repeatedly to recreate the interesting effects. The string, in full view, can be detached from the bell without arresting the child's stroking actions.

Piaget extrapolates from this vantage point when he locates the beginning of intentionality at this phase of genetic development. It is only when unforeseen events are reproduced by repetitive assimilation that the means become distinct from the ends and can be intentionally used. In other words, the complexity of an act only appears when it breaks down under environmental pressures.

The complexity, as we may recall from the beginning of this section, is tied to intentionality and calls forth awareness merely as an epiphenomenon. Moreover, using slightly different arguments, we saw that on the one hand intentionality had to be defined with respect to the meanings of actions, while on the other hand the inability to adapt utilizes generalizing assimilation to allow for future integration of the maladjusted means into a new sequence of actions. This last element will, in turn, become part of the pool of segments only if allowed and governed by repetitive assimilation. I have thus linked within one discourse the generalizing assimilation, the notions of intention, and means-and-end. Equally important, I justify Piaget's contention that goals are not established *in abstracto* and a priori, but contingently out of interactions with the milieu where consolidation through repetitive assimilation is essential.

We can now return to the main claim that invariance comes to the fore at this level. The impact of the environment is essentially registered by an adjustment in the meanings of actions. Three different levels are implied by this remark whose full details will be treated in Chapter 5. At the epistemological level, it indicates action-oriented supervision of knowledge whereby a person acting in the world has his constructed reality perpetually tested. This reality either gains more permanent features if confirmed by the consequences of actions, or it changes if some discrepancies intervene between the prediction and the given; however, to avoid having to rely on a represented reality which is subject to revision, one grants actions the privilege of having a semiotics: that is, features of that reality are part and parcel of each action. Properties are meaningful by being incorporated within acts and sets of acts. Hence, for a person to act is to be inspired by, to predict, and to anticipate the appropriate property. The world must be more or less significant relative to the property propounded by actions, in order to have any bearing on the constructed reality. At the psychological level, an individual's activities result in the right or the wrong sensorial payoff. If right, then the expected sensation matches the resultant one, and a recorded adaptation ensues with its correlative equilibrium. If wrong, then a mismatch forces some kind of adjustment of a cognitive disequilibrium. In either case, the resultant reverberates somehow and modifies the psychological makeup of the individual. At the biological level, the favorite contemporary model is that any movement of the organism provokes some stimulation whose error coefficient relative to a preset range determine a feedback and an adjustment.

The concept of action expressed on the three levels of epistemology, psychology, and biology points out clearly Piaget's filiation to the hermeneutic point of view. As a matter of fact, the features articulated above refine the postulates found in the literature on the subject.[33] They make up the hermeneutical circle of the mental and the conceptual aspects surrounding an action:

1. Movements are those of an agent's body, and are manipulated by that agent.
2. Success or failure characterizes the direction or the goal involved.
3. After instigating an activity, the agent keeps a tab on it to crosscheck its appropriate characteristics.
4. The agent is responsible for his movements and their resultants.
5. An agent links various acts into one activity.
6. To ensure that a behavior is an act, the agent ties the objective to the subjective aspects of it.

Based on his genetic findings, Piaget further articulates the structures of action. By considering in more detail the impact of discrepancies on the semiotics of actions, he assumes that the adjustment operates on the meanings. It consists in finding a new link between the pragmatics of maladjusted acts and the semantics of well-established ones. In fact, it enables the repetitive assimilation of a particular action to be ensured against obsolescence due to the adaptive mechanism which, as we just saw, favors old semantics. Recognition, henceforth, uncovers "real" constants since it appears only in case of a match-up. Recognition and repetition also specify the cognitive *invariants* that come to the fore as the common element tying the pragmatics of one act to the semantics of another.[34]

I have been describing a process that can truly be called adaptive, since it results from an assimilation and accommodation starting under endogenously provoked uses of reflexes. This genetic detour is necessary to explain the cognitive birth of invariance. It is only when the means is distinguished from the end through a mismatch, and then cemented again to other acts, that it becomes meaningful. Hence one must actually break out of hereditary tendencies to become a conscious person. For example, the invariant notion attached to grasping emerges from the dichotomy created by suckable and non-suckable grasps. As long as all grasped objects can be sucked unobtrusively, there is no need to recognize the specifics for grasping.

The environment is paramount, because instinctual drives evolve into a set of branching systems through encounters with the milieu. Thereafter, the cognitive creations of regular environmental features proceed in a convergent specificity. Hence the branching system of actions both uncovers the invariant attributes of the real, and aims at them via its various intentional acts. Thus man does not live teleologically, but has goal-directedness forced upon him by active interactions with his milieu.

If repetitive schemata result in interesting encounters due to possible mismatches, then they will provoke the child into seeking them anew. At first, the sequence of acts leading to particular features remains solidly fastened; if, however, following some specific stimuli, the schema is enacted and does not end in the accustomed way, then it will break down into "means" and "end." For instance, a comparison between grasp-suckable and grasp-nonsuckable yields a dichotomy between the grasp as a means and the suckable as an end. This explains the evolution toward objective properties. There is a progressive move from circular interplays of body-centered reflexes like grasping, sucking, and seeing, to the use of outward-oriented danglers like rubbing, swinging, and sounding.

Notwithstanding his denials, Piaget is very close to Maine de Biran when he admits that the earliest "objectivizations" occur as anticipatory behaviors succeeding unsuccessful actions. Success is the cement necessary to fasten together desires and results into one unbroken chain. Lack of achievement severs that chain. I insist on this point because it reveals the origin of intellectual progress for Piaget.

Even though progress is instigated through encounters with the environment, it is only when anticipatory failure occurs, or when goal-directed behavior is not successful, that an intellectual reworking starts. Hence, the unity of behavior must break down under environmental impact for conceptualization to take over. In harmony with an hermeneutic tenet, one can assert that an action is holistic and is not an event in the mind which causally provokes the movement of a person.

To pursue the matter of Piaget's debt to Maine de Biran, we must remember that Maine de Biran not only saw muscular efforts as generators of feelings against outside resistances, but that he also maintained that effort stood as a sign of voluntary and directed activity of the self. The active will, in its efforts against the resisting outside, was for him a source of cognitions, and even more absolutely, the origin of all moral and intellectual life. Piaget, on the other hand, utilizes the same ingredients of man's psyche, but interprets them as we saw above, in the contrasting manner of action-oriented adjustments yielding consciousness.

By answering in this manner, Piaget proves himself to be the heir to a long lineage of philosophers. Their burden was to work out the puzzle of a psychic mind interacting with a material world. His answer seems to be a synthesis of their solutions. At one end of the spectrum, there are those who postulated that at the origin of all psychical activities there was a monolithic spiritual substance which stood passively impregnated or modified from without. There, we perceive Malebranche whose occasionalist God impregnated the spirit, and also Leibniz with his preestablished harmony as the cause of modifications. In those two cases, only through an introspective discovery of objects can the subject be conscious.

At the other end of the spectrum, Maine de Biran views the "I," only conscious by forcing himself upon matter. No psychism can be activated without obstacles to actions of the self. The internal source of all volition needs the external world which, in turn, sharply distinguishes the active from the passive self which is acted upon. This is where the discussion becomes more Piagetian, because the world is suddenly a referee between the passive subject of the spiritualist and the active self of the ideologist. The dualism in Piaget's terms apparently opposes reflective thinking to a spontaneous activity. Interestingly enough, that very dualism evolved out of an initial confusion. In the eighteenth century, some authors included spontaneity into reflective thinking, and others did the inverse. For instance, Condillac posited a universal intellect which he located in instincts. But J. J. Rousseau extolled all native, innate faculties, and among them a sensually-based reason. As the dichotomy grew sharper, spontaneity was seen more on the side of matter and body, while the mind worked deliberately. It began as a refinement of Gassendi's materialistic monism, where the intelligence of de Bonald's man was served by organs. Maine de Biran took the split from there, reversed it, and described an animal invaded by reason. And before Piaget translated that view into a reflective and active mind which is inherently biologically-rooted, Goethe made sure that activity itself became the unifying force for all forms of life, be it psychic or material.

These historical asides should help us understand why Piaget's human being and his mental constructs are action-oriented. Once again, Maine de Biran anticipated this view, by asserting that the will is the source of all activities that appears in the higher human faculties by way of the external world, and through "others" in the moral sphere. An anthropological undercurrent therefore exists in all individual determination. Similarly, Piaget introduces an "energetism" in the affective flux of the logico-mathematical development of the structuring self, which needs the social "other" or the material outside to build the reciprocity or reversibility necessary for its deductions. These two openings either by the inner "energetism" or the outer "questioning" are the source of progress by successive equilibria. Through them, Piaget opposes the Cartesian Cogito who reflected the mind's closure over its own deductive products.

The particular role of affectivity in Piaget's genetic psychology further accentuates his debt to Maine de Biran. In brief, behavior is the result of the dual play of an "energetism," resting in affectivity, and a structuralization of thought processes. On the one hand, affectivity, as the embodiment of "energetism," is the source of valuation which, in its voluntary drive, yields motivation. In turn, motivation appears as a need to function whenever the real opposes the anticipated result of an action. On the other hand, intelligence, *qua* structuring activity, initiates adaptive behavior.

In Piaget, there occurs a reversal of Maine de Biran's hierarchy. For Maine de Biran, the emotions activate the faculties and thus dominate all intellectual knowledge of the world. For Piaget, even though affectivity fuels dynamically and pushes forward the assimilative-accommodative polarity of all intellectual life, it is operational thinking that seeks its equilibrium in the establishment of invariance among the flux of events. In fact, affectivity finds its stability in the establishment of unerring values created by the intellect. Stability can only be established within the constancy of the intellect's operational structures. There must therefore be a subsumption of the affective realm under the thought processes, resulting in the intellectualization of the emotional domain.

The important point is that in an orthodox interpretation of Piaget, every change of affectivity structurally duplicates the levels of intelligence. Let us take, for example, the infant's propensity to grab various toys, irrespective of their ownership. His feeling toward them is one of unadulterated joy at free play. At this early stage, his fun cannot be spoilt since he has not taken over the toys. Indeed, the object he has is "not" not somewhere else, and so his gains are not the losses of somebody else. Later on, when he has progressed intellectually, objects can be absent as well as present, and so his feelings shift accordingly. The child's affective relations will be colored by the sense of possession that entails another child not having whatever is taken. Another interesting example is offered by the sense of security needed by children; in various surveys this seems to follow a progressive evolution. In Piaget's system, feeling secure would depend on the various cognitive uses of repetitive assimilation. The numerous rhythmical motions based on repetition favor regularity, but in a crucial way they reward expectations in terms of interpersonal and private physical contacts. We identify many such motions in everyday life: swinging one's leg, drumming our fingers, mumbling to oneself, the endless jolting games of adolescents, the polite social formulae perpetually accompanying various meetings, the lengthy litany of African chance encounters.

One can judge how appropriate is the pragmatics of action which, as we saw earlier, requires recognition to precede repetition. In the present context, the expectation and subsequent sensorial payoff has interoceptive supplements which, as part of the action, constitute the secure feeling. The message, which goes beyond Piaget's structural commitment, is that the constructed reality loaded with affectivity requires a perpetual contact between our body and the world. Further examples reflecting that message could be the various therapeutic interventions such as T.V. playback, role playing, feedback techniques, and many other repetitive behaviors.

Thus, if knowledge of the world is involved, contact with the world has to be maintained. Even the invariant features, which are for Piaget the epitome of intellectual achievement, must remain tied to figurative aspects within the semiotics of actions. This conclusion is obviously a stumbling block within Piaget's genetic and cognitive psychologies. For one, the gist of their message consists in generalizing their discoveries of both the functional invariants and the successive intellectual structures. Secondly, Piaget's interpretation of motivation as a need for activities characterizes the human species.

Hence, on both counts universal man is the resultant of his studies. But my epistemological translations point to claims to knowledge which are those of an agent, and thus of a person. The problems uncovered illustrate Piaget's dual and muddled allegiance to singular development on the one hand, and to the progression of an all-embracing and rational intellect on the other.

ACTION: MEANS AND ENDS

Throughout the previous section, we investigated the nature and the types of actions used to interact with our world. Some were found to be associated with goal-directed behaviors, others carry forth open-ended intentions. From the second type emerges consciousness, while with the first comes an agent that controls each and every behavior. Our efforts were then to articulate the semiotics of action to synthesize a person's conceptualization with his psychological makeup. To pursue these efforts, we return, in this section, to Piaget's genetic studies.

The developmental phase useful for our purpose is distinguished from the preceding ones by the appearance of a new function, which Piaget calls "Secondary Circular Reaction." My earlier survey showed that the "Primary Circular Reaction" of Stage Two is used to consolidate reflexes. They originate out of established activities of an instinctual sort, such as hunger, and through haphazard motor variations get attached to sensations. Accommodation can then be localized within the kinesthetic changes which gain permanence under regular environmental influences. Thus, whereas the sensations are interpretable within the already-experienced spectrum, the means utilized to reach them are interchangeable. It is also possible for these motoric means to substitute their concomitant proprioceptive sensations for the regular stimuli and have them play a role in the semantics of further actions.

Let us retain this important development from Stage Two, which includes the interchangeability of means with constant sensorial retribution, and the semantically dual role of means and ends that exogenously selected actions can play. Subsequent stages reverse these roles, and allow the motoric segment to remain constant, while sensations vary. These possible interchanges are at the origin of the cognitive distinction of means from ends. They introduce plasticity into the hereditary mechanisms and confer increased importance on the variability of results.

Piaget describes the "secondary circular reactions" as behaviors which act on the external environment and no longer on the body itself, and which tend to preserve the result as distinct from the means utilized. Sometimes he also characterizes them as searches for these deportments that were successful by accident. It is obvious that the issue is rather diffuse for Piaget, since he indiscriminately emphasizes the new occurrences as fundamental, while insisting on the priority of the means used. Moreover, he often adds, as an afterthought, that the recognition of the end, *qua* end, can only take place when the act is repeated. This last remark induces me to conclude that he is inconsistent in his first interpretation, because as a corollary to all that has been said, new results in the sensorial domain cannot be cognitively significant. An unforeseen phenomenon must be assimilated, that is, integrated within the meaning of actions through the generalizing assimilation. Only then can it become the "end" of an action, and only then can we move from the known to the unknown. That is to say, it can at that time be properly called an expected and recognized sensation, which implies that the act has been reenacted.

At this juncture, it is useful to mention the relationship between Bergson and Piaget with respect to the absence of any genuinely new percepts in cognition. Even though the conclusions they draw from this view are diametrically opposed, which explains Piaget's relentless criticisms of Bergson,[35] they seem to agree on the relationship tying consciousness to actions.

Bergson argues that a mental act appearing as a representation must perforce impoverish the real: it cuts out the ties that connect any given objective real to its neighbors. Reality, when presented, is fastened in a continuous stream to what precedes it and what follows it, to its origin and to its effects. That conception resembles William James's stream of consciousness.[36] Our actions cut into and select certain aspects of the world and leave others behind so as to give a picture where many facets are obscured and are the source of indetermination. Instead of the Biranian self, which, through its efforts, bounces on the world, and henceforth gives a view of reality, Bergsonian actions light up selected parts, produce a reflection, and concern our needs.[37] In the immediate presentation to our senses, we choose according to organic functions, and this choice defines our consciousness of the representations thus formed.

We even find that Bergson ties consciousness to the complexity of behaviors. In a style reminiscent of claims made in the last section, he holds that the further away the response is from the stimuli, the greater the latitude for virtuality. The more complex possible acts are, the more demands are made on awareness of the real. Hence, the same pervasive appeal to action-oriented percepts underlies, in both Piaget and Bergson, any encounter with the world.[38]

Like Piaget, Bergson holds that consciousness is functionally dependent on the intermediaries that separate stimuli from the actions which count as responses to them. Cognition is crucially dependent on an active involvement of the person both in terms of his personal history and of his movements, which remain embedded in sensations.

For Bergson, the more complex our acts, the more internalized they become; the greater our conscious selectivity, the more prejudiced is our representation of reality. For Piaget, it is that very internalization of reality which gives access to it in any objective sense. While attacking Bergson's conclusions, Piaget first expresses the objectivity of all thinking as an article of faith:

> Unless one is an empiricist or an *a priorist* (or Platonist), it is difficult to see how mathematics can apply so admirably to physical reality if the logico-mathematical structures are not deeply rooted in biological organization, which is at once the origin of the subject's activity and the reason for this fundamental applicability.[39]

He later qualifies this position by specifically sketching out a rejoinder to my own analysis which views consciousness as dependent on the meanings of actions embodied in a complex intercoordination of behaviors. That is to say, consciousness is not tied to our actions on the real, as Maine de Biran would prompt us to believe. Instead, consciousness is dependent on the coordinations of these actions, which require a progressive conceptualization of the rapport between the various actions brought about by their sensorial results. One is not conscious directly of one's acts or of the objects acted upon. First, the object must submit itself to the action schemata to be intentionally aimed at, and thus "discovered."[40]

It is not the totality of one's behavior that is given in consciousness, but only the relevant and the immediate:

> For the concept of consciousness considered as a primary fact, it is necessary to substitute the dynamism of "conscious realizations" in which we perceive at first the intentions and results of acts.[41]

Hence consciousness, as a total phenomenon characterizing mental life, is discarded in favor of the partial awareness of the tail-end of action-oriented behavior or of the intention proper.

At the end of the previous section we ascribed some confusion to Piaget due to the fact that he is both a realist and that he believes in a constructed reality. To clarify this issue, we see that without the possibility of discarding his appeal to new results, there could not be any sense for the appearance of an *external* world at this stage.

The fleeting nature of a stream of unfamiliar phenomena precludes altogether the emergence of a permanent reality. Therefore, in Piaget's case, a conceptual holism transposed from his cognitivism is substituted for the commonsense realism whose leitmotif is to seek a unity under the plural world of appearances. Alchemy is one of the most famous by-products of that perennial leitmotif. (Emile Meyerson's *Identity and Reality*, particularly Chapters 11 and 12, is relevant to this view.)

Having established at the beginning of this section the genetic gains achieved in the stage of "secondary circular reactions," we must now ascertain their possible epistemological transpositions. It is precisely because the modes of cognition impose variations on the means while keeping the end constant that the child can qualify objects *qua* objects. Something that is felt, sucked, and seen has much more substance cognitively than if it is only touched or heard. One of the criteria for objectivity is accessibility to several sense organs. This puts into play various schemata that are coordinated by sharing some common sensorial ends.

The various motor means produce multiple access to a unique sensation through their interchangeability, and are the base for the stability of that sensation. These characteristics are essential at this level to a definition of the external world for the child. We should realize that the interchangeability of means does not indicate substitutions, but rather the interesting fact that a sensation can be reached, or rather achieved, via several paths. Even though the movements lead to similar results, they enter into one cognitive nexus whose epistemological outcome is wealthier properties. In order for these movements to end similarly, however, sufficient traits have to be read as common. This discloses a series of matches between expectations and payoffs. From earlier analyses, a likely interpretation permits the pragmatics of one act to be the semantics of the next, and so we have in our case one pragmatics linked intimately to several semantics. The more such links are cognitively established, the greater the stability of the corresponding properties, and the more reasonable permanence appears. Accordingly, recognition followed by simultaneous repeatability is a basis for permanence in the world.

This exact position is held by Hayek in his incisive philosophy of perception:

What this amounts to is that all the "knowledge" of the external world which such an organism possesses consists in the action patterns which stimuli tend to evoke.[42]

Sense-data must not only be available for use within the semantics of distinct actions, but they must also be linked together by being part of the end of one and coexistentially the onset of the other. In other words, recognition, leading to repetition, is the conceptual correlate to a theory of real actions. This interpretation clarifies Piaget's assertion that

through the very fact that for the nursing the bottle belongs to two series of schemata capable of giving rise to adaptations and functions independent of each other (vision and sucking) and through the fact that it realizes the coordination of these two schemata, it is necessarily endowed with a certain externality. . . . We shall speak, therefore, of recognition as function of the coordination of two schemata of assimilation.[43]

In summing up the results uncovered in Piaget's notion of secondary circular reaction, we realize that externality is not found in direct access to the remote real, but is grounded in the means utilized to reach for it. The stability and permanence proper to a determination of the world demand that the ends of actions or sensations remain constant while the means are interchanged. The flight from egocentrism that is characteristic of childhood and defines cognitive development, is rooted in the clear-cut distinction of means from ends. This in turn is paradoxically dependent on the mobility of intercoordinations of actions, which is the source of the awareness of the permanence of selected sensations. The real never happens to be there, never takes us unaware or by surprise. The world must be recognized, then repeated. In short, the world cannot but be as we know it to be. Cognitive relevance entails integration of sensations within the intentional realizability of actions schemata. Consciousness is reduced to intention and is thus dependent on the intercoordination of actions, which, because it is directed, reduces it even further to "consciousness of."

We saw earlier that the multiplicity of means linked to the same sensorial payoff is the source of the cognitive means-ends dichotomy. It is also the path followed by accomodation to specialize actions toward adapted behaviors. This specialization militates against a vague, overall awareness, and concurs in its reduction to "intentional realizability," or, more specifically, "consciousness of." These last remarks vindicate Piaget's functional dependency, uncovered through the intentionality of mental events, which revealed some close similarities to Merleau-Ponty's own "intention toward," and which we remarked upon in the previous section.

The interpretation given so far to Piaget's genetic epistemology offers an alternative to a purely behavioral reductionism, and, as a consequence, keeps the traditional status of mental predicates more or less intact. His theory of action embodies, under a vitalistic cloak rather than in a stimulus-response vein, the famous reflection by the psychologist E. G. Boring: "In the 20th century it eventually became apparent that the organism behaves first and feels afterwards."[44] Obviously not in line with either the rational Cartesian "cogito" or the sensual Rousseauist "I feel, therefore I am," this assertion established a historical contrast for Piaget's message. When translated into a philosophical setting, Piaget's psychology yields a conceptualism steeped in actions. Indeed, the web of coordinated actions progressively hardens into a stable constructed reality.

PERMANENCE, INVARIANCE, AND EXTERNALITY

In earlier sections of this chapter we showed that recognitory assimilations followed by repetitive assimilations are determining factors toward stability and permanence of sensory elements. At the same time, interchangeability and complexity proper to coordinations of actions are the source of the distinction between means and ends.

This section will attempt to make explicit the details hidden in the various modes of intercoordinations of actions that Piaget calls "organization." In brief, this latter notion synthesizes permanence and means-end into the fundamental notion of externality, which ultimately leads to both objectification and objectivization. Essentially, my goal is to clarify the epistemological status of the notion of externality as comprised within the critical idea of an external world.

At the sensorimotor level, the infant reaches a phase where he repeats movements leading to interesting results. He exerts himself in multiple ways and as he extends his activities away from the periphery of his body, he ineluctably provokes the occurrence of new phenomena. It is this very richness uncovered by the centrifugal broadening of the child's experiences that Piaget regards as the inception of never-ending accommodations. As was elaborated in the previous section, the new phenomena become cognitively relevant only through their insertion into the semantics of actions. This happens via the generalizing assimilation which, by differentiation from previous encounters, can readjust the "weight" to be attached to stimuli, and through this process accommodate the meaning of actions to the real. This is finalized when it is tried out, so to speak; furthermore it must be reinforced by two concurrent action schemas. The first is simply a recurrence of the same phenomenon. The second appears with the fulfilment of expectations within the "zooming" sequence, which makes available the proper details of an event.

Only after "reinforcement"—that is, after the real-obtained sensation has been matched to the expected one—can that sensation be properly called the semantics of an action. At this level, the accommodation operates within the sensorial domain, and more specifically within the meaning of actions.

Later on, once the real becomes strongly stabilized within the semantics of these actions, the element that will have to give in to the pressure of the environment will be the kinesthetic segment, and so accommodation will be defined in the motoric domain.

The phenomena to which the child is adapted through the generalizing assimilation are more and more remote from his body as he utilizes first sucking, then prehension, followed by vision. The important step that favors this progressive removal is the interrelationships established between the various action schemas.

Earlier we saw that the coordination of actions was possible only because various stimuli, belonging to the semantics of widely diverse actions, simultaneously make up the pragmatics of antecedent actions. This specifies Piaget's loose notion of organization which focuses on the assimilatory role of the schemas viewed as the inner functioning of the intellect. Let us take as an example the experiment, often pointed to by Piaget, which consists in the child reproducing various prehensions of a string with which he shakes a doll. Originally, the visual act pays off after a sequence which centers and coordinates several actions sufficiently to bring the details to the fore. Assuming the prehension of objects appearing in the visual field, such as the string and the doll, to be a well-established set of coordinated acts, we have to resolve the modes of sensorimotor integration subsuming the shaking of that doll by the string.

Strings and dolls are, at first, inseparably part of oculomotor movements. They graduate to items which can be "seen" when they are part of alternatives by their presence, absence, and multiple appearances. Next, the visual gazes, via the recognitory assimilation, are identifiable with the pragmatics of genuine, looking acts. These connect to other behavioral dimensions, among which are tactile sensation. Under the generalizing assimilation these sensations become an element of the semantics of oculomotor acts. Hence, we arrive at the apparently paradoxical situation of tactile sense-data leading to the expectation, and under the right circumstances the occurrence, of a visual sensation.

Mutual assimilation ensures that the reverse process results in visual data being included in the semantics of "mechano-receptor" acts, and in visual sensations shaping the pragmatics of hand actions. Under the stable sensorial conditions obtaining at the end of the repetitive phase, the motor elements become interchangeable. An oculomotor movement can, under substitution by a prehension, pro-voke a visual sense-data to be the onset (semantics), and a visual sensation to be the outcome (pragmatics), of a grasping hand gesture.

The ensuing attainment consists in the hand pulling the string to shake the doll. But this is a new phenomenon and thus not cognitively relevant until assimilated by generalization.

The doll, visually speaking, was until then part of the pragmatics of the grasp; that is, the child gripping that doll was prone subsequent-ly to look at it. At the same time, visual stimulations instigate steady oculomotor gazes resulting in sensations, and so in that case the visual doll is part of both the semantics and the pragmatics of a looking act. On the other hand, the doll, shaken by the string, is a moving target, and requires substitution of the steady oculomotor segment by, let us assume, an oscillatory scanning of the eye. Therefore, we have, under the generalizing assimilation, an adjustment first of the pragmatics of the grasping, which is stabilized as recognition of the appropriate shaking object, and second, adjustments of the semantics that permit repetition of the hand gesture under the correct visual impressions; i.e. a shaken thing. The moving doll forms the content of the terminal segment of the overall behavior and thus fulfills its purpose under the guise of a produced goal.

The semiotic model used in this example explicitly articulates Piaget's genetic framework. As a matter of fact, Piaget explains in a rather sketchy manner that the infant, having fortuitously shaken the doll by budging the hood of his cradle, will attempt to relate his own gripping to the doll's stirrings and to the hood's shifts. To achieve a mental integration appropriate for the succession of apparent motions, the child will reproduce the original accidental movement. Conse-quently, for Piaget repetitive assimilation, on the conceptual level, regulates all contingent happenings by intercoordinating schematical-ly the various sensorimotor domains.

It is central to this epistemological undertaking that a more polished conclusion be drawn, namely that both invariance and means-end differentiation are at last united in these intercoordinations of actions. The visual sensation, for instance, is obtainable at will through the recognitory and repetitive assimilations; therefore, it yields *permanence*. The visual sensation is also within the pragmatics of one act and part of the semantics of another, thus inducing *invariance*. It remains available under various interchangeable motoric elements, thereby provoking a dichotomy of *means* and *ends*. The conjoined appearance of these properties created by the use of actions is the proper base for the determination of *externality*.

Another facet, still problematic at this stage, is the effect that the three assimilatory schemes have on the characteristics of mental predicates:

- *Generalizing assimilation* introduces the unexpected into the meanings of actions. It is future-oriented, and only comes to the fore when unknown environments are encountered. In short, this assimilation reflects the open-endedness of intentionality, which must be set relative to misadaptation, and not as a function of indeterminacy. The generalizing factor is therefore a vital contributor to the competence of intellectual functions, rather than being associated with the more achievement-oriented behaviors.

- *Recognitory assimilation* represents the fulfilment of a predicted sensation. It ties the pragmatics of actions, which is the intermediary link in a sequential behavior, to the anticipated features which characterize any intentional act.

- *Repetitive assimilation* succeeds recognition, and stands as the end segment of a complex behavior that is goal-directed. Hence, the semantics, which embodies the last sensorial matching, is more directly attached to the purposefulness or notion of efficiency, also prominent in actions. This interpretation has the advantage of being stepwise more precise than Piaget's solution to the riddle expressed in the following passage: "There remains to be explained how a remote spectacle can thus be conceived as produced by the action itself. This question can be answered in one word: this discovery is made through reciprocal assimilation of the present schemata."[45]

Besides the three types of assimilation, Piaget recognizes another functional invariant, the accommodation. Its role is to incorporate all new events impinging on an individual. For this to occur, there has to be some activity of the organism which permits an adaptation through the interchangeability of its motor element.

One may recall that at the reflexive stage, the fundamental source of activities was instinctual drives, which became differentiated into distinct behaviors through their encounters with the organism's particular milieu. Thence emerged reflexes, which were reinforced by appropriate usages or rendered obsolete by misuse.

Stabilized patterns of behaviors mold the world into a relatively fixed and narrow sensorial spectrum. As soon as the automation of reactive behavior is replaced by a system that allows for more flexibility, both in the motor variations and the sensorial payoffs, reflexes graduate to actions. From there evolves the cognitive relevance of sensations within the semantics, pragmatics, and meanings of actions. Accommodation, inherited from reflexive behavior, consists mostly in the modified exercise, within a streamlined range, of the motor part of various action schemata. The sensations are to remain constant, and only the means to get at them could suffer some slight modifications; for example, the position of fingers in grasping, movement of the tongue in gustatory investigations leading always to sucking, etc. This streamlining is essential to the independence and identity of the various schemas, for fear that a vastly different movement should provoke an unrecognized sensation.

This form of streamlined accommodation was originally tightly unidirected on the sensorial level, and thus not free. The further use of generalizing assimilation grants cognitive relevance after integration to new and therefore unknown phenomena, and reveals two forms of accommodation. One operates by appropriately adjusting to the various stimuli that contingently determine the sensation forming the semantics of an action; it functions directly at the sensorial end of movements, and controls the onset of that action. The second type, to be discussed presently, is relevant to the interchangeability alluded to above.

New phenomena must be inserted in the continuous sequence of actions and concurrent sensations of an individual. One should not assume that every new event blankets all previous and present activities in order to trigger afresh untried psychophysiological mechanisms. The halting behavior of a robot might very well operate in this manner, but not the goal-directed and intentionally fluent gestures of a human.[46]

In any situation, some of the sense-data will likely be cues or stimuli within the onset (semantics) of an already settled action. Once enacted, that action confronts the environment, resulting in sensations which may or may not match those expected. As any action transforms the milieu in a direction comprising the effected sensations, a changed codification occurs that belongs to the semantics of a further action. The matching process is thus all-important for the resumption of behaviors. It was earlier qualified as the pragmatics that initiates repetitive assimilation, and will be the subject matter of the next chapter.

A perfect match sometimes proceeds from a coincidence between the onset stimulation of an act and the terminating sensations. This match ensures the cyclical repetition of a given behavior, and could eventually explain several curious phenomena such as the fixed ideas in hallucinatory reactions to sensory deprivation. It also clarifies the mysterious advent of rhythmical movements typified by stroking one's beard, drumming one's fingers, exchanging knowing glances, and nodding one's head in agreement. Among children, their favorite autorhythms are also examples. Chattering, singing nursery rhymes, swinging, and various repetitive games are similarly explained.

One could argue for a similar elucidation in cases of repetitive usages of polite social formulae which secure interpersonal contacts.[47] All these rhythms are favored by a sense of affective and cognitive security, because they rely on regularity, predictability, and permanence.

To further clarify the role played by the interchangeability of actions, it is worth noting that it consists in a modified use of a movement controlled by a semantics that is carried over as an invariant sensation from the pragmatics of an already-adapted antecedent act. For a full adaptation, the new linkage must also terminate in an adjusted pragmatics, and so on for any interlocking set of actions.

For the individual, to be closeted within recognitory and repetitive assimilation means that a catalog of motor variations with their semantics and expected outcome is progressively drawn up. Furthermore, instead of one action pertaining to one sensorial domain, there can be several of them belonging to different domains but having the same sensation within their semantics. For example, in the case of the infant who is interested in a doll shaken by a string, we presume the following sequence: (a) initially the baby strikes the string accidentally, thereby stirring the doll; (b) the baby will try to reenact the event by shaking first his hand and then the string, even though the string has been visibly disconnected.

The temporal juxtaposition of hand motions and eye scanning is converted into a psychological arrangement where the tactilo-kinesthetic result of the prehension becomes part of the semantics and therefore triggers the visual sweep. Of course the baby succeeds only after multiple trials, consisting in adjustments through the generalizing assimilation while the jerking doll remains a stimulus for the prehension of the string. Accordingly, the new vision of an oscillating doll needs an accommodation through its insertion in the meaning of an oculomotor behavior, prior to its integration into the semantics of particular visual sweeps.

In due time, the pragmatics proper is established, both for the visual and hand actions. The mutual input, constituted by the moving doll and the tactile sensation of the string, links the two actions together and, under recognitory and repetitive assimilations, firmly entrenches the shaking into the semantics of the oculomotor action. It is possible that the progressive loss of interest toward new toys is related to the insertion of their properties within the semantics of actions, which reflects a fading novelty and the birth of regularity.

The final consequence to be noted is that prehension is inserted as a means within the overall behavior, while the visual display gains its status as an end through the insertion of the grasping before the oculomotor segment. It must be stressed that the sequence in one sensorimotor domain must be broken up to incorporate a different modality. This ensures that a sensorial manifold, through which, as we have previously seen, objectivity and intentionality emerge, introduces psychological properties with all primary biological acts. Philosophically, this message, when filtered by the semiotics of action, represents a major contribution of Piaget's psychology.

We can apply our semiotics of action to the example presented above. The moving doll obtains *permanence* as it is predictively fulfilled in the recognitory schema, and becomes an *invariant* as it is transferred without changes from the pragmatics to the semantics of distinct actions schemata. Consequently, the *externality* of the event is finally obtained.

For Piaget, the fluid play of a general form of activity ultimately solidifies into divergent acts under the selective and oppressive forces of the environment.

In previous sections we showed that the temporary adjustment of new phenomena is open-ended within the meaning of action and under the generalizing assimilation. But even more to the point, the adjustment translates into a progression that is future-oriented. The insertion of new motor linkages, as exhibited by the accommodation of unexpected phenomena, was found to be the source of intentionality and of the specifically anchored "intention to." These details elucidate Piaget's insight that accommodation neither branches out systematically nor seeks out the unknown. Indeed, accommodation fixates appropriate adjustments to a reality that is both partially new and haphazard.

Meanings of actions are strictly defined in a conceptual domain.

As soon as they fasten themselves tightly to the real by adaptation, they evolve into a semantics and a pragmatics which, under *the recognitory and repetitive assimilations, ensure that actions are purposeful, goal-directed, and therefore achievement-oriented*. In other words, those actions fail to keep the open-endedness, the future-directed character of their original predictive role. Also, they eliminate what is to become a prominent feature of subsequent stages, namely the creative and enrichment capacities embodied in the potential actions of conceptualization.

The indefinite array of possible phenomena presented by the world stands as the very fuel of our mental activity. On the other hand, the absence of unexpected phenomena would, under the cyclic pressure of accommodation, freeze our behavior into fixed semantics and pragmatics of actions. We would then become creatures of habit with a lack of freedom imposed by a thorough cognitive determinism. The open-ended feature of intentions would be checked by the closure of habits, and intentionality, as a mental predicate, would be a vacuous symbol.

Significantly, one could trace to these consequences Piaget's constant assertion that in fact accommodation *opposes* assimilation. I argued earlier that accommodation forces the cycle constituted by the chain of actions to close into an adaptation to reality. Generalizing assimilation is, on the other hand, restricted to perpetually resetting the meanings of actions, and thus remains a function of the conceptual network. Accommodation transforms the conceptualization proper to meanings into a presentation of onsetting stimuli attached to the semantics of actions, and therefore spoils the freedom inherent in generalizations.

This analysis of the development of the notion of externality gives substance to what in Piaget is still implicitly a program and not yet a justified outcome of his genetic studies. In brief, the new environment is interesting for the child, both because it gains its regularity via its insertion within well established behaviors, and because of its original open-endedness. One must avoid a facile appeal to the innate curiosity of man toward the unknown emerging suddenly in the world. In fact, Piaget did, on occasion, fall prey to that cliché, despite the contradictory implications it introduces within his genetic epistemology. Indeed a totally new phenomenon is cognitively unacceptable, and it is only through a partial recognition that adjustments via accommodation operate and latch on to the unknown part. I can therefore conclude, by going beyond the letter of Piaget's writings, that *renewal is perforce imposed from the outside, while stability characterizes the inner core of cognition*.

CHAPTER 5

The "Encounter" with the World: Conflict and Creativity

In the preceding three chapters, movement, sensation, and their transposition into a semiotics of action were delineated. Hopefully the groundwork that was presented supports viable claims to knowledge of an external world. From this analysis some additional inroads were made concerning the epistemological status of permanence, invariance, purposefulness, consciousness, and intentionality. A framework was developed, rooted in Piaget's cognitive psychology and genetic epistemology, in which goal-directedness is related to the pragmatics and semantics of actions, while open-endedness is tied to intentionality and to the meaning of actions.

We have now reached a crucial cognitive crossroads relative to the child's development. Piaget claims that at each stage of the child's intellectual progression, he is in a state of either equilibrium or disequilibrium. The former reflects stability, permanence, and fulfilled anticipations, which are proper for recognitory followed by repetitive schemes. The latter state occurs when a readjustment through the generalizing assimilation is required to compensate for an unexpected event. Production of new strategies or new structures follows henceforth, and delimits the creative power of the individual. To explain this production, Piaget identifies the four factors of equilibrium, maturation, physical interaction, and social intercourse. Equilibrium predominates over the other three, making it the foremost cognitive feature. As a matter of fact, the other three factors are reducible to it because they achieve their own equilibrium states by obeying some homeostatic-type laws.[1]

To understand the intellectual progression of the child, it is therefore essential to delimit the conditions under which equilibrium and disequilibrium become manifest. This directs us to the periphery of the body, where "encounters" with the world occur. At the same time, however, this lessens the role of an intellect controlled by disembodied structures.

The polarization indicated reflects a recent trend in Piaget's writings.[2] To my mind, it brings into the open the simmering split within his genetic psychology, or more pointedly between his probabilistic and his deterministic models. On the former side, there is a study of the concepts as they appear and are related within a structural framework. Undeniably, a system of successive structures comes to the fore and resumes the common denominator between all individuals. On the side of cognitive psychology, the interest is for a functioning intellect as it relates to the world, and hence as it inhabits a person's body which seizes upon that world.

Obviously, from genetic psychology one gets the sequence of concepts which the child is alleged to master, and also a proof of his cognitive development. A dilemma arises out of deciding whether the child prospers intellectually because he successfully masters the concepts, or whether, on the contrary, he understands the various notions as a function of his own intellectual evolution. All indicators point to an association between the probabilistic approach and the first hypothesis, while the deterministic model, in favor after 1975, harmonizes with the second position.

Looking at the succession of concepts, one can assume that they can either be learned from without, grow out from within by maturation, or be the result of interactions between the individual and his environment. Denying total control to the inner human nature and also to the outer milieu, Piaget adopts interactionism as a compromise. In that case, to master a concept out of interaction suggests an individual who acts on the environment and receives some kind of message in return; but since each concept belongs to a series, one has to account for its insertion. If the chronology of mastered notions is not imposed by learning or maturation, then some other prescriptive guide has to be found, even more so in view of the Piagetian belief that the sequences are common to all children. This last reason has convinced most of those philosophers who bear some interest in Piaget's works that maturation has to be the guide. On the surface they are not overly wrong when the child's intellect is described as constructing knowledge through its structures which develop out of innate functioning. The pitfalls would have been to accept structures that furnish or shape the mind, and so adopt a learning theory.

To locate the guide that produces a universal succession of concepts, a closer look at interactionism has to be taken. If actions are involved in each and every concept, then their complexity has to be a factor. To build complexity into an activity takes time. Hence we have here a natural scale for a chronological order. Moreover, the more likely an environmental feature, the greater chance it has to link up with an active organism, and the sooner will it have cognitive significance. It follows that complexity and likelihood determine the probability for a property to be acknowledged as a concept, and also placed in the genetic order. For all that, the probabilistic approach justifies the independence of each property, and so the concepts have to be related somehow. That role is fulfilled by the structuring intellect. In fact, the greater the independence shown by properties, the tighter should be the structures over the corresponding concepts. Therein lies the view that to accept a developing cognition together with a probabilistic account entails promoting intellectual processes whose structures match logical ones.

Piaget's analyses prior to 1975 relied on a probabilistic account of the constructions inherent in intellectual development.[3] It thus makes sense that throughout his long career, he "uncovered" mental structures characteristic at each stage of the child's cognitive growth. Abiding by the probabilistic model, he had to emphasize structuralism in thinking. Some order had to be imposed on the incoming data which were not sought after by a normative mind. Indeed, the freer the entrance way, the more regimented cognitive processes had to be afterward. Therefore, the preeminence given to logico-mathematical structures reflected a reliance of the individual on probabilistic encounters with the outside world.

To illustrate this point, football can be compared to rugby. In football, structured plays are rehearsed ahead of time and the one selected is, in general, sent from the bench to be executed in a faithful manner. In rugby, interactions on the field dominate through immediate decisions and organized plays are enacted within the actual context.

The important issue had to be a concern for the structures that mobilized intelligence. Only as an afterthought did Piaget describe the intermediary steps leading from one state of equilibrium to the next.

Thus we can understand the almost miraculous advent of equilibrium states which could often be treated as sudden insight, or simply hindsight. Piagetian commentators are often perplexed by the discontinuity marking the child's progress to a new stage. They are forced to see in Piaget the structuralist, and forget the dialectics governing his developmental psychology. Yet, as was excellently treated by M. Boden, his genesis with structure stems naturally out of his structuralism without genesis and his genesis without structure.[4]

Emphasis on a probabilistic model has to be counterbalanced by a structuralist stance regarding the intellectual treatment of data. Paradoxically, the subject becomes prominent in all equilibrium achievements, and the active role played by the individual through encounters with the environment is left unaccounted for. Thus, the ultimate adequacy of the mental tools to the world appears to present an open gap. To bridge this gap, Piaget resorted in his early writings to vitalistic arguments, or to the flimsy span built out of fortuitous interactions with the milieu and governed by probabilities. The most recent writings present a different approach which is essentially deterministic. In it, actions are tightly organized so as to ensure that the milieu is verified and the environment is interrogated, obvious inference being that one can forego the need for a formalized intellect.

PIAGET'S PROBABILISTIC SYSTEM

To support his probabilistic model, Piaget argues that equilibrium is the endogenous dynamic force behind the sequential acquisition of cognitive structures.[5] Furthermore, he places the overall orientation of genetic development squarely on a probabilistic interplay at the junction of our encounters with the world. The spectrum of properties is presented in a neutral vein, while the individual's actions emphasize some of these properties over others. The selection out of what the environment has to offer is a developmental variable, which qualifies the various structural equilibria.

Seven stages defining the various probabilistic selections, and therefore the occurrences of properties, are distinguished in the formation of these equilibria. First, under the impulse of perceptual egocentrism, specific properties are singled out, and acquire a higher probability within our picture of the world than those that are ignored. Secondly, greater attention is granted to the absolute value of properties rather than to their changes in time. Thirdly, the perceptual centering over properties forces singularity, thus making an independent estimate more likely than a composite one. Fourthly, a bipolar trend appears as soon as it becomes cognitively significant for one property occurring at some point to increase the incidence of another. At a fifth stage, this last aspect progresses to an oscillatory shift of attention from one property to another. This leads naturally to the sixth phase, where the increased probability of multijointed properties overcomes their independent status. Within the seventh and last step, there is a greater likelihood of compositions among conjunct properties, and also a preponderance of their relational and dynamic features. In other words, the temporal distributions of sense-data begin to be reflected in the structural relationships of operational thought so as to achieve, for instance, reversibility of actions. To illustrate the seven stages, one can consider the evolution of the mother in the child's mind. At first she is the preponderant feature recognized in the environment, but with many other women participating in that feature. Then her status as a warm body to cuddle against takes on a unique value. It is followed by an identification period where she is the center of all attention. Next, her moods will color various reactions which the child begins to read out, and afterward to connect. There is no more the angry mother and the sweet one which can appear successively as per magic because in the sixth phase, the infant conjoined the two. Finally, he is able to see, in the mother, the person with her own characteristics.

At every level a class of actions relative to some properties is favored from among all possibilities. But the structured intellect ensures that to every action its inverse is included. That class becomes an approximately closed set under the various assimilative and accommodative constraints.

The explanatory devices employed by Piaget to justify the seven steps in the probability sequence seem ambivalent at best. For example, he insists that given two properties A and B which have different probabilities, they will suffer variations that the infant will notice, and after a while, will interpret as co-variations. This will induce a shift from focusing on one property to an alternation between A and B. This maneuver to and fro becomes oscillatory, and creates a tie between the properties such that the anterior logical relation A-or-B (the exclusive or) gives way to A-and-B.[6] For instance, a rolling object is, at first, an event distinct from a bouncing ball; however, their salient variations which tend to be co-happenings introduce more than a concomitant interest in two alternate properties. They result in a conceptualized object whose very definition includes conjoined qualities and even proportional ones.

We must note that A *and* B is reached as retroactions and anticipations force the alternate centering on A *or* B to converge into a simultaneous presentation. Piaget's argument gives rise to some confusion because, on the one hand, all probability measures apply to our behavior and therefore strongly depend on the structure predominant at the respective level. Yet, on the other hand, the pressure for sequential changes of these very probabilities is located in objects. Thus, the conflict which is supposed to start progress originates either from within the internal source of stage equilibrium or around the external probabilistic influence on the seven-step sequence. To resolve this dilemma, Piaget relied at one time on a third capacity which he attributed to a particular mental power. Since evolution means the possibility to tie various properties together, then producing single representations known as imagery or memory had to be the appropriate power. Recently a new solution was provided by relational representations, to which Piaget appeals in his inspiring works, *Mémoire et intelligence* and *L'image mentale chez l'enfant*.

Notwithstanding Piaget's various solutions, I disagree with him on the ground that he is inconsistent, and the various probabilities can be applied directly to the properties offered by reality. On the contrary, they modulate the actions leading to their receptions. This would mean that the classical learning models[7] which emphasize external pressures must be modified in favor of an internal process. In fact, Piaget seems to be of two minds when he proposes that equilibration provides the endogenous tool. Scrutiny of the seven equilibrium levels delimited earlier will clarify this issue. Obviously steps two, three, four, and five cannot be accounted for by an appeal to a reinforcing parameter. As a matter of fact, the strengthening of behaviors, on a continuous or all-or-none basis, is not the result of repetitive reinforcements if the behaviors are selectively shifted with no changes in the external conditions. Rather, it must be viewed as being influenced by the corrective aims of action-oriented conducts. In other words, the internal stability factor at play in any equilibrated phase imposes the use of familiar actions to compensate for disturbances. Lastly, within the Piagetian format, one must reject passive acquisitions by association, which do not account for the original, dynamic, and subject-biased seven levels. The argument revolves around the incompatibility of Piaget's developmental view with a conditioning description. Going back to the example of a rolling and bouncing ball, it operates at every age level in a natural setting, and no property is favored over any other. Hence, the selectivity proper to each of the seven phases is a cognitive matter and originates with the shifting action-oriented behaviors. The interactions between activities determine the complexity of properties. A rolling ball bounces only if oculomotor and grasping schemas permit it through their mutual integrations. No reinforcing schedule can bypass the semiotics of action. Indeed, it blocks for a time the cognitive awareness of the surprising variations accompanying a "super ball."

Despite Piaget's reliance on a structured intellect, confusion still reigns regarding the universal development of the seven stages detailed earlier. To simplify the issue raised by the probabilistic model, let us assume that there is a prefatory and naive Piagetian view. It holds the seven-step sequence governing the acquisition of set-of-properties to be the fruit of a child's innate talent. Foremost among its qualities is the power to be awe-struck when faced with anomalies such as the covariations of sensorial inputs. To improve on this discovery instinct, Piaget appeals to a mental probability function which can be attached incrementally to various properties as their frequency of presentation to the child's attention increases. Curiously enough, one could use similar terms to describe Skinner's operant conditioning. In a nutshell, Skinner posits that, at birth, the baby inherits a slew of potential behaviors, each with a particular situation. Owing to the various consequences, every experience provokes an increase of the probability of some behaviors and a decrease of others.[8] There is a progressive shaping of the behavioral stock by the most common and favorable environmental features. Hence, the individual reflects the regularity of the milieu, via his adapted deportments.

Yet the resemblance with Piaget is only superficial, since Skinner attaches probabilities to behavior as a result of some observationally obtained set of frequencies. Meanwhile, Piaget plunges into an explanatory network of mental predicates which include perceptions, actions, and selective attention. The distinction points up a fundamental difference between Skinner's radical behaviorism and Piaget's epigenetic cognitivism. The former relies on performance and rejects mental predicates as methodologically unsound, while the latter needs them for his cognitive constructions which in fact are competences.[9]

Skinner's inability to account for the continuous dialectical growth of intelligence lies in the overly descriptive method he retains. On the contrary, Piaget's genetic epistemology and cognitive psychology are explanatory. The sequence of probabilistic measures relative to conducts is meshed by the filtering of assimilation. This will actively work over disturbances so as to fit them structurally or accommodate them functionally in order to bring stability.

From previous discussions in this text, it is obvious that, for Piaget, the individual seeks and fashions states of equilibrium above all else. The lack of structures at any or all states imposes non-relational apperceptions, while the appearance of conservation schemes announces a craving for compensatory transformations. Trivially, unstructured appearances cannot yield properties of objects. Furthermore, the breadth of the action-field under the three assimilatory functions of recognition, generalization, and repetition in due course provides the child's actions with representations together with their nullifications. This yields, in a child, the power to undo any imposed world. That power is a kind of revolutionary abstracting process which is managed via an accommodation by differentiation and an assimilation by integration. Thus the instability introduced by the milieu is compensated. The two functions of differentiation and integration give properties the four characteristics of equilibria: extent, stability, mobility, and permanence. They are then used to yield the closed structures so familiar in Piaget's writings, such as grouping, INRC-group, etc.[10]

The four attributes just mentioned regulate actions in the following sense:

- The extent to which actions apply to new objects, and the ensuing relations
- The stability introduced by compensatory transformations so that any actions can be reversed or nullified
- The mobile freedom offered by relations in combining variously separated objects
- The constancy of established structures under the stress introduced either by new objects or by inclusion into larger systems

These features show that progressive equilibration strengthens the relational networks and extends the field of activity, but diminishes the detailing of objects. In other words, qualitative familiarity makes room for structuralization via abstraction from actions. A richer and wider cognitive universe results in an increase of relations between properties. This is correlated with an operational tightening in terms of structures brought into play, which is a manageable control by cognition; that is, *the wider the range of our experiences, the stricter the demand for invariance.*

For instance, as our investigative efforts probe further into the spatial real, we anchor that very real by tauter transformations, and favor constancy in the temporal domain. Once again, there is an appeal to a transposition that is symptomatic of Piaget's ambiguous flirtation with dualism. Conceptual meshing of isolated data demands dualism, and it is this very polarity which Piaget faces when dealing with structured thinking as opposed to the world. When leaning toward a preeminence of the world, he will emphasize the role of accommodation; but if the subject dominates, then assimilation predominates by submitting data to the cognitive schemes. Between the two extremes, an equilibrium is sought and only gets suspended as the result of various perturbations whose compensations are probabilistically settled.

The model presented so far has relied on the power of the environment to change the probability measures to be assigned to the various actions available at any one level. Nevertheless, one is hard-pressed to explain the process by which these actions are influenced by the properties they gather in the environment. The specifics remain obscure regarding the feasibility of any interactions between the environment and the intellectual tools. Singular, objective, and independent events are simply not adequate grounds for a tightly progressive evolution. In that case, the world is reified anew at every step, and perpetually confronts the organism without obvious adaptation. Thus, classical Lockean dualism surfaces again, leaving unexplained the advent of a coherent universe cemented by properties. Piaget seems to opt neither for a phenomenalist nor a representative solution, but for an internalization of the result of probabilistic processes so as to account for the constant progression toward stable states. His opposition to a phenomenalistic answer is deep-seated, and centers on his inability to grant a status to the notion of "observability" within his genetic epistemology. In effect, what I am presently arguing and what is being "flaunted in the face" of common sense, is that the notion of an observer is cognitively inadmissible within a coherent Piagetian interpretation.

IS THE WORLD PROBABLY OBSERVABLE?

Previous developments in Chapters 3 and 4 have shown that unexpected events are not meaningful, because new phenomena are not cognitively relevant. Thus, despite claims by empiricists, an objective and independent phenomenon cannot be observed. This point is important enough to justify a survey of the relevant literature. It should reveal both the role of the observer and the conditions of his observations.

Wittgenstein at first held that we "picture facts to ourselves,"[11] and drew the conclusion that the subject "does not belong to the world."[12] Later, and in a contrasting mood, he adopted in his *Philosophical Investigations* a view more germane to the one presented here, emphasizing the role of agent played by any language-game participant.

Between the two extremes presented by Wittgenstein lies a straightforward third version held by Stuart Hampshire—which resembles my own denial of the notion of an observer—on the grounds that one always experiments actively or does things with some goals in mind.[13] This point is brought out quite forcefully in the following:

> Observations are made with the intention of discovering the way things are in the world: actions are performed with the intention of changing the way things are in the world.[14]

My objections to such a view are fundamental in nature and, of course, consistent with a Piagetian epistemology. In the first place, the dualism is still implicitly present in the accepted dichotomy of action and observation. I hold that without action there can be no sensations, and thus no reaping from and no contact with the world. Secondly, intention, observation, and action are presented as independent entities to be collated according to criteria offered, in the main, by ordinary language. Despite the obvious reliance on the complexity of natural languages in which "the uses" shown by speech episodes are all important, a latent atomism still prevails. It has to be a remnant of the purification process favored by logical positivism.

It is a simple matter to illustrate this atomistic bias in related treatments of this issue.

Smart claims that the closed status of terminal behavior prevails over open processes, and therefore that "what is important in intention is not consciousness but goal-directedness."[15] He is, in fact, arguing against Hamlyn's own proposal that consciousness is part and parcel of "the conceptual scheme which centers around the concept of action."[16] The two authors disagree on the specific alliance to be effected between the crucial concepts surrounding the notion of action. Yet, despite their divergence, they both get their inspiration from everyday linguistic usages. It indicates that, even though concepts denote separate entities for them, their association is open to contradictory interpretations. Hence, due to their latent atomism, their views cannot rely only on the criteria offered by linguistic usage, but must seek elsewhere for additional support. In particular, Hamlyn shows that his choice of concepts is not only guided by some real facets of the

unifying power of an action, but also by the importance given to these
concepts within psychological studies. Therefore, his epistemological
claim that asserts the presence of consciousness in action must have
some psychological backing. And this union is not consistent with his
protests against the relevance of genetic epistemology to epistemology.[17] By borrowing his tenets relative to the concept of action
from within the commonsense universe, he cannot object to one's
establishing an analysis on other grounds; for example, based on
genetic epistemology, or even cognitive psychology. But where Hamlyn most betrays his philosophical allegiance to atomism is when he
offers his intuition as a way to make up for the lack of a common
conceptual network fitted to subtend and define the notion of consciousness and action. He permits then their associative, but independently contrived, composition.

It has been standard practice among empiricists of old, and analytical writers lately, to define objects as atomic collections of properties.
The form taken by their convictions is unequivocal, even though it
reflects an inner faith more than an elaborate epistemological composition. For example, Locke tells us that:

> when we talk of any particular sort of corporeal substances . . . the
> idea of either of them be but . . . a *collection* of those several simple
> ideas of *sensible qualities* . . . we suppose them . . . supported by some
> common subject; which support we denote by the name substance.[18]

The conventionalist Henri Poincaré confesses his inability to
account epistemologically for objects and essentially holds that sensations are united together by an indestructible cement.[19] Bertrand Russell was never able to shake off his early atomism, and still maintained,
in his later writings, that "particulars as complete complex of compre-
sence participate in the finite crisscrossing of our specific modes of
responding to the spectrum available in each sense."[20] As fine an
analytical writer as Arthur Pap does not avoid the "escapism" of
unexplained congealment: "The notion of thinghood is rooted in constant association of diverse qualities."[21]

We can cite several writers expressing themselves similarly. One
of them talks of the "capacity of the mind to synthesize the varied data
of the several senses."[22] Others use throughout a mysterious complete
pattern of "qualia."[23] Still others bring forth a totality, a compound of
sense-data.[24] To sum up the position, the phenomenalist proponent of
logical positivism holds that "seeing a red book" is reducible to the
having of sense-data, where the object is a logical construction from
those sense-data. In their account, what is still missing surrounds the

whole determination of the semantics of the logical constants which hold the sensa together, and which are, of course, not the acceptable ones from propositional logic.

Within the epistemological framework delineated in the first four chapters, I brought forth the idea that beyond Piaget's cognitive psychology there is a viable epistemology. Its main focus touches on the crucial aspects just discussed; namely, the notion of external property, which depends on a constructed reality rather than being artificially posited in the world. At the same time I brought forward enough elements to further an understanding of the notion of object beyond the relatively feeble attempts made by the representative writers just quoted.

In brief, we saw that permanence, invariance, and externality, relative to the sensorial world, demand a semiotics of action. Hence, the object, as defined by these properties, is constructed within inter-coordinations of actions. To justify the emergence of the object within the various and distinct sense modalities, a mandatory manifold behavior sets the limits of that object via its semantics, pragmatics, and meanings. Recognizable properties are linked within action schemas by being the pragmatics of one act, and part of the semantics of another.

At this point, we must return to the original intention of this section, which was to enunciate Piaget's views on the notion of observability and at the same time show that his probabilistic model is inadequate. Among the analytical writers we noted a consensus that man is an observer whose representations are conglomerates of properties. Although their commitment to man as observer is unequivocal, divergencies begin to arise concerning his attributes, his experiences, and his relations with observations. Amid the factions, Ryle's position is particularly appealing from a Piagetian point of view, since it diminishes the autonomy of the observer vis-à-vis his own observations. Doubting mental events to be authentic objects of consciousness, Ryle disputes the possible separation of sensations from their owner like an arrow which cannot take itself as a target.[25] The point is crucial because representation is rejected since there cannot be a ghost in the machine introspectively aware of his perceptual events.

Langford, quoted earlier, rejects Hamlyn's call for reason and intention in the percipient, and in so doing uses Ryle's argument that these two reified entities, as well as volition, lack identification because they are unobservable and uncommunicable. Unhappily, this exclusion suffers, in a negative sense, from the same shortsightedness shown by other analytical writers—that is, it does not settle the epistemological status of observables. To do so requires a strong conceptualist stand which dares to redefine the notion of observability. In a commonsense, sometimes called "naive," philosophy, we are mere spectators or even mirrors of phenomena. A more sophisticated approach inserts events within our universe of beliefs, and thus requires reasons to sustain its predications. It follows that behaviors, taken as events, are as much in need of justification as are actions, since they too need interpreters. Whichever causal reasoning we use to classify a physical phenomenon, it stands on a par with reasons posited for actions. That is, they both have first and foremost a conceptual status.

Langford goes on to assert that "to act is to act on something and so to change it."[26] Taking this sentence at its face value invites controversy. One acts on a state of affairs and one changes it. Of course, one does not act on an objective and independent entity, but on a state of affairs which is a representation made from an aggregate of properties. The change is operated on that aggregate wherein there is a duplication with some variations. This leads to a paradoxical identity crisis between the given, the representation, and its variations. The cloning process is such that no distinctive mark separates the original from its duplicate representation, unless one grants humans some intuitive and active power. Hence, one must seriously question whether the agent is a passive observer who feels "mere presence to." In other words, an agent cannot be an observer in the classical sense. *It follows that within Piagetian epistemology, due to the preponderance of action, no observer can simply be postulated.*

Other ambiguous paradoxes result from the analytical position sketched so far. For instance, a representation is acted on in order to achieve another tabloid, and the objective real is tied in unknown ways to the various mental projections. On the other hand, within Piagetian confines, the original set is already intentionally presented. It is tied to the subsequent set by operationally defined transformations such as retroaction or anticipation. Any identity definition is discussed within these limits.

Against G. E. Moore's commonsense conviction that there is an immediate perception of objects, the evolution of equilibrium structures from primary sensation to sensorimotor schemas shows that the more immediate the presentation, the less reliable it is. Regulation, by interactions of actions, is the source of solidification and of objectification through the invariance it creates.

In order to clarify the status of an observer as related to his observations, one must be cautious about Spinozist category confusion between the physical and the psychical domains.[27]

The Piagetian solution is to seek a continuum between psychological events within a cognitive universe. In order to achieve that goal he argues against analytic epistemology, and advocates a presentation of reality that is distinct from representation. They both have a cognitive status adequate for reflecting the dynamism of objects. Presentation as something "presented to" is mediated by actions, and so is far removed from its progeny in the objective world. Representation lacks ties to the "out there," as no causal network can be an adequate tracer to it. Hence, some kind of link has to show them to be related to objects. The semiotics of action is such a tool as it uses assimilation for sense-data, while using accommodation on cognitive schemes. The crucial epistemological step, however, comes about through the submission of accommodation to the generalizing assimilation. It creates the path justifying the intentionality inherent in action. Consequently the danger of a latent dualism is avoided, and Piaget's conceptual holism takes over. This introduces the important format where intended sensations best lend themselves to being made operational. Indeed, any retroaction or anticipation can operate within the semiotics of action without worrying about a specific sense datum with which to relate. The permanence permeates the object via the ontological tracks plotted by the intercoordinations of action, which grant it the identificational efficacy of anticipation and retroaction.

Expected sensations, loaded with our past experience, funneled by our intention within the semiotics of action, and integrated by the object created within the intercoordinations of actions, at last become presentation. Piaget pursues the matter further in his system and within the sensorimotor stage considers that these presentations are amalgamated as representations. This is a result of the presentations being subjected to repetition, recognition, and generalization. Therefore, any meaningful universe is ultimately representational and by the same token obtains its stability, invariance, and projectibility. This last stricture testifies to the continuous play of actions among perceptions, even though the former subtends presentation and the latter representation. Action *qua* action is the source of constancy, of predictability. The very fact that the real must be acted on to be cognitively significant molds it and limits its variability. From presented sense-data to represented perceptions, action is the link that generates the conceptual characters proper to properties and to objects.

The continuing search for properties likely to encompass various actions and their retroactions knits the semantic fields of cognition into clusters of permanence. They, in turn, become sources for dispositional predications so basic to an understanding of real objects.[28] As a matter of fact, the neo-Piagetian semiotic model described throughout this text is eminently suited to fulfill the epistemological requirements demanded of counterfactuals, including their normative control over any contemplated, substantial real.[29]

If we maintain the traditional status of actions as mere happenings distinguished by their causal histories, then we cannot appreciate the support brought to a purer conceptualistic position by the preceding paragraphs. Indeed, a causal approach to action is implausible, because it maintains that one does not know an action unless the other events construed as its past are given. A counter example to the causal view is offered by an avowed spy scratching his nose apparently as a warning, but in fact as a result of tingling sensations.[30] While it is true that movements do not permit a distinction between mere happenings and actions, one can still argue that within our framework complex movements guide the performance. Moreover, through the coherence obtained in the semiotics of action, they impart intentions. Of course, these movements constitute the person at that very moment, and do not originate in agents located in a mind.

Interesting consequences ensue from these views. It is held, in general, that an epistemological "encounter" with the real must be defined in an abstract world. Piaget treads that familiar ground, and I have previously expressed my concern regarding his cognitive interpretation of it. In the infant's early stage of conservation, Piaget regards abstraction as a representational centration wherein the perceptual field, while altogether available, is mined selectively. By contrast, my neo-Piagetian interpretation acknowledges a precognitive "ore" of stimuli, following which focusing actions set up a spectrum of expected and presented sensations. These in turn are filtered out via an actual encounter with the world. Hence, the conceptual centering on selected properties dominates the pure receptivity of the perceptual field, if such exists. It is equally obvious that actions precede configurational attention. Moreover, the sensorial continuum constituted by proprioceptive and exteroceptive information ties actions and goals, which are reflected by purposefulness. What follows is a distinction of the links between results of and processes of actions. Ultimately, results and processes form an operational equilibrium by reversibility via the commutative interchanges of ends and means. For instance, the object surges out of grabbing something seen, and looking for a felt thing.

For Piaget, the genetic progression of intelligence culminates in some structure in which states of affairs are linked. This intelligence is embodied in sets of transformations that, through their actualization, identify the states of affairs. Any variation from the expected sensations is probabilistically investigated and compensated for, relative to the accumulated invariants. The ontologically posited object, that is to say a full-fledged intentionally-laden state of affairs, is the nucleus for that continuous adjusted creation of invariant features. Thus, whereas specific sensations fall subservient to probable behaviors, objects conquer their status in a well-established, coordinated, and stable set of actions. At last we have found a rationale for the probabilistic matrices used by Piaget for the genesis of property and object conversations, and it is tied to a hypothetico-deductive normalization.

Another point can be made in favor of a cognitive universe which is action-dominated. For the infant, separation imposed by singular perceptual fields does not lend itself immediately to linkages, but the intercoordinations of actions that constitute sensorimotor schemas are the very grounds for objectification and its concomitant identification. The configurational primacy proper to early ages is witness to state changes, rather than to property variations which are preponderant later on. Piaget relies on accommodation for the first, and on assimilation for the second. Consequently, an orthodox interpretation ties accommodation to random encounters with objects, while assimilation introduces structures by linking together these probable encounters.[31]

A careful scrutiny exposes the shallowness of such an explanation. Probabilistic requirements depend on the number of encounters in accommodations, and also on the possible couplings between sensations as organized by assimilation. Unfortunately, the cognitive role and purpose of the various encounters are too loosely defined to tie the individual to an environment that he can call his own. Haphazard interlacing cannot account for a stream of consciousness, for genetic growth, and for homogeneous structural formation. To support these three strongly-organized mental requirements, some artificial explanation is demanded within the probabilistic model. Something like preestablished harmony or vitalistic controlling factors might be the cohesive force holding events together. This weakness is revealed by Piaget's forceful appeals to Ashby's homeostatic model, servomechanisms, phenotypical control over individual development, and biological laws.[32]

Preceding any account of the growth of intelligence, an analysis of the notion of "encounter" must be provided. Since the probabilistic account seems to have failed, we should examine the deterministic framework considered by Piaget in his recent works. Of course, he is forced by the weight of accumulated evidence in his genetic and cognitive psychology to reject his previous probabilistic explanation.

The interesting point is that one reaches the same conclusion by going beyond Piaget while building an epistemology which in fact is a transposition of a Piagetian philosophical psychology.

PIAGET'S DETERMINISTIC MODEL

In one of his latest critical volumes,[33] Piaget revamps his cognitive model by reevaluating the central notion of equilibrium. In earlier works, he emphasized operational structures rather than the construction of the object itself.[34] Equilibrium within coordinations of actions was promoted over the status of objects, thus presenting a world which, by being internally stunted, had an inherent semantic paucity. Importance was given to an intellect whose role was to structure rather than to account for, his personal knowledge of the world.

The extension, mobility, permanence, and stability characteristic of equilibrium states were qualified in a sequential manner within genetic development and not within their immediate cognitive context. Paradoxically, progress was defined probabilistically on the number of properties "encountered" and their concomitant series of possible coordinations of "couplings." This position did not account for the evolutionary progress of equilibrium itself, and as a consequence equilibration was not identified.

Earlier in the text, I construed actions to be the bulwark of all progression toward permanence and invariance. This was judged important because they at the same time indicate the stable state of achieved intellectual structures. On the other hand, the very notion of "encounter" used by Piaget to qualify accommodation betrays the latent intentionality, the aim, the reaching out for the expected. And it is in that direction that one must locate the internal transformations leading to more formal thinking.

Nowadays Piaget conjectures in terms of isomorphisms between "real" configurations and cognitive structures. This reflects his newly found confidence in modeling that replaces his earlier, rather limited, probabilistic explanations. However, I sense a move toward experimentalism in his parametric distribution between subject and object. He dutifully sets out to clarify the elaboration of the object within its causal or logico-mathematical network; that is, he analyzes first the regulations governing actions and objects, at play within stages, and then the transition from one equilibrium level to the next. To accomplish such a task, he cuts himself off from the constructive, inspiring, epistemic subject, to embark on the nacelle of ad hoc models controlling the psychological subject. It is a venturesome approach, as it leaves him an easy prey to an accusation of artificiality based on the multiplication of formal constructions that are supposed to account for all nuances. For example, in the type IA model Piaget describes many relations between the subject and observables.[35] Specifically, he distinguishes the movement of the subject (MS) from the motion of an object (MO), and also the sensation of pushing (PS) from the resistance of an object (RO). After that, he relates all of those by postulating two relations "a" and "b" such that $a = (RO \rightarrow (MS \rightarrow PS))$ and $b = ((MS \rightarrow PS) \rightarrow MO)$. Of course, $(MS \rightarrow PS)$ is an action schema and the sensation of pushing is felt by the subject as a result of the resistance of the object through a feedback loop $PS \leftrightarrows RO$.

We notice distinct symbols used to denote the sensations of the subject and properties of objects. It is plausible for a sophisticated adult to draw such a distinction, but within a genetic epistemology which ties in with knowledge, additional justification is needed. The division between subject and observables is artificially introduced and does not reflect the thorough conceptualism of the active mind. On the other hand, the model can be viewed generously as a tool to bring out necessary clarifications, and in that case we should interpret it as a working model: the interactions a and b suggest an unobservable relation between the object and the action of the subject. In turn, this aspect ultimately results in the realization of invariant ties.[36] The gist of the epistemological message provided by this model is that it centers on clarifying the direct encounters with the milieu; hence, its search for invariants is of a causal sort and related mostly to the psychological subject. Moreover, the motivation behind analyzing direct encounters is to understand equilibration and its progress—but this concept is also tied to a causal explanation.[37]

In the second model, IB, Piaget introduces logico-mathematical actions (AS) that seriate, classify, and set one-to-one mappings.[38] This model also points to the subject's application of these actions to objects through actual activities of classifying, ordering, or simply arranging (FS). It does mean that an action scheme $(AS \rightarrow FS)$ is used on objects' motion (MO). As in model IA, action schemes, $a = (RO \rightarrow (AS \rightarrow FS))$.

I have already opposed such a view of action, which allows one to separate it completely from the object and consequently cuts off its cognitive support. To foresee a modifying factor is to admit the malleability of the object, hence to have an anterior presentation of it. Therefore no transformations would be cognitively relevant if the object had not been presented before and only the solitary after-the-fact results were available. The nonmodifying agent, whose role is purely extrinsic to the object, simply does not have access to it. Such an agent, not aiming or expecting anything in particular, would be likely to seriate water as well as pebbles, with the shock of having to compare an everspreading liquid.

Piaget's salvation lies in his seemingly innocuous appeal to ghostly gestalts, embodied in the subject's application of an organized set of actions to some state of affairs. The introduction of these "good forms" guarantees the noninferential immediacy of the subject's encounters with reality. Piaget relates the various components of actions by arrows (MS→PS), which reflects his intuitions, but lacks elaborate analyses. One does not know whether these arrows represent functions, operations, or causal and logical relations.

In the neo-Piagetian perspective presented in the previous chapters, I have established that the sensation PS stands for the anticipation of an action MS, and that this intimate connection explicates the arrow (MS→PS) appearing in model IA. The resistance of the object RO is the very same expected sensation interpreted as the pragmatics of the action over the ontologically posited object within the action-chain. From an epistemological viewpoint, the equivalence between subject and object behaviors remains implausible. Yet, if we adopt it as an isomorphism between models, then we have to admit that Piaget interlaces two distinct modes of explanation. The relation "a" holding between the resistance of object and the subject's action schema corresponds to our converging feedback spiral, involving the pragmatics and semantics of actions within an eventual stable chain. Accordingly, Piaget's model IA will have to include the sequence: Stimuli→ Conceptualization→ Action→ Object→ Sensation → Stimuli→. . . .

Model IB must be rejected because of its similarity with model IA, which imposes inferentiality on the cognitive level and therefore makes feasible the immediate imposition of *gestalt* structures demanded by model IB. The immediate availability of logico-mathematical "good forms" like seriation or ordering is to be doubted, since they are subject to a gradual structuring, and thus fit inside the various models of action intercoordinations.

Piaget's genetic findings about the progression of cognitive growth direct him to include logical relations in the models, and so we obtain model IIA.[39] In it cognitive influences are strengthened by the use of a function that imposes the coordinations of actions of the subject (Coord.S) onto the coordinations of the objects (Coord.O) such that SO=Coord.S→ Coord.O. However, this function is still under the control of the object's physical features (RO→ MO), which reverberate onto the subject's action schemas (MS→ PS) or action schemes

(AS→ FS). To perform this feat a function OS is used, OS=(RO→ MO)→ (MS→ PS).

At this particular point are introduced the first few inklings of the idea that one must come to "understand" the world in order to come to terms with it. *This understanding consists in an awareness of one's own actions on the world, which, for Piaget, can only occur via a representation. Moreover, he insists that consciousness must be centripetal*, since only via an encounter with objects can we be made aware of our actions and correct their sensorial shortcomings.

This process is summarized in model IIA by the appearance of the connecting arrow OS, which essentially expresses the idea that accurate knowledge of one's own observability can only obtain via a reflection on the properties of objects.

Once again we are faced with Piaget's latent realism, which relies on Maine de Biran's notion of effort against obstacles to explain the appearance of the world. That is, only through the resistance of objects to a subject action can externality be conveyed. The numerous loopholes in that view have been surveyed at length in the opening sections of chapters 3 and 4. At the same time, one can favorably regard the assertions that representation yields consciousness and that misrepresentation of the real is corrected within a loop cycling over sensations via conceptualization of actions: Obs.O→ (MS→ PS)→ Coord.S→ Coord.O→ Obs.O. *As a consequence of my analysis of intentionality, I retain a centrifugal positing of externality, thus differing sharply with Piaget.* The origin of Piaget's emphasis on centripetence is that "consciousness of" is located at the tail end of a behavior (see chapter 4).

The relation SO ties Coord.S (subject-coordinations) to Coord.O (object-coordinations), and symbolizes the idea that the necessity obtaining in any causal net can only come from the operational set of the subject, which is the source of logico-mathematical structures. Causal tracks are not imprinted by observables, but must be introduced by the observer. I concur with this view, with the reservation that on the epistemological side there is no justification for a sharp division between subject-coordinations and object-coordinations. As a matter of fact, that split was unnecessarily introduced by Piaget's lapse into a "naive" or gross commonsense philosophy, and remains artificial. It is now reintroduced through the severed umbilical chord represented by the endogenous production of objects.

I have previously debated this issue, which can be reiterated *grosso modo* as follows: the temporal spread of events is transposed into the aphysical frame of operational linkages, thus forcing various presentations of the state of affairs. The necessity factor is to be found in the pragmatics and semantics of actions which, under the impact of inter-plays of actions, impart predictability to properties. In turn, sensorial feedbacks controlled by the environment allow a search for invariance to pay off within an appropriate semiotics of action. I must note that the process requires a hierarchy of type IIA schemas, which is exactly what Piaget ascribes to that model.

The inevitable formation of invariants firmly settles the cognitive presentation of reality within logical dimensions (consistency, coher-ence). There is a gradual formalization that perforce disregards the particularities of the world. The constructed reality expands by benefit-ting from generalizing schemas while depleting the milieu that dis-turbs the successive erections of these invariants. It is in this sense that one must interpret Piaget's subject- and object-coordinations (Coord.O, Coord.S) that are, for him, the source of "new discoveries." Again I detect an admixture of vocabularies that betrays his latent scientific realism, but clashes with a Piagetian epistemology that re-jects both "newness" and "discovery." We should realize that any progressive equilibrium is made at the expense of the complex world. As we just mentioned, the generalizing schemas differentiate into classes or seriations, and proportionally ignore the object's qualities that do not fit in. A subject coordinations means that as the milieu disturbs expected results of actions, the bothersome object is inserted in a wider spectrum of intersecting actions where the disturbance is compensated for. A hard rubber "super ball" does not fit in with the oculomotor expectations relative to bouncing objects. The compensa-tion is introduced by dispositional predicates such as elasticity, which explains a slew of operational behaviors and whose main effect is to include the unexpected bounces.

Adopting model IIA as a template, Piaget devises a hierarchy which in his eyes resolves the drawbacks of his earlier probabilistic pattern of random actions. The new design tightly links the sensations, actions, observables, and various interactions between internal and external coordinations. Moreover, it reduces possible instabilities by transposing the relevant sensations and observations into the next equilibrium plateau, thus accounting for the operational expansion of thought processes (that is, intelligence).

Obviously there is a tendency for Piaget to accept a neutral "real" opposing a structuring intelligence. Depending on the preponderance granted to either side, he offers model IA or model IB. The interrela-tionships are biased toward objects for the A models, and to mental operations for the B model, which conveys a strong rationalist stance via its logico-mathematical subjection of the real. In the B model, actions and sensations are ingredients inserted in the coordinated schemata at play. Therefore, observables are projections of the subject, since they reflect a practical and conscious will to act and must therefore be integrated in a complex behavior. Piaget goes so far as to add that objects observed through our actions inherit all our intentions.[40]

It follows that object-coordinations (Coord.O) resembles the prototype imposed by actions-coordinations, since the properties of objects are determined by the subject. Of course, Piaget sees only an isomorphism between Coord.O and Coord.S, thanks to his everpresent realism. He does not totally surrender to synthetic constructivism. He even accepts the idea that, at this level of overwhelming logico-mathematical domination, it is the object's resistance that forces a reintegration into broader structures, thus compensating for any disequilibrium. Furthermore, he admits among the various cognitive modalities the possibility of pure descriptions, and these are only conceptualized when an action differentiates the various observations.

I have questioned already the coherence of holding the view that an agent can be an observer, while mediating the world through presentations and not representations. The purity of the object is not sanctified, but rather generated by actions, and therefore the real is no tabloid to be surveyed directly. The leitmotif of the observer being a source of passivity is antithetical to the active mind propounded by an epigenetic epistemologist, but it still reappears time and time again in Piaget's writings. Against this flaw in his arguments it must be reasserted that beyond Piaget's psychology, there is a theory of knowledge where the notion of observability is redefined. To be specific, even if we admit to being an observer, our intentions are severed from any particular milieu. But more importantly, as agents our expectations are the source of transformations that grant knowledge. Action entails that whatever is acted on suffers a change. An agent, as an observer, can only be defended when he represents something to himself.

Efforts to view sensations as being intimately tied to actions lead to a further complicity between the descriptions of properties and of actions. One does not categorically impose rules or conditions that define events *ex ante*, but one hypothesizes on them *ex post*. There is no judge at that point, but there is a creator of a set of anticipations. Naturally, to anticipate entails actions that are directed at "objects," and are also performed to achieve some ends; but there is intentionality only in the conceptual domain of "virtual" actions, and not objective particulars. Herein lies a plausible justification for Brentano's reference[41] to the "intentional inexistence" of represented "objects."

Interestingly, our representations, which are the bases for sets of anticipations—sometimes called beliefs—are controlled by how the world is, while our actions, which are cognitively sealed in the presentations, depend on our mode of being. From earlier analyses, presentation precedes and generates representation; accordingly, actions yield certitude about beliefs, giving a weak form of knowledge.[42]

These remarks sharply distinguish the impact of the environment from one's personal physical constraints, and urgently impress upon us the need for the regulatory agency of equilibrium. It leads to another major facet to be belabored, namely the very process of stabilization which is built around compensations to disturbances. Piaget introduces a regulatory mode followed by cognitive structures as the outcome of an activity that scurries about swallowing up an environment which tries to impose itself on the organism. Objects *qua* objects must, for better or for worse, be inserted in the operational network in use at the respective stage. This means that properties that are created in the operational network will delimit the "intension" of various sets, thus limiting the objects contained within the extension of these sets. If the environment offers some resistance to its insertion in the operational network of actions, then there will be either a rearrangement or a reorganization. The various forms of rearrangement are either a compensatory action of the subject, or a modification of the object's properties and the subject's actions. On the side of reorganization, a more adequate structure is created so as to resolve the unexpected contradictions. Unable to control the boomerang effects of a rolling ball, the child will push it back toward him, or he will modify its speed, or still he will begin to think in terms of a system of push and pull, finally arriving at an understanding of tangential forces.

At this juncture Piaget's realism introduces an epistemological gap centered around the dualism, object-subject. It is reflected by the lack of cognitive significations given to the notions of resistance and contradiction. To fill in the gap, one has to transpose the resistance and contradiction from its birth through encounters with the milieu, to the level of structural representations. Only there can the projected significances of objects be questioned property-wise. The ensuing compensations demand, within the chain of "virtual" actions, interchanges among properties and among actions. Their variability makes up the different adaptive means at our disposal. These adaptations will be the source of new structures that will account for the cohesiveness of our experience (see Chapter 4). Undeniably, as actions become related into more complex sets of activities, there is a corresponding increase in the number of interchanges or intermingling that can be carried out. Since properties are reinforced when they belong to several behaviors, then their resistance strengthens accordingly. On that account, the wider the field of our experiences tied by relations, the tighter our control over transformations through the creation of invariants. This particular viewpoint is in fact, but not entirely in spirit, advocated by Piaget, when he grants the second level in the model B hierarchy the power to anticipate variations in what the environment has to offer. This competence precludes any surprise stemming from encounters with the real, and reveals a system of "virtual" actions which are available to the person.

To account for the progression of cognitive growth from one structure to a more abstract one, Piaget once more revises his probabilistic system. In it an encounter is probable relative to the presence of some phenomena and their disturbing effects on perceptions. In the deterministic model, for a structure to succeed another one it has to be more abstract; that is, it must contain more complex activities. This is influenced by the two factors of variability and resistance which are the internal parameters of cognitive structures. The interiorization in the adjustment process gives a greater control over the environment, and divulges a trend toward a cognitively specified reality.

At first the behaviors most probably influenced by changes in the environment are those that directly involve one particular action or the properties of objects as perceived by the subject. The main reason for this is that they are centered on single independent properties rather that those that are conjoined. In addition, the lack of relational structures in the early stages favors compensation by incremental modifications, with the milieu still in the lead. The integration of disturbing factors must wait until the individual can establish relations between properties. It is then viable to hold that the increased probability of these external factors will be not only a function of the frequency of their occurrences, but more critically subject to their insertion into various coordinations with other properties.

To be sure, the probability function has an epistemic flavor in the Carnapian sense.[43] Within the Piagetian system, the probabilities attached to events will be proportional to the "entrenchment"[44] of the corresponding properties within the relational network of actions. For instance, an element might be found to be big with respect to small objects, and then cannot be judged as small, relative to another set of larger objects, thanks to the nonrelative nature of properties at this cognitive level. (To be big is to be absolutely big.) Later, the mastery of an ordering structure will permit the element to be both big and small within the seriation. Hence, the probability of viewing various properties and their variations is dependent on the cognitive relations brought into play. Ultimately, the appearance of new structures can incorporate contrasting properties, like big and small, without contradictions. This leads to ultra stable compensations when some factors, viewed as the inverse of others, cancel out their effects, as in adding and subtracting two apples. Similarly, the altruism of some children is possibly the result of cognitive mastery. Their toys, when not in their hands, are realized to be present somewhere else, and will eventually be subjected to a compensatory action that by reciprocation will put them back in their hands.

The final outcome of intellectual progress is a certitude accompanying expectations in the sense that, no matter what happens, the result can be integrated in a structure, thus gaining normalcy and losing its accidental indeterminism. The probability of events, viewed from a logical positivist point of view, is tied to the frequency of observations, and thus remains independent and constant throughout the life of the observer. On the contrary, within our purview inspired by Piaget's deterministic model, the meanings of encounters, and thus their epistemological value, are determined by the contemporaneous cognitive structure which reads them out. Once again, the possibility of neutral and singular observations is jeopardized, as is logical atomism.[45]

Piaget's work on equilibration details the regulations which occur between the subject and the object on one side, and the actions coordinations of the subject and relations between objects on the other.[46] This work recognizes the various forms of equilibrium achievements based on external factors affecting the infant. Piaget dismisses as unproductive the assumption that in the case of physical actions there is an immediate total agreement between the subject's actions and the properties of objects. In other words, he rejects straight cognition of objective properties through one's behavior. Furthermore, he rejects mere biological immersion of the organism as a symbiotic motive force behind cognitive growth.

It is at the level of sensorimotor activities that the advent of new cognitive structures can best be explained in terms of assimilation and accommodation. Any study of equilibrium, reequilibrium, and disequilibrium relies on an analysis of the ties established between assimilation, accommodation, and objects. Moreover, such a study must be buttressed by a survey of the various relations holding between actions schemes, such as mutual assimilation of the suction, prehension, and visual schemes.

Piaget holds that the schemes lead to stable logico-mathematical structures because they are constructed by coordinations of the subject's actions. On the other hand, the schemas obtained directly from objects and including the sensorial qualities, remain open to contradictions under the impact of the varieties offered by the environment, and thus never reach a permanent equilibrium. They make up our experimental or physical knowledge, and essentially constitute our causal reasonings, which attribute effective power of one object over another.

The infant attributes rather than applies his own intellectual format to the physical relations between two objects, A and B. For instance, referring to model IA, the motion (MO) and push (PS) of one object over another force the introduction of unobservable relations between the resistance of the passive object (RO) and the action of the active one. Indeed, the only direct acquaintance we have of the passive object is of its resistance (RO) and its motion (MO). The functional relation obtaining between (RO) and (MO) is not causal unless it inserts the action MO→ PS as a condition. This happens because, according to Piaget, it is the tactilo-kinesthetic covariations that, when attributed, give us a feeling for a visual perception of causal relations.

The child seems to favor the imposition of his own action scheme on physical events in order to assimilate the real. Regarding this process, Piaget prefers that the imposition should be an attribution rather than an application. Unhappily, this does not remove all ambiguities, because both choices betray a dualistic view.

Indeed, to apply a conceptual frame on sense-data suggests either a functional dependence of the given which is transformed into a representation, or an apportionment of a pattern according to the particularities of the surroundings. On the other hand, attribution of properties requires an entity to be a recipient and implies a molding design. One can then discern form from content. According to Piaget, these are also the respective domains for development and learning. To bypass the dualism introduced by Piaget when he grants the intellect the power to attribute qualities, we should in my opinion return to the more orthodox monism characterizing his early but insightful studies.[47]

These studies suggest that the knowledge of physical reality is proportional to its progressive loss of subjective elements. For example, pain will at first pervade all things, then lodge itself back in its psychical locus. Similarly, causality, which in a previous paragraph was seen as an attribute transposed from tactilo-kinesthetic sensations, survives among physical events, only after the feelings of push, moving, and resistance, return to their psychic abode. Objectivity of some property depends on the subjectivity slowly gained by others.

Piaget's cognitive constructions always remain susceptible to disturbances for lack of initial stability. These constant victimizations of the conceptual framework lead Piaget to seek further by setting down a paradoxical inquiry: are obstacles, opposed by their nature to operationalizations, necessary conditions of intellectual growth, or are they simply occasions for the readjustment of structures? In other words, should we give preeminence to disequilibrium or to reequilibration as the motive power behind cognitive development?

The answer seems to be that conflicts always accompany actions and their intercoordinations. This is due to the gap they open through their exercise and the fact that it is to be filled in by unexpected results. Thus, whereas disequilibrium leads to a search for other possible actions, reequilibration directs the choice among actions toward a better or progressive equilibrium.

Even though I have sketched what seemed to be Piagetian epigenetic answers, the mood here is definitely vitalistic. Piaget often states that, biologically speaking, conflicts stem from the disequilibrium intrinsic to the laws governing living organisms. On the other hand, if it is within the action schemas that progress has to be defined, then cognitive constancy is the prevalent factor. For instance, presentation at time n will generate the actions under given stimulus conditions at time n+1, and will be the instrument to match the present and expected sensations at time n+1. This expectation is the source of constancy, which, if admitted, favors reequilibration of the concept relative to some object, irrespective of the variations offered by nature. The preestablished choice governs, through expectation, what is to be found. At the same time, we saw earlier in the text the source for the notion of "creativity" to be the open-endedness of intentions within the meanings of actions, that is, of those actions not yet reinforced, and thus not stabilized. This freedom, while limited, does permit adjustments and reequilibration. Careful scrutiny of this interpretation points to fruitful perspectives, both in psychology and in education. The creativity just alluded to is restrained by performance, and is funneled by the competence steering it. In brief, when viewed from the vantage point of intellectual schemes and developmental activities, performances supposedly reflect them, and by the same token betray the underlying competence that they embody. Viewed in developmental terms, competence opens several courses of action whose adjustments through the performances are reflected back into a reequilibration of that competence. Piagetian epigenesis locates an optimal difference between competence and performances, during the transitory periods where the child acts at level n, but is able to master a level n+1 structure.

The child's potential is not to be seen as a progressive orientation toward a maximal development. Instead, it is contingent on the effective enactment by performances of an intellectual structure. One can conclude that the creative potential of a child stems from the operational congruence of his competence and his performances at a given time and for a specific task. Reequilibration ensures this congruence in a "zooming" sequence of adjustments whose action-oriented basis entails getting at the world and constructing a reality.

To resolve the above-mentioned paradox as to whether obstacles are contingent causes for readjustments or rather the origin of intellectual growth, Piaget attempts to qualify carefully the regulations governing various disequilibria. They can be shaped into two formats:

1. An internal scheme that links the successive loops of the generalized model IIA:[48] (Obs.Sn. Obs.On) . (Coord.Sn+1. Obs.On+1). Any observations at time n+1 regarding the object and the corresponding feelings of the subject will verify the inferential relations and establish a tested continuum with prior observations. For instance, this empowers the child to reach one day to "the" moon and not just "a" moon.
2. The second format directly relates the object and the subject, as shown by the original model IIA, where $OS = (RO \rightarrow MO) \rightarrow (MS \rightarrow PS)$.

Within these two formats any action is definable relative to its goal, and it is with respect to that goal that one must analyze regulations. In other words, regulations modify actions in accordance with certain goals, and their effects can be formulated in three ways:

1. The means to reach a given goal can be affected so that the chain is segmented to allow for variations subordinated to that end, then various movements correct the deviations to reach it: a blanket is pulled in various ways to bring closer and to grasp an object;
2. A unidirectional effort is made to keep constant an event which has already been actuated: hands and mouth movements maintain the nursing;
3. One removes obstacles that oppose the hoped-for results: following the motion of an interesting object demands various bypasses.

These views bring forward the teleological role of regulatory processes, which is characterized in a very specific action by sensorial expectations.

Piaget comes out clearly in favor of sensations as part and parcel of all actions, and of intentionality as inherent to all actions aiming at objects. This sheds some light on the regulatory processes at work in the cyclic model IIA; namely, there is a verification of action-coordinations, both of the object and of the subject at time n, by the observables at time n-1 (Obs.Sn–1 and Obs.On–1). These regulatory processes can now be seen to lie in the matching process between the sensations anticipated by the actions making up these coordinations, and the actual set generated by the stimuli (pragmatics of the action).

In the case of disparities in the matching process, a crucial role is played by compensations. They govern the closure of logico-mathematical structure in the form of reciprocal or reversible actions, and represent inversions among physical events.

One can now specify the compensatory regulations that will realize the three possible schemes of actions mentioned above. The first requires an accommodation in the sense that the means are interchanged so as to make the fixed goal cognitively relevant. The second scheme is a simple feedback loop to keep the action going toward its goal. It adjusts positively or corrects negatively like a homeorhesic system. In the third case, conflicts force the intentional introduction of acts so as to counteract the detrimental effects of obstacles on the attainment of a specific goal. The overall effect of these various compensations is to nullify a disturbance at first with oscillatory damping convergence, and then with asymptotic increasing accuracy. The procedure is repeated until the original action evolves toward a perfect reversible action, which becomes the operation of the completed logico-mathematical structures. So for Piaget it is unequivocally from the equilibrium state that the all-important reversibility of actions originates.[49] Hence, compensations ensure some constancy, and ultimately contribute toward forging the various conservation invariants.

Piaget reminds us often that regulations specify the influence of the result of one action over subsequent acts, and that they must therefore originate in the repetitive assimilation. This begins at the sensorimotor level, from which it borrows its main traits: reproducing a movement, adjusting it by recognizing an anterior percept, generalizing by using other means and leading to different ends.

In keeping with the essential cognitive status of assimilation, and also with his basic realism, Piaget probes various reasons for the infant's apparent urge to seek new objects. He finally adopts the view that there exists a desire to assimilate, with the obvious consequence that this gives an orientation to actions and explains the never-ending opposition to nature.

With that desire, Piaget simply postulates an inner motivation which leads to the incorporation of nature in one's own cognitive realm, and in turn reduces individuals to goal-seeking servo-mechanisms relative to any one action. The resistance of nature to this incorporation forces a reenactment of the schema, so that some modifications of the last segments of the chain of actions can overcome the differential opposition in a compensatory manner.

Obstacles are thus the source of differentiations within the assimilative schemas, and therefore enhance the anticipatory power of the cognitive faculties. An increase in the discriminating ability follows, and it is brought about by all these adapted responses. The multiplicity of schemas also permits a much denser network of relations, which thus integrate the object in a wealthier semiotics of action. It is from the vantage point of this dual play that one can put into perspective the dispute between Bruner and Piaget concerning the status of the identity principle. While Bruner sees it as innate, Piaget points to it as the result of a host of other prerequisite properties. Bruner distinguishes between sensations that are a "form of the same thing" as characterizing the identity principle, and sensations that are "the same kind of thing" as the bases for an equivalence set.[50]

Within the semiotics of action, the object constructed and aimed at via the interchanges of means or motoric elements constitutes the integrated identity, while the sensorial interchanges among goals build the differentiated equivalence. They are both genetic upshots and not innate principles. As a matter of fact, the coordination of schemes increases the intension of an object, while decreasing its extension. The outcome is a more precise identification, together with a restricted equivalence set.

In order to conciliate the two opposite trends introduced by mutual integration and differentiation, Piaget brings into play a stabilizing factor. This turns out to be none other than the notion of object, through which action coordinations integrate, and which can also account for the variations in scheme usages. The danger fostered by such a view is that a potential source of parcelling emerges via the repetition of one action phase that can be opposed by the modifications of the sensorial phases. An object that is tightly meshed in the network of actions is then enlarged by the richness of the qualities bestowed on it by that very network. A compromise has to be found, which Piaget sets at a higher stage, where a general equilibrium law compensates between the system's own need for integration and the perturbations introduced by nature's own diversity. A typical example is the simple act that, from a means into a reflex activity, sets out to reach for some object. It associates thereafter with other acts to enrich the initially impoverished object. From an instinctual drive, it majors into a cognitive status.

A noticeable aspect of the construction of objects is constituted by the potency of intersections within action coordinations. Previously, when Piaget set an obstacle as the source of both retroaction and anticipation, he was in fact stating a fundamental position. He stressed that the reenactment of actions means repetition of the motoric phase of the coordinated chain of actions, and differentiation essentially indicates sensorial redistribution. In short, equilibrium must be defined in a neo-Piagetian form that means within the semiotics of action, where there is the possibility of articulations between the motoric and the sensorial phases. I prefer this formulation, which properly reflects the constructive Piagetian spirit rather than the basically dualistic orthodox view that there is a constant search for equilibration between form and content. This latter view, given preeminence by most commentators, "reflects" the classical dichotomy between figurative and operative thinking. In fact, it emphasizes the final role of logico-mathematical structures proper to scientific concepts. The former view, tied to the semiotics of action, reflects our interest in developing an epistemology. For that reason, knowledge must remain in the forefront, and this implicates the construction of a reality which is transposed from Piaget's cognitive psychology.

Moreover, my interpretation allows the origin of decentration or objectivization to be placed within the tenuous attachments of coordinated actions, which involve the interchangeability of sensorial sets and motoric phases respectively. On that score, all Piaget tells us is that the universe becomes progressively separated from us, in proportion to the various differentiations and integrations that consolidate the object into a permanent entity. Having amplified the discourse sustaining the birth of reality, I can assert that objectivity is built by the dissociation and not by the association of sensations.

The resistance of the object is merely mentioned by Piaget without elaboration. Within our framework, it can be interpreted to mean a mismatch at the sensorial end of an action, where the anticipated sensation, transposed into expected stimuli, does not match those received. Accommodation then takes place in the resetting of that sensorial goal with a better fit toward the actual reception of stimuli.

To further the epistemological gains stemming from the format, one should work out its action-oriented articulations in more detail. We note that while the environment is assimilated via recognitory, generalizing, and repetitive schemes, objects resist these assimilations owing to the initial paucity of action-oriented schemas. The broadening of experiences stems from these resistances which force the repetition of actions. But these occur in a converging or damping feedback loop manner such that only the first part of an action or motor phase is faithfully repeated, and the second or sensorial part is subjected to adaptive transformations. The process gives rise to a multiplicity of possible sensations all of which are connected with, or recursively dependent on, their initial presetting by a unique sensorimotor handle. Conversely, the very multiplicity of sensations allows for several actions to aim at any one of them. Stimuli will act as the differentiating agents to initiate the adequately accommodated action. The motor phase of the action is a source of integration and creation for specific objects, while qualities instigate the differentiation that confers a relative independence on the various senses, and at the same time bestows objectivity on a complex world. In other words, diversity among phenomena yields a proportionate objectivity. Relative to these remarks, one can note that accommodation is essentially located at the sensorial tail-end of behaviors, and is not part of the more centrally rooted assimilative action-schemes. Hence, *integration and differentiation do not conflict, since they are located within different phases of an action; the latter at the sensorial terminal, and the former within intercoordinations of actions.* However, they both are connected by a chain of actions, which means that structures are not disconnected from sensations. The operative and figurative aspects of thinking are neither form and content nor two forms of cognition, but together they construct reality. By contrast one can enunciate some very general propositions which summarize Piaget's own deterministic position. The assimilative schemes posit the structured object, while accommodation processes the physical modalities of that object. Hence, assimilation is the source of integration and structuring, and accommodation differentiates qualitatively.

Still faithful to the polarity characterizing his psychological studies, Piaget continues to separate the epistemic from the psychological subject. In terms of knowledge, this could be regrettable because its unity is split in a physical and a logico-mathematical knowledge; but if one restricts this orthodox interpretation to Piaget's attachment to scientific knowledge, then the personal knowledge of an agent can still recover its unity. Earlier discussions argued that encounters leading to a "new" knowledge require assimilation followed by accommodation. Referring to the previous paragraph, this tells us that integration precedes differentiation. On the surface, it seems paradoxical. However, in Chapter 3 we showed that repetitive and recognitory assimilations led to generalizing assimilation, and that accommodation is really part of this generalizing process. Of course, within the semiotics of action this means that sensorial configurations must be dealt with prior to motoric interplays. Finally, we can conclude that sensory integration precedes motor differentiation, and that is eminently plausible. In terms of epistemological unity instilled by the person acting on the world, and thereby constructing his reality, the line of reasoning is now open. For instance, the proprioceptive and kinesthetic effects, correlative to any movement, are part of the semiotics of a particular action leading to some sensations. Accordingly, the feelings making up the psychological subject accompany the act of the knowing person. Indeed, the agent is epistemologically and psychologically linked to his reality.

COMMENTS ON PIAGET'S DETERMINISTIC MODEL

According to Piaget, models I and II represent the structural relationships that obtain between the subject, his coordinations of actions, and the intercoordinations between objects. Evolving cognition depends on the temporally-staggered feedbacks, which carry these coordinations into a constructive spiral where more and more objects are defined with more and more details. Hence, the spreading field of phenomena surveyed is subjected to a tighter network of interrelations. This process is due to a multiplication of the number of obstacles offered by the world.

Any obstacle presented by the world entails a disequilibrium of the servo-system loops,[51] which are corrected by the three basic compensatory behaviors:

a: cancels perturbations simply by ignoring them or adjusting to them by small incremental shifts;
b: accommodates action by varying them in a qualitative scale of more or less, so as to compensate for disturbances;
c: integrates all possible variations, so as to include symmetric actions which can be the exact inverse or the reciprocals of one another.[52]

Examples of compensation a are provided by the child who forgets a disappearing object, adds traits to make sure that a toy is recognized as his, or displaces himself slightly to recover the lost perspective of a rotating game. In the case of behavior b, the swiftness of eye motion compensates for the slow hand trying to catch a super ball. As for conduct c, the child waits his turn for playing in a revolving team, or counterbalances a swing.

My main criticism is levelled at the lack of cognitive genesis supporting these constructive systems. To compensate for such a situation, I hold that if there has to be a construction, then it operates first on the object and always in a conceptual frame. Hence, it is in the very erection of the world that compensatory accommodations exist, which therefore obviates the need for a separate analysis in terms of the behaviors a, b, and c. From the start, the world enters essentially and directly into its own conceptualization, and does not need to impinge beforehand on approximate representations in order to force corrective actions. A dualistic view is inappropriate. What must be ascertained is whether or not Piaget moves in that direction when he analyzes the relations holding between his models I, II, and the compensatory behaviors. For him all perturbations hinder the various assimilatory schemes, and can only lead to a resumption of activities via some compensations which constitute a new constructed equilibrium.[53]

Thanks to a generous phraseology, this statement remains ambiguous unless it gains a specific interpretation within the confines of a semiotics of action as provided in Chapter 4. Piaget's lack of such a reduction entrenches him in a potentially deceptive defense of his constructive regulations. Indeed, he argues that motivational and effective forces push the assimilatory tools toward the world, and this only when objects of that world become functionally interesting to human needs. Moreover, objects attract operational thinking in proportion to their arrested state, which provokes both a cognitive gap and a conative need.

This is obviously a legacy of a functionalistic position, which as Piaget acknowledges, likens him to J. Dewey, E. Claparede, and S. Freud. Still, the resemblance with these authors might seem fortuitous in light of Freud's overwhelming use of maturation, and the continuous, lifelong and obstacle-free development bestowed on man by Dewey. [54] Both positions are antithetical to Piaget. Nevertheless, failing to justify man's apparent hunger for encounters with the world, he selects functional needs to sustain the dynamic constructivism proper to his inherently static structuralism. The gap separating the subject from objects is then bridged by the motivations stemming from these needs.

It is the very existence of that gap that, in many instances, fractures Piaget's attempt at drawing a conceptualistic epistemology from his genetic psychology. Of course, the fault is to be traced to his underlying scientific realism, which curiously brought him allies from within the ranks of Marxist orthodoxy. This last point is exemplified by an excerpt from the Soviet psychologist, D. Uznadze:

The development of conscious mental processes is preceded by a state which cannot in any degree be regarded as a noumenal, purely physiological state. We call this state "the set." A state of preparedness for a definite activity, its onset depending on the presence of the following conditions: a need, actually felt by a particular organism, and an objective situation for the satisfaction of this need. . . .[55]

Clearly, the position advocated is that learning and development are not shaped by experiences modifying behavior, but rather by behaviors modulating experience. Accordingly, Piaget's cognitive universe is rooted in actions, and that support should obviate the urgency for a kindred dynamogenism. Earlier, we saw that on two counts the evolution of the thinking process depends on activity. The first relies on the action precognitive support in the world, and the second is circumscribed by active construction of objects with no polarity whatsoever. Under these conditions, the world is not to be reached at the front gates, but infiltrates through the back door.

Piaget continuously flirts, however, with the idea of representation as an essential sign of intellectual maturity. In fact, its appearance terminates the sensorimotor stage, which explains the curious presence of an observer together with his observations in the cognitive models IA and IB described earlier.

From my previous analyses, it is clear that this view is not consistent with the basic Piagetian tenets characterizing the sensorimotor level. Indeed, while one could insist that cognized sensations are presentations, they are denied representational and observational status. The two main reasons for it are adduced in Chapter 4. First, sensations partake of intentions within the meanings of actions. They also specify their teleonomy within the pragmatics and semantics of performances, which force them to cohere sequentially with these meanings so as to compose the conceptual domain. Secondly, resistances to objects are the source of accommodations via the generalizing assimilation, which entails that fully constituted sensations originate obstacles within an expectant cognitive set and thus must precede the actual encounter.

Opposition to this conceptualism exists among various authors proposing more "realistic" positions. Their tenets center on the belief that observations present a direct access to the world. A clarification is necessary lest we forget Piaget's propensity for baptizing himself a realist, either as a biologist and a psychologist, which is acceptable, or as an epistemologist, which is surely misguided.

In general, the realist position starts with a physiological argument along causal lines, which proposes that stimuli originating in an object—such as light rays or odors—hit the sense organs separately. Impulses move along the nerve pathways in the direction of the central nervous system (CNS), and provoke some activity in it.

> It is immaterial here whether we then say that this activity causes sensations which, with interpretations become perceptual consciousness. . . . When and only when physiology is taken into account it may be concluded that perceptual consciousness is really adverbial, a mode of experiencing an internal activity normally but not necessarily is due to the appropriate external object.[56]

This position on the role of sensorial activity is so unrefined that not only does it not distinguish the trees in the forest, but it is even mistaken about the status of the forest as well. On the one hand, it postulates a singular objective event, causing a delimited neurophysiological process whose final correlate is a perception. It is as though the environment would selectively uncover privileged entities toward the percipient, and then impose specific physiological events. On the other hand, the psychical and psychological characteristics have to be accounted for, and this is done almost as an afterthought in the form of a consciousness that is "caused or related to brain activity."[57] That is, the adverbial awareness is connected without argument to the tail-end of a physical causal chain, in spite of the danger of identifying causal relations between body and mind with a mutual reduction of their properties. Even more extreme appears the conviction adopted here, yet opposed by many analytical writers,[58] that any discussion of mental events is restricted to the brain, not in terms of empirical conditions, but because of a conceptual analysis. For all that, it can argued that events involve the periphery of the body above and beyond the central nervous system, and a psychical chain parallels the physical sequence. This was already argued in Spinoza's coextensive mode of substance and mode of thought.[59] As a matter of hindsight, to imbue any physiological process with consciousness is to prejudge the body-mind controversies.

In addition, to alleviate the difficulties of a purely physiological argument, Hirst advances the view that

> an apparent externality . . . might be an essential feature of the content of visual, auditory, and similar sensing, since it is caused by nerves' impulses from externally activated sense organs.[60]

This is simplistic at best, and does not proffer anything further that the naive realist's viewpoint.[61] Chapter 4 in this text terminated in an elucidation of the very concept of externality, and is presented as an argument against this propounded bareness. Uznadze argues the same point by holding that:

> For any phenomenon of behavior to appear . . . (a living being) develops a relationship with this environment on the basis of the integral state of the set arising in the subject, which leads him to perform purposive actions.[62]

A further defect of the atomistic viewpoint, which altogether obviates the need for a total activity of the subject, is shown by the empiricist's insistence on the aggregate of sensations as the basis of physical objects. For instance, one analysis[63] relies on touch to yield proprioceptive data. In addition, size, shape, positions, temperatures, weight, hardness, textures, elasticity, momentum, and acceleration will be accepted only when their access is within arm's length. All these qualities are judged sufficient for a representation of physical objects. This leads to the assumption that hearing, sight, smell, and taste are not only superfluous, but are also inadequate as a separate group to produce the physical objects, thanks mainly to their fleeting nature.

To support these choices, the psychological and conceptual reifications rely implicitly on the precarious foundation of observational data. Indeed, the latest neurophysiological studies have reshuffled the sensorial conglomerate presented above. Nowadays, size, shape, and positions of limbs are derivative of proprioceptive information; temperature and hardness depend on another network equal in stature to touch and smell; acceleration and positions of body possess their own pathway in the semicircular canals and the vestibule of the ear; and very likely they somehow integrate in the CNS to modify various reflexes, such as the knee jerk.

In short, the realist position holds that what we observe must be at the periphery of our bodies, and is passively attended to in the sense that we have a mediated awareness of objects through the original use of externally imposed sense-data. If this much is admitted, then it must be precognitive in the sense that any favored channels of information, postural or other, would prejudge and encroach on the passivity of the observer. Stimuli are the only elements entering into the sensorial universe that qualify for that role. Their cohesion into sensations raises them to the cognitive level, thus giving them representational status. The whole approach precludes altogether an intermediate sense-datum that is directly given in consciousness.

A different view is offered by Piaget, who introduces the active notion of obstacle via cognitive perturbations related to the fulfilment of needs. The basic assimilatory schemas of sucking, touching, look-ing, and listening are primitively geared to satisfy bodily demands, and if halted will create perturbing lacunae.

On the surface, one can be content with such a nonspecific jump from needs that depend on the physiological demand of the human species to individualized development. A detailed analysis suggests a translation into cognitive terms proper because activities stem from perturbations. Now, perturbations arise out of a conceptual system whose vital role is to anticipate; that is, schemes are actuated as actions; the needs become transposed as the goals of these actions, to be satisfied in a conceptual domain. The enacting occasion is provoked by the weighing of stimuli, which selects the appropriate sensation (e.g, foodstuff) so as to match an environmental presentation. The repetitive, recognitory, and generalizing schemes are put into play in combination to compensate, if need be, the lacunae specifically occa-sioned by the mismatch of these expected sensations—as in turning the head to retrieve, visually, a capricious object.

Piaget's critics do not quite capture his adualism when they assert:

> It is assumed that errors in search would not necessarily imply concept deficiencies but, rather, behaviors that are inappropriate for detaining the object.[64]

They refuse to acknowledge his monolithic union of concepts, actions, sensations, and objects. In fact, in accepting an underlying empiri-cism, they express more than their dualism, they advocate the three independent domains of ideas, behaviors, and objective reality. Of course, the path chosen is psychological rather than epistemological, since they conclude:

> Then, if the object is not obtained in particular situations, we can seek explanations by further analyzing the requirements of the situations.[65]

The attribution to Piaget of dualistic views is pernicious through-out, and even inhabits the interpretation given of his notion of disturb-ance. The critics see it as the result of a child's belief yielding anticipa-tions that provoke a discovery of dissonance between his expectation and nature's offerings. He can then utilize this information to do as he pleases. The assumed freedom can only be sustained by a hidden mature judge who, in the infant's mind, compares various representa-tions of an available reality. Aquinian apologetics, with all the required interventions of God, have come to the rescue of Piaget's epistemolo-gy, via the critiques of his neo-associationistic detractors!

Nevertheless, far from going back to square one of modern theory of knowledge, Piaget is still guilty of letting dualism creep inadvertently in several explanations of his genetic studies.

In Piaget's writings, one finds that at the outset of the child's development, the observables distinguished in models I and II as Obs.O and Obs.S are undifferentiated. They do not belong to an object, nor to a subject, owing to the absence of a physical-psychological dichotomy. Specifically, qualities cannot be attributed to objects as long as they merge intimately with the body's agency. Equally important, no conscious predication is possible for lack of a subject to originate it. Piaget relates the end of egocentrism to the child's ability to sever the object from the subject. He thus lends support to the dualistic paradox adduced above. On the one hand, objectivity of properties is denied on the grounds that objects are simply not out there for these properties to be objective with. And this mishap is due to the dependence of these objects on the actions of the subject. On the other hand, observables are not related to actions, since awareness of their source in the body is not present to grant these actions a meaningful status. In fact, what Piaget is saying is that as long as the subject is not object to himself, then the umbilical cord constituted by actions cannot be cut. Accordingly, it must undermine the coming into being of the objective reality. Yet, unable to endow his body with intentionality, the infant accepts its imposed neutrality. One must reason that being respectful of Piaget's view, the child continues to use his body out of an energetic vitalism that is the only way the psychological ghost can be tied to the physical machine. Of course, there remains a gap in Piaget's notion of encounter with that physical realm. He asserts that at the beginning the body is the grounds for action, and the object and the subject *qua* object are at the end! Then he decrees that in between is the observable cut-off from actions. What is missing is an account of observability which is divorced from objects. But the logical prerequisite is for an object to be an object before being consciously observable. Piaget, holding for psychology to be a science of behavior and a science of consciousness[66] has to wait for an epistemology to give such an account.

Commentators are quick to enter the argument on the side of learning by accusing Piaget of duplicating not only St. Thomas Aquinas's innate maturation of intellectual faculties, but also Rousseau's sensualistic instincts. Both Genevese are supposed to rely on spontaneity to guide development and to reject externally imposed learning.[67]

Considering the necessity of interactions with the milieu to occasion perturbations that, via their compensations, institute cognitive growth, one cannot accept the reduction to maturationalism forced on Piaget. In addition, it is difficult to consent to the alternative offered, which advocates a piecemeal acquisition of selected behaviors. By way of illustration, let us be reminded that progress in the transplant of organs depends not on advances in surgical techniques, but on success in immunology. Similarly, the problem in cognition is not a question of the learning of methods, but the insertion of an almost foreign body into a total functioning system. If intellectual development commands the sequence of concepts, then it also controls the appearance of each and every property. In an interactionist mode, its role is to organize all encounters with the environment. Only then can one assume that the milieu reveals its features. But, those are positively given, meaning that absent features are not just out there. Similarly, actions anticipate positive properties and seek to confirm them rather than hunt for the properties which are not there. The clash is therefore between two asserted attributes, one offered by the world and the other expected by the agent. Only out of clashing encounters can a lack of some feature emerge. But for it to be interpreted as a disequilibrium requires a conceptual intervention. Further conscious actions are then taken to compensate for the error or lacuna, and to ascertain what is actually given by the environment. The mind actively pursues the world and adjusts after interaction with it. As long as the environment renews itself, cognitive disequilibria occur, properties evolve, and the constructed reality is enriched.

CHAPTER 6

Conclusion

To sum up Piagetian constructivism, one can trace four cognitive progressions.

The first evolution distributes the various structures according to the operational complexity that intervenes in the construction of the object and its properties. The more impregnated the conceptualization is with cognitive schemes, the more immunized against contradictions remain the invariant features, and thus the more lasting and appropriate is the erected reality.

The second sequence predicts stabler equilibrium and richer knowledge as cognitive schemes expand away from direct sensorial encounters. By ascending in the hierarchy of intellectual structures, a scheme avoids exogenous corrections. This is due in part to the formal level blotting out the concrete one as assimilation prevails over accommodation. In other words, implications proper to the assimilative role of intelligence overshadow accommodative explanations.

A third progression establishes a link between the relational complexity of schemes and the awareness of objects thus determined. As directed actions open up new linkages through adjustments, more meanings enrich the object's schema and the intentions attached to it. Indeed, perturbations require adjustments, that is, nullification by a refined conceptualization that incorporates them as variations inside a closed system encompassing their reversal. The evolution is from conflicts that remain blurred and can even be ignored, before they successfully alter one's consciousness through their intricate composition.

Finally, the fourth progression strengthens reality within a formal frame that continuously casts off its qualitative content, normally of a psychical nature. It is not a complete loss, as the affective domain retrieves these qualities and, by actually stripping objects, awakens feelings, emotions, interests, attitudes, and the whole sensual spectrum, in chronological order. Consciousness gains intensity with the skeletal consolidation of the real, while it forgets these fleeting multi-dimensions. Reality is not harmed by the advent of a fully constituted subjectivity, because it profits from an accrued stability. It is more predictable, especially amidst the purified cognitive schemes that embody the formal level.

Paradoxically, by severing itself from the sensorial periphery of the human body and submitting to cognitive structures, reality becomes more articulated, durable, and refined. It does so via the coordinations, differentiations, interactions, and interlocking of actions. Accordingly, constructivism supports a reality which is not a medley of represented fragments supplied by some faculties that reproduce particular surroundings. There is no frontal opposition to the world resulting in a mental amalgam of predicates, but on the contrary that world comes from within the intercoordination of acts to spoil the intentions inherent in our actions.

The real is built within the network of intellectual operations, which not only reflect all possible actions but also present the sensations which constitute their sequel. Maintaining the constant influence of sensations in all activities, even those that involve intercoordinations of actions, distinguishes personal knowledge of the world from scientific knowledge.

Looking at Piaget's protocols that report actual experiments, one is struck by his selection of logical factors at the expense of those that are affective, sensorial, sociocultural, and linguistic. As a result, many possible interpretations are eliminated from the start. It does suggest that formal structures are filtering the data coming from the exercized tasks. The message is clear: Piaget favors a hypothetico-deductive model where scientific concepts dominate all progressive understanding by the child. On that account, intellectual evolution, as described above by the fourth progression, summarizes scientific knowledge. Its details are worked out by Piaget's genetic psychology and genetic epistemology. What most concerned us throughout this text was the many dimensions of personal knowledge which are not provided by structured understanding. Missing are the intentions and the achievement-oriented or consciousness aspects of a person's actions. To find them we have to delve into Piaget's cognitive psychology and delineate an epistemology.

The task includes dissecting the cognitive processes that, when mastered by the child, subtend both his scientific and logico-mathematical thinking. In epistemological terms, the methods of science and reasonings in logic are articulated out of the more basic elements that produce our conceived and perceived reality. Hence, prior to a "sophisticated" discussion of abstract scientific concepts, one is well advised to unearth the vital components of the everyday world. Classically this effort amounts to giving the grounds for claiming some kind of knowledge about the real.

In accordance with the last few remarks, this text had to transpose Piaget's cognitive terminology into an epistemological discourse. Most importantly, the very notion of observation, so prominent in his latest equilibration model, had to be discarded altogether. Indeed, intellectual progression, defined relative to a constructed reality, originates in deformations or corrections, and so the beliefs it sustains do not depend on observations. One must not forget that any primitive perception is subject to operational modifications before its cognitive insertion. However, this assimilative process, while a modification, is not a creation.

As a first approximation, one discerns a Piagetian theory of knowledge, which is a loose version of Kant's epistemology. For instance, to depict the Piagetian account of perception, all we would need is Kant's notion of intuition, which is an immediate intentional representation. To give perceptions the status of knowledge, one modifies and relates them, and for that purpose Kant's categories rule over intuitions to bestow upon them the homogeneity of our knowing being. Moreover, they organize the perceptions to determine the existential conditions of objects, thus giving a unified stream of comprehension that obviates a dualistic appeal to a representational mere copy. Piaget pursues a similar vein when he postulates an implicative network where virtual actions are defined within structures. These are homogeneously controlled by rules for action sequences such as reversibility or association. At the same time, the limits of possible worlds are set, and because they preexist with the structures, one cannot get to know the true nature of things (noumenon). The real world escapes us as we approach it.

To escape this all-too-Kantian conclusion, a neo-Piagetian epistemology was presented in Chapters 2 to 5. The notions of reflex, behavior, activity, and deportment were interpreted within a semiotics of action.

On a purely descriptive level, an action is a sequence of movements fastened together. The problem is to ascertain the elements that link the separate segments. One begins with reflexes as the original cognitive sequences encountered in the development of the individual. They are broken down under environmental duress (accommodation). The parts are reassembled under repetitive, recognitory, and generalizing schemes, and appear along the heterogeneous modalities of motor differentiation (visual, auditory). They intercoordinate, which in a cognitive sense means that they assimilate one another. For instance, the oculomotor movement is fastened to kinesthetic sensations and consequently integrates them within the visual modality. In turn, any coordination defines an action as a sequence in one domain leading to the intersection with another domain. The integrated sensation at that intersection becomes a goal for the sequence of acts which, by that very fact, is goal-directed. The sensation has turned into an aim for that string of events and is also the basis for the semantics of any particular object. Indeed, if enough action-sequences coordinate, then their intersections, made up of sensations, stabilize. Further, as goals for directed behaviors, they assume the conceptual attributes of an object. Hence one can say that the object appears at the intersection of sensorimotor activities. An object stands as the precondition of a sequence of movements that actualizes itself in a sensation belonging to another distinct sensorial modality. Even though the object is born within an intersection, its properties are dependent on various acts. Terminating one of them, they attach themselves to other acts, suggesting that the object of which they are a part is a source of continuity by its ability to start other acts. Presented objects are loaded with intentions as the very condition of their possible actualization through actions, and this mostly because every action aims at their properties. Objects take a perceptual and sensorial format only within action schemas.

An interesting aside stems from this interpretation. Any property aimed at by an action, is in the cognitive domain, a sensation reached by an activity. Furthermore, a corresponding physical description would mention a movement linked to some sense datum. Effectively, the talk could be reduced to a signifier which in some way is always connected to its significant. Since no knowledge is defined out of the range of actions, a significant, no matter how far removed, is connected to the sign that represents it. Even with linguistic expressions, a chain of actions maintains the contact. Piaget places a further restriction on symbols whose resemblance to the significant imposes a parallel development. Since imitation is the original tool linking the signified to the signifier, the development of action must permit the right movement to imitate the thing to be represented by the mirroring symbolism. Body control seems essential to obtain a viable semiotic function for behavior. In some odd ways, recalling the extreme behaviorism of John Watson, symbolic representation also demands the internal play of virtual action. Of course, the fundamental difference is that action, with all the concomitant conceptual aspects, is involved in a comparison process rather than mere behavior and possible transformations.

It is obvious that the intersection of actions, as locus of permanence, in an ontological sense precedes the cognitive status in terms of sensations, and the semantical determination of the object in terms of properties. In addition, the intercoordination of actions introduces, above and beyond sensations, the notion of "otherness." Indeed, the sequence of motor elements must ultimately result in a sensation caused in a distinct and differentiated modality. The sensorial terminal thus introduced appears as if imposed from the outside. Nevertheless, the motor apparatus cannot be regarded as provoking the birth of these sensations from the inside, so to speak. *For these reasons, the outer world is given in the very intentionality of human actions.* In a crucial way there is an intimate bond that gradually links various activities to some features in the world; only then can these features be called stimuli and thereafter sensations. Within those bonds, activities are specified and tuned, with resulting attributes only when reproduced by repetitive assimilation. A conceptual interpretation of this phenomenon translates the bond between an activity and a stimulating feature of the world into a meaningful relationship. That is, the feature is meaningful to a behavior if there is a link through a concurrent stimulus and a sensation.

An act is viewed as a conglomerate of several sense modalities, of which one plays the role of the tactilo-kinesthetic phase while others stand as an expected sensorial set. The concomitant "aiming at" has to be of the objective world, since it fulfills itself through the act as described above.

Knowledge can only obtain by being the grounds of a pseudodomain. To aim is to anticipate and consequently to force the use of certain channels that we have called assimilatory schemes. It is frivolous to introduce objectivity by arguing that partial sensual fulfilment of a prophecy yields an obstacle either through opposition or differentiation. Accommodation is a cheap substitute for "out-ness." The

very roots of objectivity are entrenched in the requirement that fulfilment of property expectancies must be imposed at the junction of two
sense-modalities. Each is a determinant of the semantics of the object,
and each is a source of "otherness" and "out-ness" to the other.
Symmetry is coming back to haunt the cognitive source of the external
world. This last remark reflects the role played by actions within
mental schemas. They link in a one-to-one, many-one, and one-many
combinations the various sensations whose epistemological status
emerges as properties within the semiotics of action. We are not simply
dealing with figurative knowledge since traits such as directedness,
consciousness, open-endedness, and intention are inherent in the
actions involved. Furthermore, the chains of actions do not transform
various states of the environment, thus they do not constitute structures in the Piagetian sense of autoregulated sets of transformations.
As it should be, logico-mathematical understanding, based on structures, appears to be an undue restriction at this stage.

Neither can we be satisfied with morphisms and categories which
represent the core of Piaget's last writings. Prior to his work on
equilibration, and this up to 1978, Piaget gave preeminence to the
transformational capability of actions. Apparently it gave him enough
ammunition to account for the acquisition of scientific concepts (space,
conservation, causality) and the evolution of intellectual structures
(grouping, INRC). His analysis of equilibration uncovered a major
gap in man's encounters with the world, and thereof a flaw regarding the ability to transform objects. Specifically, before a transformation can be accomplished, the action must be applied to something
and the various conditions of the object must be acknowledged.
Hence states must be correlated, connected, and compared. In brief,
correspondences and even mappings through applications of actions
precede all transformations, thus his appeal to morphisms and categories.

Once again the solution offered concentrates on logico-
mathematical thinking with its concern for a scientific treatment of
reality, but personal knowledge, whether it is creative or achievement-
oriented, is thwarted by such curtailing formal frameworks. The epistemological traits coloring all actions that we have been anxious to
delineate throughout this text are not accounted for. Even more
troublesome, the individual who does the comparing and introduces
morphisms smacks of a new ghost in the machine and runs counter to
the Piagetian conceptual monism.

Piaget's dilemma grows out of his favoritism for mathematical
structures, and at the same time his dependence on the child's own
systemic development. Since the knowledge of whose evolution

Piaget is most proud is scientific knowledge, it is the formal tools underlying its construction that constitute his cognitive psychology. His bias forces him to "read out" of psychological experiments a growth leading to logico-mathematical structures. In that way, he suffers from the same prejudice as ordinary language philosophers, namely a reliance on the one standard given by adult thinking. In Piaget's case, it is that of the scientist, while for the philosophers, it is the mature way of common sense.

The neo-Piagetian position defined throughout this text centers on the origin of our sense of externality. What I found remains a contrast to Kant's own elaborations. The chapter on transcendental aesthetics in Kant's *Critique of Pure Reason* treats space as the medium for our perception of objects. Perception through intuition, which is immediate intentional representation, utilizes sensations whose contribution only yields knowledge of appearances. On the other hand, conception through reason, which declares off limits the nonintelligibility of spatial thinking, henceforth sets the boundaries for the thing-in-itself. Appearances are marked, and are converts of "out-ness" because the underlying objects are determined by and in space, which is the foundation for outer experience. Beyond the space-time determination of the sensible thing lies the object. What is missing in Kant is an analysis concerning the object that genuinely betrays itself through its appearance. For Piaget's conceptualism, that betrayal is an article of faith, and is used through the processes of equilibration to construct a viable reality. On that account Hamlyn seems mistaken when he reduces Piaget to Kant simply because the latter uses his categories to grant objectivity to man's intuitions (perceptions). The dualism in Piaget is an aspect of his scientific bias and does not reflect properly a neo-Piagetian theory of knowledge. With that remark in mind, Piaget could not have repeated Kant's famous dictum that "thoughts without content are empty, intuitions without concepts are blind."

Nevertheless, the comparison is worth pursuing for the light it sheds on a philosophical psychology built from but beyond Piaget. For Kant, a perception is the determination of the object as conceived through categories which set up the possibilities of its experience. Similarly for Piaget the very schematism of operational thought posits the object as supporting the exercise of various schemas. Corresponding mental structures characterize the network of "virtual" actions, and this corresponds to Kant's productive imagination, the realm of which is the transcendental apperception. To this last domain can be attributed the central role of generator of concepts. Reproductive imagination, on the other hand, is in the sensible domain of imagery, and corresponds to the schemes of recognition and of generalization that, in Piaget, are revealed by the "secondary circular reactions." In addition, generalization contains the important accommodative modulators that operate under environmental impacts.

The schism in Kant between generative and reproductive imagination, in which one belongs to understanding and the other to intuition, is thus strengthened by genetic epistemology. Piagetian thinking places the former in a logico-mathematical framework, and the latter in the determination of practical schemas which stand closest to the sensible domain. Piaget refines Kant's dichotomous view of imagination by distinguishing several types of structural determinations of the sensible. For instance, among the identifiable types are simple repetitious encounters through reproduction, the extension of environmental determination via a generalizing scheme, and lastly the integration of the sensible in the reflective abstraction which portends "imagination" proper and is actuated within the recognitive scheme of the practical phases.

In Kant, the unity of experience forces time as the internal form of intuition to subsume space as a form of outer intuition. In Piaget the necessity that is introduced by spatial structures and that characterizes the epistemic subject, dominates the possible variations among temporally distributed acts of the psychological subject. In other words, the chronology of events is defined through action schemas which grant all the temporal characters of the descriptive network, but those events must be transferred as formal properties to obtain the explicative and implicative spatial structure. In fact, the transfer from the outer time-distribution of phenomena to the inner spatial organization of objects is gradual. Firstly, an empirical abstraction gives some figurative representation by operating on temporally distributed percepts. After that, a pseudoempirical abstraction acts in real time and in real place to organize objects in a planned manner. Lastly, reflective abstraction works out, within a spatial framework, the invariant properties of the world, such as order and number.

As mentioned above, Piaget's writings fail to knit together the modifying action scheme and what is supposed to be modified. Either observations are represented and then can only be modified by "virtual" actions, or observables are acted upon with the status of being really "out there" and appear at some point as the given in a changed form. Moreover, coordination of actions is considered to operate only within a representable domain, and cannot reach the objective real. Under these circumstances, intentionality becomes essential to the self reaching out toward the world. Piecemeal applications of operative schemes onto the actual percept destroy the continuity of experiencing and its projections within a future real. The present, as simple encounter, is undifferentiated. It cannot be the world, it cannot be the subject. It is just the specious instant without polarity, because consciousness of the object as distinct from the subject is absent.

Encounters at the surface of the skin without mediation only give us fleeting impressions. One needs intercoordination of actions to obtain permanence and invariance. The use of operational structures over temporal sequences grants us a homogeneous spatial construction of the real. Paradoxically an inward retrieval in relational schemas simultaneously empowers one to reach out far into the world. Hence, depth requires time, as Erwin Straus so aptly pointed out in his far-reaching article, "The Upright Posture."

Piaget distinguishes two types of observables: those that are directly dependent on, or a part of, actions, and those involving objects. Again we are faced with a latent dualistic realism that inserts itself in the loose net of his action-oriented conceptualism. Admittedly, operational intelligence rules over the given, but one is nevertheless supposed to give ontological preference to that given. A coherent position cannot break down the real into an aggregate of observables, which would be psychologically unified and then as a whole, be purposefully acted upon. Distinctions, differentiations, and integrations must be drafted within the semiotics of action and certainly not at the terminal post where man meets nature.

This last aspect is particularly convincing about Piaget's great difficulties regarding the insertion of observables in the "implicative" network of coordinations. In fact, he is always in need of distinguishing actions coordinations from physical ones. To avoid too much "chumminess" and even confusion between conceptual implications and the causal network of actions, Piaget has to appeal to error factors and to conflicts. Both kinds of obstacles impart to percepts an endogenous contribution toward the operational streamlining of equilibration. The thought process can either oversee mistaken observations, or steer toward false perceptions, essentially because it does not properly insert them in the relevant context.

To my mind, both cases avoid the given and treat the intentional. They clearly prevent objective observables from entering the semantics of the cognitive domain intact, where the semantics of action represents all properties of objects. One should accept that this view countermands Piaget's orthodox characterization of language as accommodative representations. My interpretation does not appeal to representation as an imitation because linguistic behaviors, in a social context, impose the links of a semantics of actions. Those behaviors are not contained in the objective situation. They are created and reflect the juxtaposition of images proceeding respectively from the sound of words and views of objects. These two dimensions are sensory modalities which enter the semiotics of action. It is not a mere coincidence that the symbolic function appears around the same period as the notion of object permanence.

My emphasis is on the action mode as a homogeneous foundation that bridges the dichotomous chasm separating logico-mathematical from physical reasoning. In this text, it is knowledge of the world that we try to account for. Accordingly, we leave aside such "advanced" understanding as the scientific, the logical, and the mathematical. The epistemology that most concerns us is, in a classical vein, the one that analyzes the means we use to get to know reality, namely action and sensation.

One should not forget that in Piaget, due to his scientific realism, implication is opposed to causation, and that it remains a thorn in the side of his holistic constructivism. Intrinsic to the role of action, there is a blending of the sensorially given and the structurally imposed. It has a classical antecedent in Aristotelian physics with its necessary powers of objects that pertain to the intellectual dimension. It also creates a path between causal and implicative reasoning. The forcefulness of the former is genetically related to the necessity of the latter. The tight bond of action and sensation that I have argued for throughout this text bridges the Piagetian gap between the intellect and its encounter with the world. Still one must be prudent in ensuring that all action sequences have a conceptual interpretation, lest they be extended within the temporal stream that runs exclusively in a physical domain. Missing that step would mean that sensation could not be transposed as properties.

The bridge is conceptualized by the intellectual progression which has its roots in conflicts. Thinking does not consist in visions but overtakes through controlled actions. Act by act or link by link the gap between anticipation and payoff is closed by adjustments with an ensuing equilibrium. For instance, unrewarded predictions follow an incompatibility between the physical schema, which reads perceptions, and the deductive scheme, which anticipates. Progress evolves from conflicts being reabsorbed under the predominance of the implicative assimilation. For Piaget, integration between activities always wins over differentiation among acts. Factual information, which could be the source of externally rooted contradictions, submits to the coherent accuracy of intentional acts whose mishaps are compensated for within the initial design. But conflicts also initiate new linkages whose orientation ensures adaptation. Going forward obliterates any loss that one could blame on contradictory results stemming from a static position.

Projectibility of goals underlies time, and within Piagetian epistemology we are thus within the physical realm. This exactly reverses the Kantian format, wherein time is of the internal mode while space seriates the external domain. It also explains the ambivalence of Piaget's concrete state, which is characteristically called concrete to emphasize the temporal element, but at the same time deals directly with states of affairs that are part of the spatial domain. Hence the needed progression from a decisional level, requiring successive strategies, to a more advanced judgmental phase relying on a simultaneous perspective.

For Piaget, the modus operandi of intelligence throughout its genetic development is representability by repetition of presentations. It brings the world nearer and distributes it on a simultaneous spatial plane. By contrast, spatial representability introduces the possibility of conflicts with the temporal immediacy of each sensation and action. Externality is surreptitiously introduced to tie the loose epistemological end of objects which, as obstacles, escape actions. So, Piaget has no alternative but to introduce a discontinuity between coordinations of actions and conjunctions of objects: the first are the progenitor of logico-mathematical structures, while the second are the origin of physical networks.

Extending Piaget's epistemology to personal knowledge via the semiotics of action, the intentionality of our acts obviates this discontinuity, and binds the world in a much tighter cognitive grip. In fact, there is no need to confront properties of objects with predicates introduced by the subject. Objects are constructed, not transformed. To admit an inert real, manipulated at arms length, is not a viable proposition in Piaget's conceptual holism. The modified and the original, if such is cognitively definable, are but two distinct constructs whose relations must be established within some semiotics of action. But, as intercoordinations of actions become more complex, so do the interrelations between the constructs with an obviously enriched and stable object. Paradoxically, the more remote one is from one's immediate sensorial experiences, that is from one's body, the tighter one's control over reality. This could explain why intentionality, which inhabits all our actions, is also the source of a kind of dirigisme which obsesses our existence. Indeed, we are utilitarian, governed by purposes. On epistemological grounds, there is no such thing as loafing through life.

The monopoly of the subject dominates in Piaget and represents the final step in a conceptual development where invariance is achieved. The fact, strikingly evident in Piaget's works, that invariants are uncovered via recognitory matchings, and therefore lie within one's field of actions, explains the preeminence of the subject. Nevertheless, Piaget's diffuse realism forces him to posit a given reality as a substratum for our behavior, which he always sees as being applied to some concrete entity. Piaget, the scientist does not have the same ontology as Piaget, the epistemologist.

As a matter of fact, within Piaget's realism, there is a tacit admission of purely mental predications to be applied to the world. It is the world that spoils our intentions and is the source of adjustments, since knowledge is presentational and consistent. Maladjustment originates from the milieu and is assimilated into cognition as variations that open up toward other consistent realities.

Piaget's studies uncover several intermediary steps that precede the closed system reequilibration. At first, by disregarding irregularities, the child pursues his endeavor without obstruction. Later, he repeats his behavior while surveying the incongruities. Still later, the actions field is extended, to include perturbation as one of the alternatives. Finally, a set of imaginary acts is envisioned, which precludes the particular conflict by comprising all alternatives and their converses which close the set.

Curiously enough, the child who initially disregards obstacles is affectively involved, and this seems to result, as far as this interpretation is concerned, from a Piagetian ambiguity: namely, innate behaviors operate out of a need that, when interfered with, is felt as a lacuna. Experimental results have shown that displeasure raises perceptual thresholds, which in our case means that lacunae blindfold the child with respect to properties affixed to the perturbation. In Piaget's perspective, this is even more pertinent, considering that consciousness appears with and is proportionate to the interlockings of cognitive schemas. In fact, the mediation is by the interiorization of actions, and is thus not directly fastened to behavior.

It is clear that Piagetian conceptualism advances a cognitive option to explain ignorance. It is not simply lack of knowledge, but rather the sign of a limited imagination toward a spectrum of actions, that makes a given object inconceivable. In short, ignorance is an active and evolving boundary to our thought processes, and not a passive vacuum to be filled in at random. Ignorance is to be likened to space-time perpetually created at the boundary of the expanding universe.

For Piaget, it is due to regulation that thinking escapes logical incongruities, because it brings forth virtual actions which, by transforming real or imagined properties, produce temporary equilibria. Progress consists in improving these equilibria by increasing their resistance to disturbances. This is made possible by enlarging the compensatory domain from a strict object-subject transaction to coordinations between actions, and then to differentiated schemes inside an overall system. Equilibrium results from the fact that all properties, all actions, and all schemes demand and obtain a negation, an inversion, and a reversal.

A fresh twist is given to assimilation, which constructs by extending or articulating cycles, and to accommodation, which compensates by adjusting to objects. Regulation is enacted within and by accommodation, while construction is caused by assimilation. In short, the dynamism that colors intellectual development is originally internal, and progress toward equilibrium proceeds from the outside.

In a typically paradoxical manner, Piaget manages to reverse both Hegelian and Marxian dialectics, in which progress is incipient to man. This is consistent with the conceptual requirements of constructivism which, beyond bare sequential structures, solicit regulative procedures to ensure their invariance in the individual and their resurgence from man to man. Again, we detect the biologist bridling each individual attempt with universal laws. Moreover, a rationalistic stroke paints over the notion of a natural progress toward knowledge by depicting reality in the colors of the stable precision of cognitive structures.

At the origin of conflicts, we had located the chronic positive assertion of properties introduced by actions. The child goes beyond this limitation by including the negations, reversals, and converses of his acts. Equilibrium appears in the system formed by these correlated actions, and becomes more stable, thanks to the increased resistance to perturbations within the set of anticipations. There is a reorganization, where deliberate actions define Piagetian intellectual operations and sustain a hierarchy of properties. An appropriate example is the progressive mastering of the concept of length. At first, perceptual centrations freeze the attention of the infant on the initial and terminal states. Later the child notices dimensional variations of the string linked to the degree of convexity, which remains an isolated quality. It is only when he is able to imagine some virtual acts on the object that his thinking grasps the transformations, relations, and correspondences between properties. Thus reflective abstraction produces invariance when the interplay between acts transcends the perceptual to reach the transformational.

The crucial processes dominating cognitive development clearly identify the role of regulation and reflective abstraction. This becomes even truer with Piaget's demand for a consciousness proportional to the degree of conceptualization used in the construction of reality. The further one is from the sphere of direct performances, the richer and more vibrant is one's awareness of objects. Knowledge, being intimately secured to cognitive systems, is in everlasting production. On this particular point Piaget is akin to Skinner, because they both hold that at every step of his existence man embodies all of his past. Of course, Skinner the behaviorist observes this past in the series of deportments, while Piaget the clinician uncovers it in the presentation of reality. In short, man is historical, and never acts as a neophyte. Could it be that we are given an epigenetic version of the principle of sufficient reason?

All the possible worlds, imposed through adjustments to stimuli and not by imagination, are alternatives that can be moved to and fro on the transformational paths framing invariance. The Cartesian ghost in the machine can again be fathomed, but with a modern consuming need for the real which is a source for his growth. Piaget cannot contain his classical dualistic prejudice, which compels him to postulate the ever-present availablity of the world. Any missing element can ultimately be grabbed, given the right assimilative tool. Our cognitive structures are enslaved by that world, and must inevitably submit to it. Under animal magnetism, man converges upon reality, which is immutable and waiting. This is why Piaget the biologist is reluctant to grant to us, human beings, deliberate choice or intentional abstraction.

Still, Piagetian thought concedes some autonomy via the semiotics of action, and its concomitant lacunae, which are the preludes of his constructivism. While intentionally perceiving, man coherently furrows into the reals. He does not omit, he discriminates. The wealth of sensations is successively constructed from the impacts of stimuli and not directly with these stimuli as sense-data. In a word, sense-data have no cognitive status and even less an epistemological value. The environment is a catalyst which leaves the construction and the anticipation to man. As a result, man's aim does not fail from a faulty grasp, but from a paucity of semantical wealth. Man's intent does not overestimate or depreciate, it acts pointedly and deliberately; still, it can be thwarted.

Convinced of late that perceptual renewal of man's reality enforces permanent contact with the world, Piaget has moved away from structure to favor procedure. Accordingly, his functional cognitive psychology is contributing to a theory of knowledge to a greater extent than his structural genetic epistemology. The choice makes sense since action is more than a simple junction with the world—it originates all constructed realities. Obviously, Piaget has adopted a structuralist constructivism to replace his earlier "constructivist structuralism." The shift is imposed by the continuity inherent in action, which contrasts too brutally with the discontinuity of state-related structures.

Another crucial quality brought about by action schemas, and not contained within structures, is their forceful goal-directed orientation. Thus, to account for their cognizance of some reality, intellectual structures would have to be procedural; procedures, on the other hand, do not need to be structural.

Any behavior being oriented tacks upon itself the colors of a strategy which aims at a goal. Any structure shaping this strategy will have to be formalized, and so described out of context. The point made is crucial because it indicates the presence of the epistemic subject. In other words, whereas in pre–1978 Piagetian writings the epistemic subject was the overall type governing structured thinking and common to individuals at a given level, it is nowadays the structured part of thinking that is similar among people. Under these conditions, personal knowledge dominates logico-mathematical knowledge relative to epistemological inquiries. The emphasis is at all times on the constructed reality and thus its permanent contact with the world.

A consistent constructivism holds that no matter how strenuous our actions toward the real, it still remains unapproachable. In a metaphysical vein it is permissible to discuss the conditions of realizability of an entity created *ex nihilo*. But, epistemology requires a consistent discourse in which the real must be called forth justifiably, and may not simply appear mysteriously like a dolmen to heliotropize our actions. Actions do not apply to things, nor do they add to or strictly modify them. They are the bearers of the semantics, pragmatics, and meanings of the object. They are the grounds for its externality and thus its place in a reality.

The operational framework is purposefully the world itself. It is not imposed externally, since there is nothing cognitively significant to be transformed from without. In an essential way, the real is genetically related to the earliest sensorial aspects, having evolved toward a homogeneous system of predictable invariants. Henceforth, it must be atemporal and acausal. Reality is not abstracted from, because it is intended to be as it is, gaining its worldly status in that very gesture of intention. It forces identity between the properties of the coordinations-of-objects and the properties of actions, instead of begging the mind to establish, as a mere spectator, some isomorphisms. But this identification is genuine, since objects are defined for and by actions, and therefore one cannot impugn the embryonic causal network for the lack of objectivized transformations of objects. Knowledge is tied to a continual anticipation by conceptual system of persistent properties, which reflects interiorized transformations by actions rather than a sequence of internalized potential acts. In short, Piaget's conceptualism, which carries a hermeneutic message, also means the determination of the external real in terms of permanence, of means-ends dichotomy, and of cognitive invariance, under conditions that can only obtain within the intercoordination of actions and make sense through the semiotics of action. Finally, in a seemingly trite way, thinking, knowledge, and reality cannot be a matter of foresight, without hindsight. A person sums up his past experiences through every act. Thus, his mind evolves as one with his body, and being that of an agent can only be his own.

Notes
Glossary
Bibliography
Index

Notes

In citing works in the notes, shortened references have been used. Full publication information may be found in the bibliography.

CHAPTER 1. PIAGET'S THEORY

1. Piaget, *The Child's Conception of the World*.
2. Siegel, "Piaget's Conception of Epistemology," pp. l6–22.
3. James, *Essays in Radical Empiricism*.
4. Mach, *The Analysis of Sensations*.
5. The following writings of Piaget most prominently detail the progression of the child's intellectual development: *The Construction of Reality in the Child*, (and B. Inhelder) *The Growth of Logical Thinking from Childhood to Adolescence, The Origins of Intelligence in Children*, and *The Early Growth of Logic in the Child*.
6. Wittman, "The Concept of Grouping in Jean Piaget's Psychology," pp. 125–146.
7. Piaget, *Recherches sur l'abstraction réfléchissante I*, p. 133.
8. These studies have excellent surveys of the four stages: Tran-Thong, *Stades et concept de stade de développement de l'enfant dans la psychologie contemporaine*, ch.1; Maier, *Three Theories of Child Development*, ch. 3; and Furth, *Piaget and Knowledge: Theoretical Foundations*.

9. Furth, *Piaget and Knowledge*, p. 245.
10. Piaget, *Les notions de mouvement et de vitesse chez l'enfant*, p. 107.
11. Piaget, *Le possible et le nécessaire*.
12. Murray (ed.), *The Impact of Piagetian Theory on Education, Philosophy, Psychiatry, and Psychology*, p. 71.
13. Piaget, *Structuralism*, p.114.
14. Piaget, *Genetic Epistemology*, p.15.
15. Piaget, *Les mecanismes perceptifs*, p.21
16. Piaget and B. Inhelder, *L'image mentale chez l'enfant*, p.431
17. Piaget, *Introduction à l'epistémologie génétique*, vol. 3, p. 123.
18. Piaget, Jonckheere, and Mandelbrot, *La lecture de l'expérience*, p.57.
19. Piaget, *Le jugement et le raisonnement chez l'enfant*, p. 142.
20. Meyerson, *Identity and Reality*.
21. Piaget and Inhelder, *La représentation de l'espace chez l' enfant*, p. 544.
22. Piaget, *The Psychology of Intelligence*, p. 109.
23. Piaget, *Traité de logique*, p. 23.
24. Hamlyn, *Experience and the Growth of Understanding*, ch. 2.
25. Piaget, *Sagesse et illusions de la philosophie*, ch. 4.
26. Green, Ford, and Flamer, *Measurement and Piaget*, p. 118.
27. Bergling, *The Development of Hypothetico-Deductive Thinking in Children*, p. 55.
28. Piaget, *Classes, relations et nombres*, p. 264.
29. This useful terminology is developed further in Lindsay and Norman, *Human Information Processing*, pp. 515–520.
30. Piaget, *Traité de logique*. (This work is charcterized by the point of view shown in this paragraph.)
31. Piaget and Inhelder, *The Growth of Logical Thinking*, p. 299.
32. This point of view reflects the position adopted by Przelecki, *The Logic of Empirical Theories*.
33. Furth, "Piagetian Theory and the Helping Profession."
34. Papert, Piaget, and Grize, *La filiation des structures* (see the chapter entitled "From Grouping to Boolean Algebra").
35. Piaget, *Traité de logique*, pp. 208–212; Watanabe, *Knowing and Guessing* (this volume gives details on the various structures); and Dienes, *Thinking in Structures*.
36. Piaget, "Correspondences and Transformations," pp. 17–28.
37. Brown and Desforges, *Piaget's Theory*, pp. 94–100; and Ennis, "Conceptualization of Children's Logical Competence," in Siegel and Brainerd (eds.), *Alternatives to Piaget*, pp. 201–260.
38. See, for example, Vuyk, *Piaget's Genetic Epistemology 1965–1980*, pp. 212, 303–304.
39. These comments were inspired by two excellent works: Bunge, *Foundations of Physics*, and Kyburg, *Philosophy of Science: A Formal Approach*.
40. Bergling asserts: "No study explicitly testing the validity of the logical model of Jean Piaget has been found." Bergling, *The Development of Hypothetico-Deductive Thinking*, p. 4.

41. Siegel and Brainerd, *Alternatives to Piaget.*
42. Mounoud, *Structuration de l'instrument chez l'enfant,* p. 19.
43. Piaget, "Review of Bruner's Studies in Cognitive Growth," pp. 532–533.
44. Hamlyn, "Epistemology and Conceptual Development."
45. An appropriate exponent of this school is: Price, *Thinking and Experience.*
46. Piaget, *La construction du réel,* p. 82.
47. Russell, *Human Knowledge: Its Scope and Limits.*
48. Piaget, *Biologie et connaissance,* p. 248. An orthodox Piagetian treatment of this topic is found in Nicolas, *Jean Piaget* , ch. 5.
49. Overton and Gallagher, *Knowledge and Development,* vol. 1, p. 41; Bronckart, *Theories of Language,* p. 50; and Bergling, *The Development of Hypothetico-Deductive Thinking,* p. 57.
50. Piaget, *The Psychology of Intelligence,* p. 114.
51. Hamlyn, *Theory of Knowledge;* Ayer, *The Problem of Knowledge;* and Ross, *The Appeal to the Given.*
52. Piaget, *Introduction à l'epistémologie génétique,* vol.1, p. 253.
53. Piaget, *Le jugement et le raisonnement chez l'enfant,* p. 143.
54. Maslow, *Toward a Psychology of Being.*
55. This theme is developed in: Piaget, *Plays, Dreams, and Imitation in Childhood.*
56. Piaget, *Les relations entre l'affectivité et l'intelligence dans le développement mental de l'enfant,* p. 157.
57. Inhelder, Garcia, and Vonèche, *Epistémologie génétique et equilibration,* pp. 15, 58.
58. Cowan, *Piaget with Feeling,* p. 52.
59. Turner, *Realism and the Explanation of Behavior.*
60. Hunt, "Intrinsic Motivation and Its Role in Psychological Development." pp. 189–282; Bringuier, *Conversations libres avec J. Piaget,* p. 80; and Ripple and Rockcastle (eds), *Piaget Rediscovered,* pp. 92–94.
61. Skinner, *About Behaviorism.*
62. Piaget, *The Psychology of Intelligence,* pp.3–7.
63. Vaihinger, *The Philosophy of As If,* p. 68.
64. Ibid., pp. 159, 221.
65. The resemblance to Piaget can be examined in the faithful interpretation of Pascual-Leone, "Principle of Equilibration," in Gallagher and Easley (eds.), *Knowledge and Development,* vol. 2, p. 269.
66. Bringuier, *Conversations libres avec J. Piaget,* p. 57.
67. Flavell, *The Developmental Psychology of Jean Piaget,* p. 420.
68. Hunt, *Intelligence and Experience,* p. 263.
69. Cowan, *Piaget with Feeling,* p. 163.
70. Mays, "Genetic Epistemology and Theories of Adaptive Behavior," pp. 45–65.
71. Burloud, *De la psychologie à la philosophie,* pp. 34–35.
72. Peters, *The Concept of Motivation,* p. 102
73. Piaget, *L'équilibration des structures cognitives,* ch. 1; Piaget and Henriques, *Recherches sur la généralisation,* p. 243; and Mischel (ed.), *Cognitive Development and Epistemology,* pp. 311–356.

74. Piaget, *Biologie et connaissance*, p. 248.
75. Mach, *The Analysis of Sensations*, pp. 22, 369.
76. Hamlyn, "Epistemology and Conceptual Development ," p. 3.
77. Hamlyn, *Experience and the Growth of Understanding*, pp. 11, 19.
78. Przelecki, *The Logic of Empirical Theories*, ch. 4–5.
79. Piaget and Inhelder, *Mémoire et intelligence*.
80. Overton and Gallagher, *Knowledge and Development*, vol.1, pp. 41, 60.
81. Piaget, *Le possible et le nécessaire*.
82. Vuyk, *Piaget's Genetic Epistemology 1965–1980*, p. 58.
83. Royce and Rozeboom, *The Psychology of Knowing*.

CHAPTER 2. A SEMIOTICS FOR ACTION

1. Piaget, *The Origins of Intelligence in Children*, pp. 24–25. *See also, Adaptation vitale et psychologie de l'intelligence*, p. 86.
2. Piaget, *Six Psychological Studies*, p.10.
3. Piaget, *The Origins of Intelligence in Children*, p. 32.
4. Flavell, *The Developmental Psychology of Jean Piaget*, p. 17.
5. Maier, *Three Theories of Child Development*, pp. 99–100.
6. Piaget, *Biologie et connaissance*, p. 254; also, *The Origins of Intelligence in Children*, p. 175.
7. Flavell, *The Developmental Psychology of Jean Piaget*, p. 79.
8. Piaget, *Biologie et connaissance*, p. 253.
9. Furth, *Piaget and Knowledge*, p.44.
10. Maier, *Three Theories of Childhood Development*, p. 104.
11. Piaget, *Plays, Dreams and Imitation in Childhood*, p. 8.
12. Piaget, *Biologie et connaissance*, p. 256.
13. Piaget, *Insights and Illusions of Philosophy*, p. 155.
14. "Cue" is interpreted in the functionalist sense as presented in Brunswick, "Probabilism."
15. Piaget, *Origins of Intelligence in Children*, p. 48.
16. Bringuier, *Conversations libres avec Jean Piaget*, p. 211.
17. Peirce, *Collected Papers*, 5:488 (references to this work are given by volume and then paragraph); and Morris, *Signs, Language and Behavior* (New York: Prentice-Hall, 1946).
18. Details about these notions are found in Peirce, *Collected Papers*, 2:228, 2:244–250, 2:306, 2:309, 5:464–496.
19. Piaget, *Origins of Intelligence in Children*, p. 48.
20. This volume covers the probabilistic model: Piaget, Apostel, and Mandelbrot, *Logique et équilibre*; another volume deals with the deterministic model: Piaget, *L'équilibration des structures cognitives*.
21. Vuyk, *Piaget's Genetic Epistemology 1965–1980*, p. 178.
22. Piaget, "Essai sur la nécessité," pp. 235–251. and Piaget, *Le possible et le nécessaire*.
23. Piaget, *Psychology of Intelligence*, p. 98.

24. Piaget, *Origins of Intelligence in Children*, p. 74.
25. Piaget, "Piaget's Theory," p. 717.
26. Gibson, "On Theories for Visual Perception," p. 78.
27. Piaget, *Origins of Intelligence in Children*, p. 87.
28. Ibid., p. 131.
29. Ben-Zeer, "J. J. Gibson and the Ecological Approach to Perception," pp. 107–139.
30. Piaget, *Biologie et connaissance*, p. 257; Piaget, Apostel, and Mandelbrot, *Logique et équilibre*, p. 117; and Piaget's reductionist thesis is defended in Cellerier, Papert, and Voyat, *Cybernétique et épistémologie*.
31. To follow the main arguments read: Koestler, *Beyond Reductionism;* Turner, *Psychology and the Philosophy of Science*, ch. 6–7; and Royce and Rozeboom, *The Psychology of Knowing*.
32. Glees, *Experimental Neurology*, p. 252. Additional details can be found in Pribram, "Neurological Notes in Knowing," p. 456.
33. Flavell, *The Developmental Psychology*, p. 99.
34. Ibid., p. 92.
35. Tran-Thong, *Stades et concept de stade de développement de l'enfant dans la psychologie contemporaine*, p. 29.

CHAPTER 3. THE OBJECT: AN EPISTEMOLOGICAL STUDY

1. MacNamara, "Stomachs Assimilate and Accommodate, Don't They?" pp. 167–172.
2. Piaget, *The Psychology of Intelligence*, pp. 107–108.
3. Joske, *Material Objects*, p. 8.
4. Mundle, *Perception*.
5. Garnett, *The Perceptual Process*, p. 50.
6. Piaget, *Psychologie et épistémologie*, p. 58.
7. Ross, *The Appeal to the Given*, p. 170.
8. Ayer, *The Problem of Knowledge*, pp. 113–116.
9. Hamlyn, *Theory of Knowledge;* and Price, *Perception*.
10. Piaget, *Psychologie et épistémologie*, p. 35.
11. Ayer, *The Problem of Knowledge*, ch. 3.
12. Moore, *A Defence of Common-Sense in Contemporary British Philosophy*, pp. 193–223.
13. Piaget, *Introduction à l'épistémologie génétique*, vol.1, p. 33.
14. Furth, *Piaget and Knowledge*, pp. 68–82.
15. Descartes, "Meditations on First Philosophy."
16. Berkeley, *A Treatise Concerning the Principles of Human Knowledge;* section 1, p. 33.
17. Hume, *A Treatise on Human Nature;* Book 1, part 4.
18. Piaget, *The Construction of Reality in the Child*, p. 6.
19. Gouin-Decarie, *Intelligence and Affectivity in Early Childhood*, p. 35.
20. Piaget, *The Origins of Intelligence in Children*, p. 140.

21. Destutt de Tracy, *Oeuvres complétes,* vol. 4, pp. 212–220.
22. Maine de Biran, quoted in Michotte, *The Perception of Causality,* p. 11.
23. Locke, quoted in Royal Institute of Philosophy Lectures, *Knowledge and Necessity, Perception and Action,* p. 93.
24. Maine de Biran, *Mémoire sur l'habitude,* vol. 2, p. 103.
25. Bréhier, *Histoire de la philosophie,* vol. 3, pp. 626–627.
26. Piaget, *Introduction à l'epistemologie génétique,* vol. 2, p. 341.
27. Piaget, *Les mécanismes perceptifs,* p. 441.
28. Piaget, "Motricité, perception et intelligence," pp. 10–14.
29. Piaget et al., *Les liaisons analytiques et synthétiques dans les comportements du sujet,* pp. 43–45.
30. Piaget, *The Child's Conception of Causality,* p. 126.
31. Piaget, *Insights and Illusions of Philosophy,* pp. 144–145.
32. Michotte, *The Perception of Causality,* p. 276.
33. Piaget, *The Construction of Reality in the Child,* p. 226.
34. Piaget, *Introduction à l'épistémologie génétique,* p. 271.
35. Piaget, *Insights and Illusions of Philosophy,* pp. 154–155.
36. Yolton, "Perceptual Consciousness," pp. 37–39.
37. Ibid., p. 48.
38. Piaget, *The Construction of Reality in the Child,* p. 6.
39. Piaget, *The Origins of Intelligence in Children,* p. 143.
40. Ornstein, *The Psychology of Consciousness,* p. 31.
41. Gouin-Decarie, *Intelligence and Affectivity,* pp. 24–25.
42. Piaget, *Les relations entre l'affectivité et l'intelligence dans le développement mental de l'enfant,* p. 59.
43. Piaget, *The Construction of Reality in the Child,* p. 8; see also Piaget, *The Origins of Intelligence in Children,* p. 143.
44. MacMurray, *The Self as Agent,* p. 89.
45. Ibid., p. 93.
46. Piaget, *Recherches sur les correspondances.*

CHAPTER 4. THE EMERGENCE OF THE EXTERNAL WORLD

1. James, *Essays in Radical Empiricism.*
2. Moore, *A Defence of Common-Sense in Contemporary British Philosophy,* pp. 193, 223.
3. Merleau-Ponty, *Phénoménologie de la perception,* p. 160.
4. Kohen-Raz, *Psychobiological Aspects of Cognitive Growth.* See particularly ch. 4, which introduces neurological findings supporting a biosemiotic model.
5. MacMurray, *The Self as Agent.*
6. Moroz, "The Concept of Cognition in Contemporary Psychology," pp. 177–211.
7. Gyr, "Perception as Reafference and Related Issues in Cognition and Epistemology," pp. 267–284.
8. Gurwitsch, *The Field of Consciousness.*

9. Boden, *Minds and Mechanisms.*

10. Gibson, *The Senses Considered as a Perceptual System.*

11. An example of this opposition is given by: Hamlyn, *Theory of Knowledge.*

12. Piaget, *The Origins of Intelligence in Children,* pp. 147–148.

13. Tolman, *Purposive Behavior in Animals and Men,* ch. 1.

14. Piaget, *Insights and Illusions of Philosophy,* p. 154.

15. Watson, *Behaviorism,* pp. 4–6.

16. Hayek, *The Sensory Order,* pp. 132–134.

17. See, for example: Feigenbaum and Feldman (eds.), *Computers and Thought;* Miller, Galanter, and Pribram, *Plans and the Structure of Behavior;* George, *Brain as a Computer;* Ashby, *Design for a Brain;* Rosenblatt, "The Perceptron," pp. 386–408; McCullough, *Embodiments of Mind;* and Arbib, *Brains, Machines and Mathematics.*

18. See, for example: Dreyfus, *What Computers Cannot Do,* particularly pp. 16, 102, 155, 193; Mischel, "Psychology and Explanation of Human Behavior," pp. 578–594; Taylor, *The Explanation of Behavior:* Straus, *The Primary World of Senses:* and Spicker, *The Philosophy of the Body.*

19. Piaget, *The Origins of Intelligence in Children,* p. 148.

20. Quine, *From a Logical Point of View,* ch. ii, section 6, p. 42.

21. An extensive treatment of this point is contained in Dreher, "A Study of Human Action."

22. See R. Taylor, *Action and Purpose.*

23. Merleau-Ponty, *Phénomenologie de la perception,* p. 160.

24. Ibid., p. 243; also, *La structure du comportement,* pp. 7, 48.

25. Hamlyn "Epistemology and Conceptual Development," pp. 16–22.

26. Merleau-Ponty, *Phénomenologie de la perception* and *La structure du comportement.*

27. Merleau-Ponty, *The Primacy of Perception,* ch. 1, pp. 3–12.

28. See, for example, Hook (ed.), *Dimensions of Mind.* See also Mischel, *Cognitive Development and Epistemology,* and Hamlyn, *Theory of Knowledge.*

29. See the various definitions of consciousness (sixteen in all) in Miller, *Unconsciousness.*

30. Piaget, *L'equilibration des structures cognitives.*

31. Pai, *Teaching, Learning and the Mind.*

32. Piaget, *The Origins of Intelligence in Children,* p. 154.

33. Gauld and Shutter, *Human Action and Its Psychological Investigation,* p. 43.

34. See a similar model in Sziracki, "Mental and Biological Assimilation and Accommodation," pp. 67–73.

35. Piaget, *Insights and Illusions of Philosophy,* ch. 3, 4.

36. James, *Essays in Radical Empiricism.*

37. Bergson, *Matière et mémoire,* p. 25.

38. Ibid., p. 62.

39. Piaget, *Insights and Illusions of Philosophy,* p. 99.

40. Piaget, *Introduction à l'épistémologie génétique,* vol. 2, p. 271.

41. Piaget, *Insights and Illusions of Philosophy,* p. 160.

42. Hayek, "The Primacy of the Abstract," in Koestler (ed.), *Beyond Reductionism,* p. 316.

43. Piaget, *The Origins of Intelligence in Children*, pp. 60–61.
44. Boring, *Sensation and Perception in the History of Experimental Psychology*, p. 563.
45. Piaget, *The Origins of Intelligence in Children*, p. 173.
46. The context for this position is covered in Weiss, *Sports: A Philosophical Inquiry*.
47. Maier, "Piagetian Principles."

CHAPTER 5. THE "ENCOUNTER" WITH THE WORLD: CONFLICT AND CREATIVITY

1. Piaget, "Equilibre et structure d'ensemble," p. 5; and Kamii, "Piaget's Interactionism," in Schwebel (ed.), *Piaget in the Classroom*, pp. 216–230.
2. Piaget, *Recherches sur les correspondances*; Piaget, *Success and Understanding*; and Inhelder and Piaget, "Procédures et structures," pp. 165–176.
3. Piaget, *Logique et équilibre*; and Inhelder, Garcia, and Vonèche, *Epistémologie génétique et équilibration* (see Introduction).
4. Boden, *Jean Piaget*, p. 16.
5. This point is the subject of: Piaget, *Logique et équilibre*.
6. Ibid., pp. 67–68.
7. See, for example, G. Miller, *Mathematics and Psychology* and Wann, *Behaviorism and Phenomenology*.
8. Skinner, *About Behaviorism*, p. 197.
9. Nelson, "Behaviorism Is False," pp. 411–452; Fodor, *Psychological Explanation*, ch. 2; and Turner, *Realism and the Explanation of Behavior*, ch. 6, 7.
10. The relations between equilibrium and structure are analyzed in Mouloud, *La psychologie et les structures*.
11. Wittgenstein, *Tractacus Logico-Philosophicus*, vol. 5, p. 632.
12. Wittgenstein, *Philosophical Investigations*, vol. 1, p. 7.
13. Hampshire, *Thought and Action*, pp. 47–53.
14. Langford, *Human Action*, p. 71.
15. Smart, "Causality and Human Behavior," pp. 143–148.
16. Hamlyn, "Causality and Human Behavior," pp. 125–142.
17. Mischel (ed.), *Cognitive Development and Epistemology*, pp. 3–25.
18. Locke, *An Essay Concerning Human Understanding*, Book 2, ch. 23, sections 1–6.
19. This opinion colors his work: Poincaré, *La valeur de la science*.
20. Russell, *My Philosophical Development*, p. 170.
21. Pap, *Introduction to Philosophy of Science*, p. 378.
22. Weigel and Madden, *Knowledge*, p. 17.
23. Lewis, *Mind and the World Order*.
24. Goodman, *The Structure of Appearance*, p. 129.
25. Ryle, *The Concept of Mind*, ch. 7.
26. Langford, *Human Action*, p. 96.
27. Kashap, *Spinoza*.

28. Goodman, *Fact, Fiction and Forecast.*

29. Van Fraasen, "Theories and Counterfactuals," pp. 237–264.

30. Frankfurt, "The Problem of Action," pp. 157–162.

31. Piaget, Apostel, and Mandelbrot, *Logique et équilibre,* pp. 105, 116.

32. One finds such appeals throughout: Piaget, *Biologie et connaissance,* ch. 2, section 5; Cellérier, *Cybernétique et épistémologie.* Note the interesting chapter 2 in Kohen-Raz, *Psychobiological Aspects of Cognitive Growth.*

33. Piaget, *L'équilibration des structures cognitives.*

34. Piaget, *Logique et équilibre.*

35. Piaget, *L'équilibration des structures cognitives,* p. 55.

36. See the analyses of various models in Moroz, "The Concept of Cognition in Contemporary Psychology" and Gyr, "Perception as Reafference."

37. Vuyk, *Piaget's Genetic Epistemology,* pp. 68, 158.

38. Piaget, *L'équilibration des structures cognitives,* p. 57.

39. Ibid., p. 59.

40. Ibid., p. 65.

41. Brentano, "The Distinction Between Mental and Physical Phenomena," p. 50.

42. This topic is thoroughly dealt with in Hintikka, *Knowledge and Belief,* pp. 19–21.

43. This special interpretation given to probability of events within the context of knowledge and perception is investigated in Carnap, *Meaning and Necessity.*

44. "Entrenched properties" is introduced in Goodman, *The Structure of Appearance,* ch. 4, 6.

45. In defense of logical atomism, see Russell, *Logic and Knowledge* and Wittgenstein, *Tractacus Logico-Philosophicus.*

46. Piaget, *L'équilibration des structures cognitives,* part 3, and Piaget, *Le comportement, moteur de l'évolution,* p. 92.

47. Piaget, *The Child's Conception of the World.*

48. Piaget, *L'équilibration des structures cognitives,* p. 62.

49. Ibid., pp. 76, 170.

50. A different analysis relating identity to conservation appears in Bruner, Goodnow, and Austin, *A Study of Thinking,* ch. 2, 8.

51. Extreme caution is in order regarding the use in genetic psychology of a terminology borrowed from cybernetics. This use betrays a sympathy for model making of the nervous system, and thus suffers from the same accusation of gratuity. To grasp the complexity inherent in such a task, see Tsien, *Engineering Cybernetics;* Arbib, *Brains, Machines and Mathematics;* and Roberts, "Biochemical Maturation of the Central Nervous System."

52. Piaget, *L'équilibration des structures cognitives,* pp. 71–75.

53. Ibid., pp. 84–85. See also Inhelder, Garcia, and Vonèche, *Epistémologie génétique et équilibration,* p. 16.

54. One can consult the good synthesis in Wynne, *Theories of Education,* pp. 187–259.

55. Uznadze, *The Psychology of Set,* p. 90. Also particularly akin to Piaget's views are the notions presented by Uznadze on pp. 127, 153, and 209.

56. Hirst, "The Difference Between Sensing and Observing," p. 40.
57. Ibid.
58. See particularly Smart, *Philosophy and Scientific Realism,* and Ryle, *The Concept of Mind.*
59. Kashap, *Spinoza.*
60. Hirst, "Sensing and Observing," p. 40.
61. Mundle, *Perception,* p. 25. This is a lucid survey of the various positions on this topic.
62. Uznadze, *The Psychology of Set,* p. 209.
63. Mundle, *Perception,* p. 170.
64. Siegel and Brainerd (eds.), *Alternatives to Piaget,* p. 10.
65. Ibid.
66. Bringuier, *Conversations libres avec J. Piaget,* p. 18.
67. Siegel and Brainerd, *Alternatives to Piaget,* p. 80.

Glossary

ACCOMMODATION. The modification of a cognitive scheme as a result of specific encounters with the environment.

ACTION. An oriented and deliberate movement that is accompanied by sensory qualities and that transforms or compares objects.

ADAPTATION. The process by which the anticipation of a system of actions is matched by the result obtained from the environment. It is often expressed as the balanced state occurring between accommodation and assimilation.

AFFECTIVITY. The moving force activating the uses of a set of actions.

AFFERENT. Leading inward or toward something (for example, the nerve impulse moving toward the central nervous system).

APODICTIC. Relating to an assertion that is universally valid and necessary. This concept is central to Kant's philosophy.

ASSIMILATION. The use and imposition of a cognitive scheme on the data presented by the environment.

ASSOCIATIONISM. A philosophical position or a psychological theory. The former holds that complex concepts result from the association of simpler ideas or properties; the latter views perceptions as the linking of spatio-temporally contiguous sensations.

ASYMPTOTIC. Relating to the continuous convergence of one thing toward another where the junction is never completed.

CAUSALITY. The attribution of a cognitive structure to events.

CENTRATION. Focusing one's attention onto one aspect of a situation and disregarding the others.

COGNITIVE PSYCHOLOGY. The study of intellectual functions and their roles in organizing the acquisition of knowledge.

COMPARING. A basic cognitive function that matches or maps various features of objects.

COMPENSATION. An action that undoes another by inversion or neutralizes its effects by reciprocity.

CONATION. The power to act, desire, will, and decide.

CONCEPT. The set of properties assimilated by a cognitive structure that is therefore tied to a system of actions, their transformations, and their results.

CONSERVATION. The constancy in a property of an object that results from a cognitive judgment and that is maintained despite the physical changes of that object.

COORDINATION. The functional use of cognitive schemes that links various actions in a systematic manner.

DECENTRATION. The progressive ability to consider various possibilities and to coordinate several aspects of a situation within a scheme or schema.

DEVELOPMENT. The gradual formation of action systems and cognitive structures that uncover invariant features of the world and are thus able to deal with more and more global situations.

DISEQUILIBRIUM. A state of imbalance that gives rise to compensatory actions.

DYNAMOGENISM. A view that relates increased mental activity to sensory stimulations.

EFFERENT. Leading away from something (for example, a nerve impulse moving away from the central nervous system).

EGOCENTRISM. The state of an individual who, at any given moment, does not distinguish between psychical and physical events, or between objective and subjective domains.

EPIGENESIS. The thesis that development starts with a global activity and evolves causally toward various organized specializations.

EPIPHENOMENON. A secondary phenomenon that emanates and accompanies the main process without influencing its evolution.

EPISTEMIC SUBJECT. The common structural traits that form an equilibrium and that individuals share at a given cognitive level.

EPISTEMOLOGY. A branch of philosophy that, interpreted as a theory of knowledge, centers on the validity of claims to knowledge. For Piaget, those claims touch mostly the domain of scientific concepts.

EQUILIBRATION. The functional trend of intelligence toward balancing action sets so as to compensate for an everchanging environment. It is a crucial developmental process in Piaget's cognitive psychology.

EQUILIBRIUM. A balanced state where all actions are compensated. Thus it contains only operations. It is an important structural element of Piaget's genetic psychology.

EXOGENOUS. Relating to an influential factor that originates in the external environment.

EXTENSION. The class of exemplars denoted by a term.

EXTEROCEPTIVE. Relating to the ability to react to sensations that originate in the external environment.

FIGURATIVE. Relating to the static and total description of an event in terms of the perceptual data accommodated by an action set. This is found mainly in imitation, perception, memory, and imagery.

FUNCTION. An innate and invariant manner of using cognitive schemes. The main functions are assimilation, accommodation, organization, equilibration, and the processes of transforming, comparing, and repeating.

GENETIC EPISTEMOLOGY. The analysis of a person's claims to knowledge as a function of his successive views of reality and the cognitive mechanisms used to build them.

GENETIC PSYCHOLOGY. The study of the chronological development of concepts.

HERMENEUTICS. A procedure whereby an explanation is given by interpreting the context surrounding the event to be explained. For a person, it entails relying on his psychological and conceptual reasons, and is tied to his actions.

HEURISTICS. A manner of discovering and proving whereby one relies on guesses, intuition, practical strategies, and ways of organizing.

HOMEORHESIS. A process favoring a development that seeks equilibration despite various deviations.

HOMEOSTASIS. A stable system that returns to equilibrium despite disturbances.

IMAGE. The internal construction of an event where figurative elements are organized by an action system. It has static and imitative attributes that allow it to play a symbolic role in cognition.

IMITATION. The reproduction of gestures that resembles a given situation and models it through accommodations.

INTELLIGENCE. Thinking that is regulated by cognitive structures and evolves with their gradual development in order to be better adapted.

INTENSION. The group of properties that determines the meaning of a term.

INTENTION. A mental predicate that characterizes one's purpose, beliefs, and directed actions.

INTERIORIZATION. The intellectual presentation of an object that shows its logico-mathematical properties. In other words, the presentation exhibits the properties of action coordinations rather than the perceptual results of an action. It characterizes the operational thinking of the epistemic subject.

INTERNALIZATION. The mental representation of an object showing its figurative elements. It characterizes the psychological subject where strategies to connect or compare objects (or events) are put into play.

INTEROCEPTIVE. Relating to the ability to react to sensations originating within one's organism.

KNOWLEDGE. The presentation and representation of various realities that originate in a progressive construction by cognitive structures, schemes, and schemas. It is identified with logico-mathematical and physical intelligence that transform and compare objects.

LACUNA. The need to complete through new actions the exercise of a cognitive scheme that is disturbed and arrested by the environment.

LEARNING. The acquisition of specific items, either abilities or memories, that occurs through appropriate encounters between cognitive schemas and the environment.

LOGICO-MATHEMATICAL KNOWLEDGE. The operational aspect of intelligence that consists of a reflection on action coordinations.

MATURATIONISM. A thesis that states that physiological and psychological changes are due to a preestablished plan.

MEDIATE. To function as an intermediary or act through an intervening agent.

MEMORY. The progressive reorganization of figurative elements as a function of equilibrated intellectual schemes.

NEED. The conative and emotional feeling that accompanies the functional use of schemes or schemas until equilibrium is achieved.

NOMOLOGICAL. Relating to laws of the mind or having lawlike characters.

OBJECTIFICATION. The process of attributing properties to real objects.

OBJECTIVIZATION. The process of rendering a property independent of the observer.

ONTOLOGICAL. Relating to the claims attached to one's commitment to real entities.

ONTOGENETIC. Relating to the development of a particular individual rather than a species.

OPERATION. Imagined reversible action that yields the transformation of an object and thus contributes to its structured interiorization or concept.

ORGANIZATION. A balanced action system forming a cognitive structure and ensuring the conservation of properties and the integration of all new elements.

PERCEPTION. The conscious and accomodated result of applying a set of actions to a given situation.

PERMANENCE. The quality of a property or object that exists in its own right and is thus independent of immediate sensory determinations.

PHENOTYPIC. Relating to a property that appears after some inherited traits interact with the environment.

PHYLOGENETIC (OR PHILOGENIC). Relating to the development of a species as opposed to that of an individual.

PHYSICAL KNOWLEDGE. Acquaintance with the world based on reflections surrounding the discovery of results of actions rather than reflections on constructions within action coordinations.

PLAY. Assimilative activities that operate via the relatively free use of a cognitive scheme and produce variations around a deferred imitation used as a symbol.

PRESENTATION. The concepts that are built out of conserved properties. It constitutes the understanding of the epistemic subject.

PROCEDURE. An action sequence that is aimed at a goal and, in order to succeed, is tied to a particular context. It yields strategies appropriate for the solution of problems that can be transferred through comparisons by the psychological subject.

PROPRIOCEPTION. The process of receiving sensations from within the organism, either from the muscles or the joints.

PSYCHOLOGICAL SUBJECT. A self-conscious individual who, guided by the need for equilibration, finds strategies to resolve problematic situations.

PSYCHOLOGIZE. To interpret in psychological terms.

REALISM. The biased view of a person who extends his own psychical characteristics to physical phenomena.

REALITY. The progressively constituted universe as conceived through the use of cognitive structures.

REASONING. The intellectual process of comparing and transforming objects and their properties.

REFLECTED ABSTRACTION. Being aware of one's action.

REFLEXIVE ABSTRACTION. Being aware of one's use of a cognitive structure.

REGULATION. The readjustment of an action by compensating for a lacuna or an obstacle.

REIFY. To regard something as an objective entity.

REPRESENTATION. The accommodated result of using cognitive schemas that refer to perceptually given events. This symbolic process permits comparisons by the psychological subject.

REVERSIBILITY. The intellectual process of going back and forth along the path of an action. One is then able to annul mentally by constructing the inverse of a property or finding the reciprocal of a relation.

SCHEMA (PLURAL: SCHEMAS OR SCHEMATA). The figurative features of an action set. It yields the representation of an object by cognitively connecting sensory elements.

SCHEME. The common and generalizable properties exhibited through the various usages of one type of action. The result has logico-mathematical properties that relate and regulate by anticipating various situations.

SEMIOTICS. A representative system that is made up of symbols and signs that signify events, and is found in language, games, deferred imitation, images, and drawings.

SENSATION. The result of an actual encounter with the world that becomes conscious only when mediated by cognitive schemas.

SENSE-DATA. The most basic elements given by the senses, but that have no conscious cognitive status in Piaget's system.

SENSORIMOTOR. Relating to the simultaneous presence of a movement and its sensorial components.

SIGNIFICATION. The symbolic result of applying cognitive schemes to objects. The set of actions applicable constitutes the real meaning of the object.

STRUCTURE. A system of operations that is equilibrated, closed, and atemporal. In the genetic psychology of Piaget, a sequence of structures has to be mastered to show a progressive intelligence and understanding.

SYSTEM. A group of organized and reversible actions whose transformations can be temporally distributed and regulated by a feedback loop that is influenced by the environment.

TACTILO-KINESTHETIC. Relating to the touchlike sensations given through the motions of muscles.

TELEOLOGICAL. Relating to processes whose direction is determined by a goal.

TELEONOMY. A process that is future-oriented.

THINK. To compare and transform objects through the use of interiorized actions. The cognitive structures, schemes, and schemas, thus applied, ensure that the events, temporally distributed, are simultaneously reflected upon.

TRANSFORMATION. The cognitive function that modifies the characteristics of objects or situations.

WORLD. The universe "out there" that is postulated by common sense. For Piaget, the epistemic subject approaches the world asymptotically via his successive realities.

Bibliography

ABBREVIATIONS

EEG   Etudes d'épistémologie génétique (series)
PUF   Presses Universitaires de France
RKP   Routledge & Kegan Paul

Arbib, M. A. *Brains, Machines and Mathematics.* New York: McGraw-Hill, 1964.
Ashby, W. R. *Design for a Brain.* London: Chapman and Hall, 1952.
Atkinson, J. W. "Strength of Motivation and Efficiency of Performance." Symposium of Theory of Achievement Motivation. American Psychological Association. September, 1963.
Ayer, A. J. *The Problem of Knowledge.* Baltimore: Penguin, 1964.
Bart, W. "A Generalization of Piaget's Logical Mathematical Model for the Stage of Formal Operations." *Journal of Mathematical Psychology* 8, no. 4 (1971).
Ben-Zeer, A. "J. J. Gibson and the Ecological Approach to Perception." *Studies in History of Philosophy of Science* 12, no. 2 (1981): 107–139.
Bergling, K. *The Development of Hypothetico-Deductive Thinking in Children.* New York: Wiley & Sons, 1974.
Bergson, H. *Matière et Mémoire.* Paris: Alcan, 1926.
Berkeley,G. *A Treatise Concerning the Principles of Human Knowledge, Section 1.* Cleveland: The World Publishing Co., 1963.
Boden, M. A. *Jean Piaget.* Brighton, Sussex: Harvester, 1979.
————. *Minds and Mechanisms: Essays in Philosophical Psychology.* Hassocks, Sussex: Harvester, 1980.

Boring, E. G. *Sensation and Perception in the History of Experimental Psychology.* New York: Appleton Century, 1942.

Bréhier, E. *Histoire de la philosophie.* Tome II: *La philosophie moderne.* Paris: PUF, 1957.

Brentano, F. "The Distinction Between Mental and Physical Phenomena." In *Realism and the Background of Phenomenology,* edited by R. M. Chisholm. Glencoe, Ill.: Free Press, 1960.

Bringuier, J. C. *Conversations libres avec J. Piaget.* Paris: R. Laffont, 1977.

Bronckhart, J. P. *Theories of Language.* Brussels: Dessart, 1977.

Brown, G., and Desforges, C. *Piaget's Theory.* London: RKP, 1979.

Bruner, J., Goodnow, J. R., and Austin, G. A. *A Study of Thinking.* New York: Wiley & Sons, 1956.

Brunswick, E. "Probabilism." *Psychological Review,* 62 (1955).

Bunge, M. *Foundations of Physics.* New York: Springer Verlag, 1967.

Burloud, A. *De la psychologie à la philosophie.* Paris: Hachette, 1951.

Carnap, R. *Meaning and Necessity.* Chicago: University of Chicago Press, 1956.

Cellerier, G., Papert, S., and Voyat, G. *Cybernétique et epistémologie.* EEG XXII. Paris: PUF, 1967.

Chomsky, N. *Language and Mind.* New York: Harcourt Brace, 1968.

Cowan, P. *Piaget with Feeling.* New York: Holt, Rinehart, 1978.

Descartes, R. "Meditations of First Philosophy." In *The Philosophical Works of Descartes,* translated by E. S. Haldane and G. R. T. Ross. Cambridge: Cambridge University Press, 1931.

Destutt de Tracy. *Oeuvres complètes: eléments d'idéologie.* Paris: Levy, 1826.

Dienes, Z. *Thinking in Structures.* New York: Humanities, 1965.

Dreher, J. H. "A Study of Human Action." Ph.D. Thesis. University of Indiana, 1971.

Dreyfus, H. L. *What Computers Cannot Do.* New York: Harper & Row, 1972.

Feigenbaum, E. A., and Feldman, J., eds. *Computers and Thought.* New York: McGraw-Hill, 1963.

Flavell, J. H. *The Developmental Psychology of Jean Piaget.* New York: Van Nostrand, Reinhold, 1963.

Fodor, J. *Psychological Explanation.* New York: Random House, 1968.

Frankfurt, H. "The Problem of Action." *American Philosophical Quarterly* 15, no. 2 (1978): 157–162.

Furth, H. G. *Piaget and Knowledge: Theoretical Foundations.* Englewood Cliffs, N.J.: Prentice-Hall, 1969.

————. "Piagetian Theory and the Helping Profession." Address to the Sixth Interdisciplinary Conference. Los Angeles: University of Southern California Press, 1977.

Gallagher, J. M., and Easley, J. A. eds. *Knowledge and Development.* Vol. 2. New York: Plenum, 1978.

Garnett, A. C. *The Perceptual Process.* Madison: University of Wisconsin Press, 1965.

Gauld, A., and Shutter, J. *Human Action and Its Psychological Investigation.* London: RKP, 1977.

George, F. A. *Brain as a Computer.* New York: Pergamon, 1962.

Gibson, J. J. *The Senses Considered as a Perceptual System*. Boston: Houghton Mifflin, 1966.

————. "On Theories for Visual Space Perception." *Scandinavian Journal of Psychology* 2 (1970): 78.

Glees, P. *Experimental Neurology*. Oxford: Clarendon Press, 1961.

Goodman, N. *Fact, Fiction and Forecast*. London: Oxford University Press, 1965.

————. *The Structure of Appearance*. Indianapolis: Bobbs-Merrill Co., 1966.

Gouin-Decarie, T. *Intelligence and Affectivity in Early Childhood*. New York: International Universities Press, 1965.

Granger, G-G. *Pensée Formelle et sciences de l'homme*. Paris: Aubier (Ed.) 1967.

Green, D., Ford, M., and Flamer, G. *Measurement and Piaget*. New York: McGraw-Hill, 1971.

Gurwitsch, A. *The Field of Consciousness*. Pittsburgh: Duquesne University Press, 1964.

Gyr, J. W. "Perception as Reafference and Related Issues in Cognition and Epistemology." In *The Psychology of Knowing*, edited by J. Royce. New York: Gordon & Breach, 1972.

Hamlyn, D. W. "Causality and Human Behavior." *SPAS* 38(1964): 125–142.

————. *Theory of Knowledge*. New York: Doubleday, 1970.

————. "Epistemology and Conceptual Development." In *Cognitive Development and Epistemology*, edited by T. Mischel. New York: Academic Press, 1971.

————. *Experience and the Growth of Understanding*. London: RKP, 1978.

Hampshire, S. *Thought and Action*. New York: Viking, 1960.

Hayek, F. A. *The Sensory Order*. Chicago: University of Chicago Press, 1952.

Hintikka, J. *Knowledge and Belief*. Ithaca, N.Y.: Cornell University Press, 1962.

Hirst, R. J. "The Difference Between Sensing and Observing." In *The Philosophy of Perception*, edited by G. J. Warnock. London: Oxford University Press, 1969.

Hume, D. *A Treatise on Human Nature*. Book I. Oxford: Clarendon Press, 1888.

Hunt, J. McV. *Intelligence and Experience*. New York: Ronald Press, 1961.

————. "Intrinsic Motivation and Its Role in Psychological Development." In *Nebraska Symposium on Motivation*. Lincoln: University of Nebraska Press, 1965.

Inhelder, B., Garcia, R., and Vonéche, J. *Epistémologie génétique et équilibration*. Paris: Delachaux et Niestlé, 1976.

Inhelder, B., and Piaget, J. "Procédures et structures." *Archives de Psychologie* 47(1979):165–176.

James, W. *Essays in Radical Empiricism*. New York: Dutton, 1971.

Joske, W. D. *Material Objects*. New York: St. Martin's, 1967.

Juvet, G. *L'axiomatique et la théorie des groupes*. Actes du Congrés International de Philosophie Scientifique, Vol. VI. Paris: Haman, 1936.

Kashap, P. *Spinoza*. Berkeley: University of California Press, 1972.

Kamii, C. "Piaget's Interactionism." In *Piaget in the Classroom*, edited by M. Schwebel. New York: Basic Books, 1973.

Koestler, A. *Beyond Reductionism*. Boston: Beacon Press, 1969.

Kohen-Raz, R. *Psychobiological Aspects of Cognitive Growth.* London: Academic Press, 1977.

Kohlberg, L. "Development as the Aim of Education." *Harvard Educational Review* 42, no. 4 (1972).

Kyburg, H. *Philosophy of Science: A Formal Approach.* New York: Macmillan, 1968.

Langford, G. *Human Action.* New York: Doubleday, 1971.

Le Ny, J. F. *Le conditionnement et l'apprentissage.* Paris: PUF, 1975.

Lewis, C. I. *Mind and the World Order.* New York: Scribners, 1929.

Lindsay, P. H., and Norman, D. A. *Human Information Processing.* New York: Academic Press, 1972.

Locke, J. *An Essay Concerning Human Understanding,* edited by A. C. Fraser. New York: Dover Publishing, 1959.

Mach, E. *The Analysis of Sensations.* New York: Dover, 1959.

MacMurray, J. *The Self as Agent.* London: Faber & Faber, 1957.

MacNamara, J. "Stomachs Assimilate and Accommodate, Don't They?" *Canadian Psychological Review* 17, no. 1 (1976): 167–172.

Maier, H. W. *Three Theories of Child Development.* New York: Harper & Row, 1969.

————. "Piagetian Principles Applied to the Beginning Phase in Professional Helping." In *Piagetian Theory and Its Implications for the Helping Professions.* Vol. I, Seventh Conference. Los Angeles: University of Southern California Press, 1978.

Maine de Biran, *Mémoire sur l'habitude.* Vol. 2. Paris: Tisseranol, 1922.

Maslow, A. H. *Toward a Psychology of Being.* Princeton, N.J: Van Nostrand, 1962.

Mays, W. "Genetic Epistemology and Theories of Adaptive Behavior." In *Philosophical Problems in Psychology,* edited by N. Bolton. New York: Methuen, 1979.

McCulloch, W. *Embodiments of Mind.* Boston: MIT Press, 1965.

Merleau-Ponty, M. *Phénomenologie de la perception.* Paris: Gallimard, 1945.

————. *The Primacy of Perception.* Evanston, Ill.: Northwestern University Press, 1964.

————. *La structure du comportement.* Paris: PUF, 1967.

Meyerson, E. *Identity and Reality.* New York: Dover Press, 1962.

Michotte, A. *The Perception of Causality.* London: Methuen, 1963.

Miller, G. *Mathematics and Psychology.* New York: Wiley & Sons, 1960.

Miller, G. A., Galanter, E., and Pribram, K. *Plans and the Structure of Behavior.* New York: Holt, Rinehart, 1960.

Miller, J. G. *Unconsciousness.* New York: Wiley & Sons, 1942.

Mischel, T. "Psychology and Explanation of Human Behavior." *Philosophical and Phenomenological Research* 23 (1963): 578–594.

————, ed. *Cognitive Development and Epistemology.* New York: Academic Press, 1971.

Moore, G. E. *A Defence of Common-Sense in Contemporary British Philosophy.* Series 2. Edited by J. H. Muirhead. London: G. Allen Publishers, 1925.

Moroz, M. "The Concept of Cognition in Contemporary Psychology." In *The Psychology of Knowing*, edited by J. R. Royce and W. Rozeboom. New York: Gordon & Breach, 1972.

Morris, C. *Signs, Language, and Behavior.* New York: Prentice-Hall, 1946.

Mouloud, N. *La psychologie et les structures.* Paris: PUF, 1965.

Mounoud, P. *Structuration de l'instrument chez l'enfant.* Paris: Delachaux, 1970.

Mundle, W. K. *Perception: Facts and Theories.* London: Oxford University Press, 1971.

Munsinger, H. *The Genetics of Epistemology.* Proceedings of the Sixth Interdisciplinary Conference on Piaget. Los Angeles: University of Southern California Press.

Murray, F. B., ed. *The Impact of Piagetian Theory on Education, Philosophy, Psychiatry and Psychology.* Baltimore: University Park Press, 1979.

Nelson, R. "Behaviorism Is False." *Journal of Philosophy*, 16, no. 14 (1969): 417–452.

Nicolas, A. *Jean Piaget.* Paris: Seghers, 1976.

Ornstein, R. N. *The Psychology of Consciousness.* San Francisco: Freeman, 1972.

Overton, W. F. and Gallagher, J. M. *Knowledge and Development.* Vol. 1. New York: Plenum, 1977.

Pai, Y. *Teaching, Learning, and the Mind.* Boston: Houghton Mifflin, 1973.

Pap, A. *Introduction to Philosophy of Science.* New York: Free Press, 1962.

Papert, S., Piaget, J., and Grize, J. B. *La filiation des structures.* EEG XV. Paris: PUF, 1963.

Peirce, C. S. *Collected Papers*, edited by Charles Hartshorne and Paul Weiss. 5 vols. Massachusetts: Harvard University Press, 1931–1935.

Peters, R. S. *The Concept of Motivation.* London: RKP, 1971.

Piaget, J. *The Child's Conception of Causality.* London: RKP, 1930.

_____. *Classes, relations et nombres.* Paris: Vrin, 1942.

_____. *Les notions de mouvement et de vitesse chez l'enfant.* Paris: PUF, 1946.

_____. *Traité de logique.* Paris: A. Colin, 1949.

_____. *Introduction à l'épistémologie génetique.* 3 vols. Paris: PUF, 1950.

_____. *Essai sur les transformation des opérations logiques.* Paris: PUF, 1952.

_____. "Equilibre et structure d'ensemble." *Bulletin Psychologique* no. 6 (1952).

_____. *The Construction of Reality in the Child.* New York: Basic Books, 1954.

_____. "Motricité, perception et intelligence." *Enfance* 2 (1956): 10–14.

_____. *Le jugement et le raisonnement chez l'enfant.* Neuchâtel: Delachaux, 1956.

_____. *Le jugement moral chez l'enfant.* Paris: PUF, 1957.

_____. *The Psychology of Intelligence.* London: RKP, 1959.

_____. *Les mécanismes perceptifs.* Paris: PUF, 1961.

_____. *Play, Dreams and Imitation in Childhood.* New York: Norton & Co., 1962.

_____. *Les relations entre l'affectivité et l'intelligence dans le développement mental dans l'enfant.* Paris: Centre de documentation universitaire, 1962.

_____. *The Origins of Intelligence in Children.* New York: Norton & Co., 1963.

————. *The Early Growth of Logic in the Child.* New York: Harper & Row, 1964.

————. *Sagesse et illusions de la philosophie.* Paris: PUF, 1964.

————. *Biologie et connaissance.* Paris: Gallimard, 1967.

————. *Six Psychological Studies.* New York: Random House, 1967.

————. "Review of Bruner's Studies in Cognitive Growth." *Contemporary Psychology* 12 (1967): 532–533.

————. *The Child's Conception of the World.* Totowa, N.J.: Littlefield, 1969.

————. *Psychologie et epistémologie.* Paris: Gauthier, 1970.

————. "Piaget's Theory." In *Carmichael's Manual of Child Psychology*, edited by P. H. Mussen. New York: Wiley & Sons, 1970.

————. *Genetic Epistemology.* New York: Norton & Co., 1971.

————. *Insights and Illusions of Philosophy.* New York: Meridian, 1971.

————. *Structuralism.* New York: Harper Torchbooks, 1971.

————. *Adaptation vitale et psychologie de l'intelligence.* Paris: Herman (Ed.), 1974.

————. *L'équilibration des structures cognitives.* Paris: PUF, 1975.

————. *Le comportement, moteur de l'évolution.* Paris: Gallimard, 1976.

————. "Essai sur la nécessité." *Archives de Psychologie* 45 (1977): 235–251.

————. *Recherches sur l'abstraction refléchissante.* Vol. I. EEG XXXIV. Paris: PUF, 1977.

————. *Success and Understanding.* London: RKP, 1978.

————. "Correspondences and Transformations." In *The Impact of Piagetian Theory on Education, Philosophy, Psychiatry, and Psychology*, edited by F. B. Murray, Baltimore: University Park Press, 1979.

————. *Recherches sur les correspondances.* Paris: PUF, 1980.

————. *Le possible et le nécessaire*, Vol. *L'évolution des possibles chez l'énfant.* Paris: PUF, 1981.

Piaget, J., Apostel, L., and Mandelbrot, B. *Logique et équilibre.* EEG II. Paris: PUF, 1957.

Piaget, J., Apostel, L., Mays, W., and Morf, A. *Les liaisons analytiques et synthétiques dans les comportements du sujet.* EEG IV. Paris: PUF, 1957.

Piaget, J., and Beth, E. *Epistémologie, mathématique et psychologie.* EEG XIV. Paris: PUF, 1961.

Piaget, J., Beth, E., and Mays, W. *Epistémologie génétique et recherche psychologique.* EEG I. Paris: PUF, 1957.

Piaget, J., and Henriques, G. *Recherches sur la généralisation.* Paris: PUF, 1978.

Piaget, J., and Inhelder, B. *La représentation de l'espace chez l'enfant.* Paris: PUF, 1948.

————. *The Growth of Logical Thinking from Childhood to Adolescence.* New York: Basic Books, 1958.

————. *L'image mentale chez l'enfant.* Paris: PUF, 1966.

————. *Mémoire et intelligence.* Paris: PUF, 1968.

Piaget, J., Jonckheere, A., and Mandelbrot, B. *La lecture de l'expérience.* EEG V. Paris: PUF, l958.

Piagetian Theory and the Helping Professions. Proceedings of Annual Conferences 1 to 7. Los Angeles: University of Southern California Press, 1974 to 1978.

Poincaré, H. *La valeur de la science*. Paris: PUF, 1921.

Pribram, K. "Neurological Notes in Knowing." In *Psychology of Knowing*, edited by J. Royce and W. Rozeboom. New York: Gordon & Breach, 1972.

Price, H. *Perception*. London: Methuen, 1932.

_____. *Thinking and Experience*. Cambridge, Mass.: Harvard University Press, 1962.

Przelecki, M. *The Logic of Empirical Theories*. London: RKP, 1969.

Quine, W. *From a Logical Point of View*. New York: Harper Torchbooks, 1963.

Ripple, R. E., and Rockcastle, V. N., eds. *Piaget Rediscovered*. Ithaca, N.Y.: Cornell University Press, 1964.

Roberts, E. "Biochemical Maturation of the Central Nervous System and Behavior." In *The Central Nervous System and Behavior*, edited by M. Brazier. New York: Macy Foundation, 1960.

Rosenblatt, F. "The Perceptron." *Psychology Review* 65 (1958): 386–408.

Ross, J. J. *The Appeal to the Given*. London: G. Allen, 1970.

Rotman, G. *Jean Piaget: Psychologist of the Real*. Hassocks, Sussex: Harvester, 1977.

Royal Institute of Philosophy Lectures. *Knowledge and Necessity, Perception and Action*. New York: St. Martins, 1970.

Royce, J. R., and Rozeboom, W., eds. *The Psychology of Knowing*. New York: Gordon & Breach, 1972.

Russell, B. *Human Knowledge: Its Scope and Limits*. New York: Knopf, 1948.

_____. *Logic and Knowledge*, edited by R. Marsh. London: G. Allen, 1956.

_____. *My Philosophical Development*. London: G. Allen, 1959.

Ryle, G. *The Concept of Mind*. London: Hutchinson, 1949.

Schwebel, M. *Piaget in the Classroom*. New York: Basic Books, 1973.

Siegel, H. "Piaget's Conception of Epistemology." *Educational Theory* 28 (1978): 16–22.

Siegel, L., and Brainerd, C., eds. *Alternatives to Piaget*. New York: Academic Press, 1978.

Skinner, B. *About Behaviorism*. New York: Knopf, 1974.

Smart, J. J. C. *Philosophy and Scientific Realism*. London: RKP, 1963.

_____. "Causality and Human Behavior." *SPAS* 38 (1964): 143–148.

Spicker, S. F. *The Philosophy of the Body*. Chicago: Quadrangle, 1970.

Straus, E. *The Primary World of Senses: A Vindication of Sensory Experience*. New York: Free Press, 1963.

Sziracki, M. "Mental and Biological Assimilation and Accommodation." *Canadian Psychological Review* 19, no. 1 (1978): 67–73.

Taylor, C. *The Explanation of Behavior*. London: RKP, 1964.

Taylor, R. *Action and Purpose*. Englewood Cliffs, N.J.: Prentice-Hall, 1966.

Tolman, E. C. *Purposive Behavior in Animals and Men*. New York: Appleton-Century-Crofts, 1932.

Tran-Thong, V. *Stades et concept de stade de développement de l'enfant dans la psychologie contemporaine*. Paris: Vrin, 1967.

Tsien, H. S. *Engineering Cybernetics*. New York: McGraw-Hill, 1954.

Turner, M. B. *Psychology and the Philosophy of Science.* New York: Appleton-Century-Crofts, 1967.

_____. *Realism and the Explanation of Behavior.* New York: Appleton-Century-Crofts, 1971.

Uznadze, D. *The Psychology of Set.* New York: Consultant Bureau Publishing, 1966.

Vaihinger, H. *The Philosophy of As If.* New York: Harcourt Brace, 1925.

Van Fraasen, B. "Theories and Counterfactuals." In *Action, Knowledge, and Reality,* edited by H. Castaneda. Indianapolis: Bobbs-Merrill, 1975.

Vuyk, R. *Piaget's Genetic Epistemology 1965–1980.* New York: Academic Press, 1981.

Wann, T. W. *Behaviorism and Phenomenology.* Chicago: University of Chicago Press, 1964.

Watanabe, S. *Knowing and Guessing.* New York: Wiley & Sons, 1969.

Watson, J. B. *Behaviorism.* New York: Norton, 1958.

Weigel, G., and Madden, A. G. *Knowledge.* Englewood Cliffs, N.J.: Prentice-Hall, 1961.

Weiss, P. *Sports: A Philosophic Inquiry.* Carbondale, Ill.: Sourthern Illinois University Press, 1971.

Wittgenstein, L. *Philosophical Investigations.* London: Blackwell, 1953.

_____. *Tractacus Logico-Philosophicus.* London: RKP, 1961.

Wittman, E. "The Concept of Grouping in Jean Piaget's Psychology." *Educational Studies in Mathematics* 5 (1973): 125–146.

Witz, K. G. "On Piaget's Grouping I and Representation of Cognitive Processes and Cognitive Structure in Children." (In Manuscript.)

Wynne, J. *Theories of Education.* New York: Harper & Row, 1963.

Yolton, J. W. "Perceptual Consciousness." In *Knowledge and Necessity, Perception and Action.* Vol. 3 of Royal Institute of Philosophy Lectures (1968–1969). New York: St. Martin's, 1970.

Index